Andrew Cain is Professor of Classics at the University of Colorado at Boulder. He has authored five books, including *The Letters of Jerome: Asceticism, Biblical Exegesis, and the Construction of Christian Authority in Late Antiquity* and *The Greek* Historia monachorum in Aegypto: *Monastic Hagiography in the Late Fourth Century.* He has also co-edited two volumes, is the translator of Fathers of the Church 121 (St. Jerome, *Commentary on Galatians*), and serves as Editor of the *Journal of Late Antiquity.*

D1035462

THE FATHERS
OF THE CHURCH

A NEW TRANSLATION

VOLUME 139

THE FATHERS OF THE CHURCH

A NEW TRANSLATION

RUFINUS OF AQUILEIA

INQUIRY ABOUT THE MONKS IN EGYPT

Translated by

ANDREW CAIN

University of Colorado

THE CATHOLIC UNIVERSITY OF AMERICA PRESS
Washington, D.C.

Library of Congress Cataloging-in-Publication Data
Names: Rufinus, of Aquileia, 345–410. | Cain, Andrew, translator, editor.
Title: Inquiry about the monks in Egypt / Rufinus of Aquileia ; translated by
Andrew Cain, University of Colorado. Other titles: Historia monachorum in
Aegypto. English. Description: Washington, D.C. : The Catholic University of
America Press, 2019. | Series: The Fathers of the church, a new translation ;
Volume 139 | Includes bibliographical references and index.
Identifiers: LCCN 2019013232 | ISBN 9780813232645 (cloth : alk. paper)
Subjects: LCSH: Monasticism and religious orders—Egypt—History—
Early church, ca. 30–600. | Desert Fathers—Biography. |
Monks—Egypt—Biography.
Classification: LCC BR195.M65 H5713 2019 | DDC 271.00932—dc23
LC record available at https://lccn.loc.gov/2019013232

CONTENTS

INDICES

ACKNOWLEDGMENTS

This book grew out of my ongoing, intersecting interests in the anonymous Greek *Historia monachorum in Aegypto,* an understudied *tour de force* of late antique monastic hagiography, and in Rufinus of Aquileia, an undervalued Latin literary figure of the late fourth and early fifth centuries. I wish to express my sincere thanks to Carole Monica Burnett, staff editor at The Catholic University of America Press, with whom I have had the great pleasure of working on now two books in the FOTC series, for the many invaluable suggestions she offered while editing the manuscript.

ABBREVIATIONS

AAAd	*Antichità Altoadriatiche*
ABR	*American Benedictine Review*
ACW	Ancient Christian Writers (New York: Paulist Press)
AncSoc	*Ancient Society*
ANRW	*Aufstieg und Niedergang der römischen Welt*
APB	*Acta Patristica et Byzantina*
ASE	*Anglo-Saxon England*
BASP	*Bulletin of the American Society of Papyrologists*
BSac	*Bibliotheca Sacra*
CCR	*Coptic Church Review*
CCSL	Corpus Christianorum, Series Latina
ChH	*Church History*
CollCist	*Collectanea Cisterciensia*
CQ	*Classical Quarterly*
CSEL	Corpus Scriptorum Ecclesiasticorum Latinorum
DACL	*Dictionnaire d'archéologie chrétienne et de liturgie*
DOP	*Dumbarton Oaks Papers*
ET	*Église et Théologie*
FAM	*Filologia Antica e Moderna*
FOTC	Fathers of the Church (Washington, DC: The Catholic University of America Press)
GHM	*Greek Historia monachorum in Aegypto*
GRBS	*Greek, Roman, and Byzantine Studies*
HSCP	*Harvard Studies in Classical Philology*
JAS	*Journal of Archaeological Science*
JbAC	*Jahrbuch für Antike und Christentum*
JEA	*Journal of Egyptian Archaeology*
JECS	*Journal of Early Christian Studies*
JHSex	*Journal of the History of Sexuality*
JJP	*Journal of Juristic Papyrology*
JLA	*Journal of Late Antiquity*
JRA	*Journal of Roman Archaeology*
JRS	*Journal of Roman Studies*

JThS	*Journal of Theological Studies*
LHM	*Latin Historia monachorum in Aegypto*
LICS	*Leeds International Classical Studies*
LO	*Lex Orandi*
M&L	*Music & Letters*
MEFRA	*Mélanges de l'École Française de Rome (Antiquité)*
MonStud	*Monastic Studies*
NovTest	*Novum Testamentum*
NT	New Testament
OC	*Oriens Christianus*
OCA	*Orientialia Christiana Analecta*
OLP	*Orientalia Lovaniensia Periodica*
OT	Old Testament
P&P	*Past & Present*
PEQ	*Palestine Exploration Quarterly*
PG	Patrologia Graeca, ed. J.-P. Migne, Paris, 1857–66
PL	Patrologia Latina, ed. J.-P. Migne, Paris, 1878–90
PP	*La Parola del Passato*
RBén	*Revue Bénédictine*
RBS	*Regulae Benedicti Studia*
RCCM	*Rivista di Cultura Classica e Medievale*
RdE	*Revue d'Égyptologie*
REAug	*Revue des Études Augustiniennes*
RHE	*Revue d'Histoire Ecclésiastique*
RhM	*Rheinisches Museum für Philologie*
RLAC	*Reallexikon für Antike und Christentum*
RMon	*Revue Monastique*
RPL	*Res Publica Litterarum*
RQ	*Restoration Quarterly*
RSR	*Revue des Sciences Religieuses*
SCO	*Studi Classici e Orientali*
SecCent	*Second Century*
SOCC	*Studia Orientalia Christiana: Collectanea*
StLit	*Studia Liturgica*
StudPatr	*Studia Patristica*
SVTQ	*St. Vladimir's Theological Quarterly*
TZ	*Trierer Zeitschrift für Geschichte und Kunst des Trierer Landes und seiner Nachbargebiete*
VChr	*Vigiliae Christianae*
ZAC	*Zeitschrift für Antikes Christentum*
ZKG	*Zeitschrift für Kirchengeschichte*
ZPE	*Zeitschrift für Papyrologie und Epigraphik*

BIBLIOGRAPHY

Rufinus's Life and Writings

Adkin, N. "Rufinus Terentianus." *RPL* n.s. 9 (2006): 142–44.
———. "Rufinus Vergilianus." *Orpheus* n.s. 27 (2006): 1–4.
———. "Rufinus Ciceronianus." *RBén* 117 (2007): 5–8.
Amacker, R., and Junod, É., eds. and trans. *Pamphile et Eusèbe de Césarée, Apologie pour Origène.* 2 vols. (Paris, 2002).
Amidon, P., trans. Rufinus of Aquileia. *History of the Church.* FOTC 133. Washington, DC: The Catholic University of America Press, 2016.
Bammel, C. H. "The Last Ten Years of Rufinus' Life and the Date of his Move South from Aquileia," *JThS* n.s. 28 (1977): 372–429.
———. "Rufinus' Translation of Origen's *Commentary on Romans* and the Pelagian Controversy." *AAAd* 39 (1992): 131–49.
———. "Problems of the *Historia monachorum*." *JThS* n.s. 47 (1996): 92–104.
Barkley, G. W., trans. Origen. *Homilies on Leviticus 1–16.* FOTC 83. Washington, DC: The Catholic University of America Press, 1990.
Bohlin, T. *Die Theologie des Pelagius und ihre Genesis.* Uppsala: Lundequist, 1957, 87–103.
Brooks, E. C. "The Translation Techniques of Rufinus of Aquileia (343–411)." *StudPatr* 17 (1982): 357–64.
Bruce, B. J., trans. Origen. *Homilies on Joshua.* FOTC 105. Washington, DC: The Catholic University of America Press, 2002.
Carlini, A. "Le Sentenze di Sesto nella versione di Rufino. Vel enchiridion si Graece vel anulus si Latine." In *Studi forogiuliesi: In onore di Carlo Guido Mor*, ed. G. Fornasir, 109–18. Udine: Deputazione di storia patria per il Friuli, 1984.
Chadwick, H. "Rufinus and the Tura Papyrus of Origen's Commentary on Romans." *JThS* n.s. 10 (1959): 10–42.
Corte, F. della. "L'Anulus Sexti di Rufino." *AAAd* 31 (1987): 195–205.
Crouzel, H. "Rufino traduttore del *Peri Archon* di Origene." *AAAd* 31 (1987): 129–39.
———. "I prologhi di Rufino alle sue traduzioni di Origene." *AAAd* 39 (1992): 109–20.
Dively Lauro, E. A., trans. Origen. *Homilies on Judges.* FOTC 119. Washington, DC: The Catholic University of America Press, 2010.

Duval, Y.-M. "Rufin d'Aquilée émule de Jérôme de Stridon." In *Dieu(x) et hommes: Histoire et iconographie des sociétés païennes et chrétiennes de l'antiquité à nos jours. Mélanges de Françoise Thelamon*, ed. S. Crogiez-Pétrequin, 163–85. Rouen: Publications des Universités de Rouen et du Havre, 2005.

————. "Le texte latin des *Reconnaissances clémentines:* Rufin, les interpolations et les raisons de sa traduction." In *Nouvelles intrigues pseudo-clémentines*, ed. F. Amsler, A. Frey, C. Touati, and R. Girardet, 79–92. Prahins: Éditions du Zèbre, 2008.

Fedalto, G. "Rufino di Concordia: Elementi di una biografia." *AAAd* 39 (1992): 19–44.

Grappone, A. *Omelie origeniane nella traduzione di Rufino: Un confronto con i testi greci.* Rome: Institutum Patristicum Augustinianum, 2007.

Heine, R., trans. Origen. *Homilies on Genesis and Exodus.* FOTC 71. Washington, DC: The Catholic University of America Press, 1982.

Hill, K. D. "Rufinus as an Interpreter of Origen: Ascetic Affliction in the *Commentarii in Epistulam ad Romanos.*" *Augustiniana* 60 (2010): 145–68.

Hoppe, H. "Rufin als Übersetzer." In *Studi dedicati alla memoria di Paolo Ubaldi*, ed. A. Gemelli, 133–50. Milan: Vita e pensiero, 1937.

Humphries, M. "Rufinus's Eusebius: Translation, Continuation, and Edition in the Latin *Ecclesiastical History.*" *JECS* 16 (2008): 143–64.

Lawson, R. P., trans. Origen. *The Song of Songs, Commentary and Homilies.* ACW 26. New York: Paulist Press, 1957.

Lo Cicero, C. "Rufino, Basilio e Seneca: Fra aemulatio e arte allusive." *FAM* 14 (1998): 177–82.

————. "Φρόνημα σαρκός: Tertulliano e Rufino." In *Terpsis: In ricordo di Maria Laetitia Coletti*, ed. M. S. Celentano, 295–311. Alexandria: Edizioni dell'Orso, 2002.

————. "I cristiani e la traduzione letteraria: Il caso di Rufino di Aquileia." In *Forme letterarie nella produzione latina di IV–V secolo: Con uno sguardo a Bisanzio*, ed. F. Consolino, 91–126. Rome: Herder, 2003.

————. *Tradurre i greci nel IV secolo: Rufino di Aquileia e le omelie di Basilio.* Rome: Herder, 2008.

Marti, H. "Rufinus' Translation of St. Basil's Sermon on Fasting." *StudPatr* 16 (1985): 418–22.

Mitchell, S. "The Life and *Lives* of Gregory Thaumaturgus." In *Portraits of Spiritual Authority: Religious Power in Early Christianity, Byzantium and the Christian Orient*, ed. J. W. Drijvers and J. W. Watt, 99–138. Leiden: Brill, 1999.

Moreschini, C. "Rufino traduttore di Gregorio Nazianzeno." *AAAd* 31 (1987): 227–85.

————. "La traduzione di Rufino dalle *Omelie* di Basilio: Motivi e scopi di una scelta." In *La traduzione dei testi religiosi*, ed. C. Moreschini and G. Menestrina, 127–47. Brescia: Morcelliana, 1994.

————. "Motivi romanzeschi e interessi cristiani nelle *Recognitiones* dello Pseudo Clemente tradotte da Rufino." *Koinonia* 35 (2011): 179–96.

Muraru, A. "Strategies of Translation in Late Antiquity: Rufinus and the Bilingual Readers of Origen's *Homilia in Exodum* 9." *Adamantius* 17 (2011): 297–302.

Murphy, F. X. *Rufinus of Aquileia (345–410): His Life and Works.* Washington, DC: The Catholic University of America Press, 1945.

Neil, B. "Rufinus' Translation of the *Epistola Clementis ad Iacobum.*" *Augustinianum* 43 (2003): 25–39.

Noce, C. "Some Questions about Rufinus' Translation of Origen's *Homiliae in Leviticum.*" *StudPatr* 43 (2006): 451–58.

Oulton, J. E. L. "Rufinus' Translation of the *Church History* of Eusebius." *JThS* 30 (1929): 150–74.

Pace, N. *Ricerche sulla traduzione di Rufino del* De principiis *di Origene.* Florence: La Nuova Italia, 1990.

Porta, P. C. "L'omelia sul Levitico 5,1: Origene e Rufino a confronto." *Orpheus* 13 (1992): 52–76.

Salvini, A. "Sulla tecnica di traduzione dal greco in latino nelle *Homiliae Morales* di Basilio-Rufino." *SCO* 46 (1998): 845–89.

Scheck, T., trans. Origen. *Commentary on the Epistle to the Romans, Books 1–5.* FOTC 103. Washington, DC: The Catholic University of America Press, 2001.

———, trans. Origen. *Commentary on the Epistle to the Romans, Books 6–10.* FOTC 104. Washington, DC: The Catholic University of America Press, 2002.

———, trans. Pamphilus. *Apology for Origen.* Rufinus. *On the Falsification of the Books of Origen.* FOTC 120. Washington, DC: The Catholic University of America Press, 2010.

Schulz-Flügel, E., ed. *Tyrannius Rufinus, Historia monachorum sive De vita sanctorum patrum.* Berlin: De Gruyter, 1990.

Silvas, A. M. "Rufinus' Translation Techniques in the *Regula Basili.*" *Antichthon* 37 (2003): 71–93.

———. *The Asketikon of St. Basil the Great.* Oxford: Oxford University Press, 2005.

———, trans. *The Rule of St. Basil in Latin and English: A Revised Critical Edition.* Collegeville, MN: Liturgical Press, 2013.

Simonetti, M. "Osservazioni sul *De benedictionibus patriarcharum* di Rufino di Aquileia." *RCCM* 4 (1962): 3–44.

Thelamon, F. *Païens et chrétiens au IVe siècle: L'apport de* l'Histoire ecclésiastique *de Rufin d'Aquilée.* Paris, 1981.

———. "Rufin historien de son temps." *AAAd* 31 (1987): 41–59.

———. "Apôtres et prophètes de notre temps: Les évêques et les moines présentés comme apôtres et prophètes contemporains dans l'*Histoire Ecclésiastique* de Rufin." *AAAd* 39 (1992): 171–94.

Torben, C. *Rufinus of Aquileia and the* Historia Ecclesiastica, *Lib. VIII–IX, of Eusebius.* Copenhagen, 1989.

Trettel, G. *Rufino di Concordia, Storia di monaci. Traduzione, introduzione e note*. Rome: Città nuova editrice, 1991.
Vessey, M. "Jerome and Rufinus." In *The Cambridge History of Early Christian Literature*, ed. F. Young, L. Ayres, and A. Louth, 318–27. Cambridge: Cambridge University Press, 2004.
Villain, M. "Rufin d'Aquilée, commentateur du Symbole des Apôtres." *RSR* 31 (1944): 129–56.
Vogüé, A. de. *Histoire littéraire du mouvement monastique dans l'antiquité, 3: Jérôme, Augustin et Rufin au tournant du siècle (391–405)*. Paris: Cerf, 1996.
Wagner, M. M. *Rufinus the Translator. A Study of his Theory and his Practice as Illustrated in his Version of the* Apologetica *of St. Gregory Nazianzen*. Washington, DC: The Catholic University of America Press, 1945.
Winkelmann, F. "Einige Bemerkungen zu den Aussagen des Rufinus von Aquileia und des Hieronymus über ihre Übersetzungstheorie und -methode." In *Kyriakon: Festschrift Johannes Quasten*, ed. P. Granfield and J. Jungmann, 532–47. Münster: Verlag Aschendorff, 1970.

The Greek *Historia monachorum in Aegypto*

Cain, A. "The Style of the Greek *Historia Monachorum in Aegypto*." *REAug* 58 (2012): 57–96.
———. "The Greek *Historia monachorum in Aegypto* and the *Life of Antony*." *VChr* 67 (2013): 349–63.
———. *The Greek* Historia monachorum in Aegypto: *Monastic Hagiography in the Late Fourth Century*. Oxford: Oxford University Press, 2016.
Festugière, A.-J. "Le problème littéraire de l'*Historia monachorum*." *Hermes* 83 (1955): 257–84.
———, ed. *Historia monachorum in Aegypto. Édition critique du texte grec*. Brussels: Société des Bollandistes, 1961.
Frank, G. "The *Historia monachorum in Aegypto* and Ancient Travel Writing." *StudPatr* 30 (1997): 191–95.
———. "Miracles, Monks and Monuments: The *Historia monachorum in Aegypto* as Pilgrims' Tales." In *Pilgrimage and Holy Space in Late Antique Egypt*, ed. D. Frankfurter, 483–505. Leiden, 1998.
Frank, S., trans. *Mönche im frühchristlichen Ägypten (Historia Monachorum in Aegypto)*. Düsseldorf, 1967.
Gascou, L. "La vie de Patermouthios moine et fossoyeur (*Historia Monachorum* X)." In *Itinéraires d'Égypte. Mélanges M. Martin*, ed. C. Décobert, 107–14. Cairo: IFAO, 1992.
Horst, P. W. van der, trans. *Woestijn, begeerte en geloof. De Historia monachorum in Aegypto (ca. 400 na Chr.)*. Kampen, 1995.
Moschos, D. "Kontinuität und Umbruch in mittelägyptischen Mönchsgruppen nach der *Historia monachorum in Aegypto*." *JbAC* 12 (2008): 267–85.

Preuschen, E. *Palladius und Rufinus. Ein Beitrag zur Quellenkunde des ältesten Mönchtums.* Giessen: J. Rickersche Buchhandlung, 1897.

Reitzenstein, R. Historia monachorum *und* Historia Lausiaca. *Eine Studie zur Geschichte des Mönchtums und der frühchristlichen Begriffe Gnostiker und Pneumatiker.* Göttingen: Vandenhoeck & Ruprecht, 1916.

Russell, N., trans. *The Lives of the Desert Fathers: The* Historia monachorum in Aegypto. With introduction by B. Ward. Kalamazoo: Cistercian Publications, 1980.

Tóth, P. "Lost in Translation: An Evagrian Term in the Different Versions of the *Historia monachorum in Aegypto.*" In *Origeniana, IX,* ed. G. Heidl and R. Somos, 613–21. Leuven: Peeters, 2009.

———. "Honey on the Brim of the Poison [*sic*] Cup: Translation and Propaganda in Rufinus' Latin Version of the *Historia monachorum in Aegypto.*" In *Greek into Latin from Antiquity until the Nineteenth Century,* ed. J. Glucker and C. Burnett, 117–29. London: Routledge, 2012.

Woods, D. "An Imperial Embassy in the *Historia monachorum.*" *JThS* n.s. 48 (1997): 133–36.

Evagrius of Pontus

Bamberger, J. E., trans. *Evagrius Ponticus: The Praktikos, Chapters on Prayer.* Kalamazoo: Cistercian Publications, 1981.

Bitton-Ashkelony, B. "The Limit of the Mind (ΝΟΥΣ): Pure Prayer according to Evagrius Ponticus and Isaac of Nineveh." *ZAC* 15 (2011): 291–321.

Bunge, G. "Évagre le Pontique et les deux Macaires." *Irénikon* 56 (1983): 215–27, 323–60.

———, trans. *Evagrios Pontikos: Briefe aus der Wüste.* Trier: Beuroner Kunstverlag, 1986.

———. "The Spiritual Prayer: On the Trinitarian Mysticism of Evagrius of Pontus." *MonStud* 17 (1987): 191–208.

———. *Das Geistgebet: Studien zum Traktat* De oratione *des Evagrios Pontikos.* Cologne: De Gruyter, 1987.

———. "La montagne intelligible: De la contemplation indirecte à la connaissance immédiate de Dieu dans le traité *De oratione* d'Évagre le Pontique." *StudMon* 42 (2000): 7–26.

Casiday, A. "*Apatheia* and Sexuality in the Thought of Augustine and Cassian." *SVTQ* 45 (2001): 359–94.

———. "Gabriel Bunge and the Study of Evagrius Ponticus: Review Article." *SVTQ* 48 (2004): 249–98.

———. *Reconstructing the Theology of Evagrius Ponticus.* Cambridge: Cambridge University Press, 2013.

Clark, E. A. *The Origenist Controversy: The Cultural Construction of an Early Christian Debate.* Princeton: Princeton University Press, 1992.

Corrigan, K. *Evagrius and Gregory: Mind, Soul and Body in the 4th Century.* Farnham: Ashgate, 2009.

Driscoll, J. *"Apatheia* and Purity of Heart in Evagrius Ponticus." In *Purity of Heart in Early Ascetic and Monastic Literature: Essays in Honor of Juana Raasch,* ed. H. A. Luckman and L. Kulzer, 141–59. Collegeville, MN: Liturgical Press, 1999.

————. *Steps to Spiritual Perfection: Studies on Spiritual Progress in Evagrius Ponticus.* New York: Paulist Press, 2005.

Dysinger, L. *Psalmody and Prayer in the Writings of Evagrius Ponticus.* Oxford: Oxford University Press, 2005.

Elm, S. "The *Sententiae ad Virginem* by Evagrius Ponticus and the Problem of the Early Monastic Rules." *Augustinianum* 30 (1990): 393–404.

————. "Evagrius Ponticus' *Sententiae ad Virginem.*" *DOP* 45 (1991): 265–95.

Frankenberg, W., ed. *Evagrius Ponticus.* Berlin: Weidmann, 1912.

Guillaumont, A. *Les 'Képhalaia Gnostica' d'Évagre le Pontique et l'histoire de l'origénisme chez les grecs et chez les syriens.* Paris: Éditions de Seuil, 1962.

————. *Un philosophe au désert: Évagre le Pontique.* Paris: J. Vrin, 2004.

Hausherr, I. *Les leçons d'un contemplatif: Le traité de l'Oraison d'Évagre le Pontique.* Paris: Beauchesne, 1960.

Konstantinovsky, J. *Evagrius Ponticus: The Making of a Gnostic.* Aldershot: Ashgate, 2009.

Maier, B. *"Apatheia* bei den Stoikern und *Akedia* bei Evagrios Pontikos: Ein Ideal und die Kehrseite seiner Realität." *OC* 78 (1994): 230–49.

Ousley, D. *Evagrius' Theology of Prayer and the Spiritual Life.* Diss., Univ. of Chicago, 1979.

Parmentier, M. "Evagrius of Pontus' *Letter to Melania.*" In *Forms of Devotion: Conversion, Worship, Spirituality, and Asceticism,* ed. E. Ferguson, 272–309. New York: Routledge, 1999.

Sinkewicz, R. E., trans. *Evagrius of Pontus: The Greek Ascetic Corpus.* Oxford: Oxford University Press, 2003.

Somos, R. "Origen, Evagrius Ponticus, and the Ideal of Impassibility." In *Origeniana septima,* ed. W. A. Bienert and U. Kühneweg, 365–73. Leuven: Peeters, 1999.

Stewart, C. "Evagrius Ponticus and the Eight Generic *Logismoi.*" In *In the Garden of Evil: The Vices and Culture in the Middle Ages,* ed. R. Newhauser, 3–34. Toronto: Pontifical Institute of Medieval Studies, 2005.

Vitestam, G., ed. *La seconde partie du traité qui passe sous le nom de La Grande Lettre d'Évagre le Pontique à Mélanie l'Ancienne.* Lund: CWK Gleerup, 1964.

Vivian, T. "Coptic Palladiana II: The Life of Evagrius (*Lausiac History* 38)." *CCR* 21 (2000): 8–23.

Zöckler, O. *Evagrius Pontikus: Seine Stellung in der altchristlichen Literatur- und Dogmengeschichte.* Munich: Beck, 1893.

Egypt and Egyptian Monasticism

Adams, C. *Land Transport in Roman Egypt.* Oxford: Oxford University Press, 2007.

Alston, R., and R. D. Alston. "Urbanism and the Urban Community in Roman Egypt." *JEA* 83 (1997): 199–216.

Amélineau, E. *De Historia Lausiaca quaenam sit huius ad monachorum Aegyptiorum historiam scribendam utilitas.* Paris: Leroux, 1887.

Ashley Hall, H. "The Role of the Eucharist in the Lives of the Desert Fathers." *StudPatr* 39 (2006): 367–72.

Badilita, C., and A. Jakab, eds. *Jean Cassien entre l'Orient et l'Occident.* Paris: Beauchesne, 2003.

Bagnall, R. *Egypt in Late Antiquity.* Princeton: Princeton University Press, 1995.

Bagnall, R., and D. Rathbone, eds. *Egypt from Alexander to the Early Christians.* Los Angeles: Getty Publications, 2004.

Bauer, J. B. "*Vidisti fratrem vidisti dominum tuum* (Agraphon 144 Resch und 126 Resch)." *ZKG* 100 (1989): 71–76.

Baumeister, T. "Ägyptisches Lokalkolorit in der *Historia monachorum in Aegypto.*" In *Aegyptus Christiana: Mélanges d'hagiographie égyptienne et orientale dédiés à la mémoire du P. Paul Devos bollandiste,* ed. U. Zanetti and E. Lucchesi, 165–74. Geneva: Patrick Cramer, 2004.

Behlmer, H. "Visitors to Shenoute's Monastery." In *Pilgrimage and Holy Space in Late Antique Egypt,* ed. D. Frankfurter, 341–71. Leiden: Brill, 1998.

Bonneau, D. *La crue du Nil, divinité égyptienne, à travers mille ans d'histoire.* Paris: Klincksieck, 1964.

———. "Les fêtes de la crue du Nil: Problèmes de lieux, de dates et d'organisation." *RdE* 23 (1971): 49–65.

Bonnerue, P. "*Opus* et *labor* dans les règles monastiques anciennes." *StudMon* 35 (1993): 265–91.

Bowman, A. K., et al., eds. *Oxyrhynchus: A City and its Texts.* London: Egypt Exploration Society, 2007.

Brakke, D. "The Problematization of Nocturnal Emissions in Early Christian Syria, Egypt, and Gaul." *JECS* 3 (1995): 419–60.

———. "Ethiopian Demons: Male Sexuality, the Black-Skinned Other, and the Monastic Self." *JHSex* 10 (2001): 501–35.

———. "The Making of Monastic Demonology: Three Ascetic Teachers on Withdrawal and Resistance." *ChH* 70 (2001): 32–41.

Budge, E. A., ed. *Paradisus partum.* Vol. 2. Oxford: Clarendon Press, 1904.

Bunge, G., and A. de Vogüé, eds. *Quatre ermites égyptiens d'après les fragments coptes de l'*Histoire Lausiaque. Bégrolles-en-Mauges: Abbaye de Bellefontaine, 1994.

Burton-Christie, D. *The Word in the Desert: Scripture and the Quest for*

Holiness in Early Christian Monasticism. New York: Oxford University Press, 1993.

Calandra, E. "La città e il nome: Progetto politico e utopia nella fondazione di Antinoe." In *Utopia e utopie nel pensiero storico antico,* ed. C. Carsana and M. Schettino, 133–59. Rome: Bretschneider, 2008.

Chitty, D. *The Desert a City.* Oxford: Blackwell, 1966.

———, trans. *The Letters of Ammonas, Successor of Saint Antony.* Oxford: SLG Press, 1979.

Clackson, S. J. *Coptic and Greek Texts relating to the Hermopolite Monastery of Apa Apollo.* Oxford: Griffith Institute, 2000.

Coquin, R. G. "Les origines de l'Epiphanie en Égypte." *LO* 47 (1967): 139–70.

———. "Apollon de Titkooh ou/et Apollon de Bawît?" *Orientalia* n.s. 46 (1977): 435–46.

Courtès, J. M. "The Theme of 'Ethiopia' and 'Ethiopians' in Patristic Literature." In *The Image of the Black in Western Art from the Early Christian Era to the "Age of Discovery": From Demonic Threat to the Incarnation of Sainthood,* vol. II/1, ed. D. Bindman and H. L. Gates, 199–214. Cambridge, MA: Harvard University Press, 2010.

Davril, A. "La Psalmodie chez les pères du désert." *CollCist* 49 (1987): 132–39.

Dechow, J. F. *Dogma and Mysticism in Early Christianity: Epiphanius of Cyprus and the Legacy of Origen.* Macon, GA: Mercer University Press, 1988.

Dietz, M. *Wandering Monks, Virgins, and Pilgrims: Ascetic Travel in the Mediterranean World, A.D. 300–800.* University Park: Penn State University Press, 2005.

Driver, S. *John Cassian and the Reading of Egyptian Monastic Culture.* London: Routledge, 2002.

Evelyn-White, H. G. *The Monasteries of the Wadi'n Natrun, 2: The History of the Monasteries of Nitria and Scetis.* New York: Metropolitan Museum of Art, 1932.

Frankfurter, D. *Religion in Roman Egypt: Assimilation and Resistance.* Princeton: Princeton University Press, 1998.

Gindele, C. "Bienen-, Waben- und Honigvergleiche in der frühen monastischen Literatur." *RBS* 6/7 (1981): 1–26.

Goehring, J. E. *The Letter of Ammon and Pachomian Monasticism.* Berlin: De Gruyter, 1986.

———. "Hieracas of Leontopolis: The Making of a Desert Ascetic." In *Ascetics, Society, and the Desert: Studies in Early Egyptian Monasticism,* ed. J. E. Goehring, 110–36. Harrisburg: Trinity Press International, 1999.

Gould, G. *The Desert Fathers on Monastic Community.* Oxford: Oxford University Press, 1993.

———. "Lay Christians, Bishops, and Clergy in the *Apophthegmata patrum.*" *StudPatr* 25 (1993): 396–404.

Guillaumont, A. "Le problème des deux Macaires dans les *Apophtheg-mata patrum.*" *Irénikon* 48 (1975): 41–59.
————. "Histoire des moines aux Kellia." *OLP* 8 (1977): 187–203.
————. "Les fouilles françaises des Kellia, 1964–1969." In *The Future of Coptic Studies,* ed. R. M. Wilson, 203–8. Leiden: Brill, 1978.
Guillaumont, A., and R. Kasser. "Fouilles suisses aux Kellia: Passé, présent, et future." In *The Future of Coptic Studies,* ed. R. M. Wilson, 209–19. Leiden: Brill, 1978.
————. "Le problème de la prière continuelle dans le monachisme ancient." In *Études sur la spiritualité de l'Orient chrétien,* ed. A. Guillaumont, 131–41. Bégrolles-en-Mauges: Abbaye de Bellefontaine, 1996.
Hausherr, I. "Hésychasme et prière." *OCA* 176 (1966): 255–306.
Hermann, A. "Der Nil und die Christen." *JbAC* 2 (1959): 30–69.
Hohlwein, N. "Déplacements et tourisme dans l'Égypte romaine." *Chronique d'Égypte* 15 (1940): 253–78.
Johnson, D. W. "Coptic Reactions to Gnosticism and Manichaeism." *Le Muséon* 100 (1987): 199–209.
Jullien, M. "A la recherche de Tabenne et des autres monastères fondés par saint Pachôme." *Études* 89 (1901): 238–58.
Keenan, J. G. "Evidence for the Byzantine Army in the Syene Papyri." *BASP* 27 (1990): 139–50.
————. "Soldier and Civilian in Byzantine Hermopolis." In *Proceedings of the 20th International Congress of Papyrologists, Copenhagen, 23–29 August 1992,* ed. A. Bülow-Jacobsen, 444–51. Njalsgade: Museum Tusculanum Press, 1994.
Koenen, L. "Manichäischer Mission und Klöster in Ägypten." In *Das römisch-byzantinische Ägypten,* 2, ed. G. Grimm, 93–108. Mainz: Philipp von Zabern, 1983.
Krause, M. *Das Apa-Apollon-Kloster zu Bawit: Untersuchungen unveröffentlicher Urkunden als Beitrag zur Geschichte des ägyptischen Mönchtums.* Diss., Karl-Marx-Universität, 1958.
Krause, M., and K. Wessel. "Bawit." In *Reallexikon zur byzantinische Kunst,* I, ed. K. Wessel and M. Restle, 569–83. Stuttgart: Hiersemann, 1966.
Krüger, J. *Oxyrhynchus in der Kaizerzeit: Studien zur Topographie und Literaturrezeption.* Frankfurt: Peter Lang, 1990.
Kyrtatas, D. J. "Living in Tombs: The Secret of an Early Christian Mystical Experience." In *Mystery and Secrecy in the Nag Hammadi Collection and Other Ancient Literature: Ideas and Practices,* ed. C. H. Bull, L. Lied, and J. D. Turner, 245–57. Leiden: Brill, 2012.
Layton, R. *Didymus the Blind and his Circle in Late-Antique Alexandria: Virtue and Narrative in Biblical Scholarship.* Urbana: University of Illinois Press, 2004.
Lembke, K., C. Fluck, and G. Vittmann. *Ägyptens späte Blüte: Die Römer am Nil.* Mainz: Philipp von Zabern, 2004.
Louf, A. "Spiritual Fatherhood in the Literature of the Desert." In

Abba: Guides to Wholeness and Holiness East and West, ed. J. R. Sommerfeldt, 37–63. Kalamazoo: Cistercian Publications, 1982.

Luijendijk, A. *Greetings in the Lord: Early Christians and the Oxyrhynchus Papyri.* Cambridge, MA: Harvard University Press, 2008.

MacCoull, L. S. B. "*Stud. Pal.* XV 250ab: A Monophysite Trishagion for the Nile Flood." *JThS* n.s. 40 (1989): 129–35.

Mayerson, P. "The *modius* as a Grain Measure in Papyri from Egypt." *BASP* 43 (2006): 101–6.

McKinnon, J. W. "Desert Monasticism and the Later Fourth-Century Psalmodic Movement." *M&L* 75 (1994): 505–21.

McNary-Zak, B. *Useful Servanthood: A Study of Spiritual Formation in the Writings of Abba Ammonas.* Kalamazoo: Cistercian Publications, 2010.

Meyer, M., ed. *Ancient Christian Magic: Coptic Texts of Ritual Power.* San Francisco, 1994.

Minnen, P. van. "P.Oxy. LXVI 4527 and the Antonine Plague in the Fayyum." *ZPE* 135 (2001): 175–77.

Nugent, A. "Black Demons in the Desert." *ABR* 49 (1998): 209–21.

O'Connell, E. R. "Transforming Monumental Landscapes in Late Antique Egypt: Monastic Dwellings in Legal Documents from Western Thebes." *JECS* 2 (2007): 239–73.

Papaconstantinou, A. "Les évêques byzantins d'Oxyrhynchus." *ZPE* 111 (1996): 171–74.

Regnault, L. *Abba, dis-moi une parole.* Solesmes: Abbaye St-Pierre, 1984.

———. *La vie quotidienne des Pères du désert en Égypte au IVe siècle.* Paris: Hachette, 1990.

Rich, A. D. *Discernment in the Desert Fathers: Διάκρισις in the Life and Thought of Early Egyptian Monasticism.* Waynesboro: Paternoster, 2007.

Seston, W. "L'Égypte manichéenne." *Chronique d'Égypte* 14 (1939): 362–72.

Sheridan, M. "John of Lycopolis." In *Christianity and Monasticism in Middle Egypt,* ed. G. Gabra and H. Takla, 123–32. Cairo: The American University in Cairo Press, 2015.

Shortland, A. "Natron as a Flux in the Early Vitreous Materials Industry: Sources, Beginnings, and Reasons for Decline." *JAS* 33 (2006): 521–30.

Snowden, F. *Blacks in Antiquity: Ethiopians in the Greco-Roman Experience.* Cambridge, MA: Harvard University Press, 1970.

Stroumsa, G. "The Manichaean Challenge to Egyptian Christianity." In *The Roots of Egyptian Christianity,* ed. B. Pearson and J. Goehring, 307–19. Philadelphia: Augsburg Fortress Publishers, 1986.

Tardieu, M. "Les manichéens en Égypte." *BSFE* 94 (1982): 5–19.

Teja, R. "*Fuge, tace, quiesce:* El silencio de los Padres del desierto." In *Religión y silencio: El silencio en las religiones antiguas,* ed. S. Montero and M. Cruz Cardete, 201–7. Madrid: Publicaciones UCM, 2007.

Thompson, D. J. *Memphis under the Ptolemies*. Princeton: Princeton University Press, 1988.

Torp, H. "La date de la fondation du monastère d'Apa Apollo de Baouit et de son abandon." *MEFRA* 77 (1965): 153–77.

———. "Le monastère copte de Baouit: Quelques notes d'introduction." In *Acta ad archaeologiam et artium historiam pertinentia*, ed. H. Torp, 1–8. Rome: Institutum Romanum Norvegiae, 1981.

Veilleux, A. "Monasticism and Gnosis in Egypt." In *The Roots of Egyptian Christianity*, ed. B. A. Pearson and J. E. Goehring, 271–306. Philadelphia: Augsburg Fortress Publishers, 1986.

Vergote, J. "L'expansion du manichéisme en Égypte." In *After Chalcedon: Studies in Theology and Church History*, ed. C. Laga and J. Munitiz, 471–78. Leuven: Katholieke Universiteit, 1985.

Vivian, T. "'Everything Made by God is Good': A Letter concerning Sexuality from Saint Athanasius to the Monk Amoun." *ET* 24 (1993): 75–108.

Voytenko, A. "Paradise Regained or Paradise Lost: The Coptic (Sahidic) Life of St. Onnophrius and Egyptian Monasticism at the End of the Fourth Century." In *Actes du huitième congrès international d'études coptes*, II, 635–44. Leuven: Peeters, 2007.

Waddell, H. *The Desert Fathers*. Ann Arbor, 1957.

Ward, B., trans. *The Sayings of the Desert Fathers: The Alphabetical Collection*. Kalamazoo: Cistercian Publications, 1984.

———. *Harlots of the Desert: A Study of Repentance in Early Monastic Sources*. Kalamazoo: Cistercian Publications, 1987.

Ware, K. T. "Silence in Prayer: The Meaning of Hesychia." In *One Yet Two Monastic Traditions East and West*, ed. B. Pennington, 22–47. Kalamazoo: Cistercian Publications, 1976.

Whitehorne, J. "The Pagan Cults of Roman Oxyrhynchus." *ANRW* II, 18.5, 3050–91.

Wipszycka, E. *Moines et communautés monastiques en Égypte (IVe–VIIIe siècles)*. Warsaw: Journal of Juristic Papyrology, 2009.

Wipszycka, E., and T. Derda. "L'emploi des titres abba, apa et papas dans l'Église byzantine." *JJP* 24 (1994): 23–56.

Worp, K. A. "A Checklist of Bishops in Byzantine Egypt (A.D. 325–c.750)." *ZPE* 100 (1994): 283–318.

Wortley, J. "The Spirit of Rivalry in Early Christian Monachism." *GRBS* 33 (1992): 383–404.

———. "*De latrone converso*: The Tale of the Converted Robber." *Byzantion* 66 (1996): 19–43.

———, ed. and trans. *The Anonymous Sayings of the Desert Fathers. A Select Edition and Complete English Translation*. Cambridge: Cambridge University Press, 2013.

Miscellaneous

Adams, J. N. *The Latin Sexual Vocabulary.* Baltimore: Johns Hopkins University Press, 1982.

———. "Words for 'Prostitute' in Latin." *RhM* 126 (1983): 321–58.

Alexander, D. *Saints and Animals in the Middle Ages.* Woodbridge: Boydell, 2008.

Amerise, M. *Girolamo e la senectus: Età della vita e morte nell'epistolario.* Rome, 2008.

Anderson, B. W. "The Slaying of the Fleeing, Twisting Serpent: Isaiah 27:1 in Context." In *Uncovering Ancient Stones: Essays in Memory of H. Neil Richardson,* ed. L. M. Hopfe, 3–15. Winona Lake, IN: Eisenbraums, 1994.

Antin, P. *Recueil sur saint Jérôme.* Brussels: Latomus, 1968.

Arnon, I. *Crop Production in Dry Regions, Volume I: Background and Principles.* London: Leonard Hill, 1972.

Ashbrook Harvey, S. *Asceticism and Society in Crisis: John of Ephesus and the 'Lives of the Eastern Saints.'* Berkeley: University of California Press, 1990.

———. "On Holy Stench: When the Odor of Sanctity Sickens." *StudPatr* 35 (2001): 90–101.

Bambeck, M. "*Puer et puella senes* bei Ambrosius von Mailand: Zur altchristlichen Vorgeschichte eines literarischen Topos." *RomForsch* 84 (1972): 257–313.

Barnes, T. D. "Proconsuls of Africa, 337–361." *Phoenix* 39 (1985): 144–53.

———. "Praetorian Prefects, 337–361." *ZPE* 94 (1992): 249–60.

Barrett-Lennard, R. J. S. *Christian Healing after the New Testament: Some Approaches to Illness in the Second, Third and Fourth Centuries.* Lanham: University Press of America, 1994.

Battenfield, J. R. "YHWH's Refutation of the Baal Myth through the Actions of Elijah and Elisha." In *Israel's Apostasy and Restoration: Essays in Honor of Roland K. Harrison,* ed. A. Gileadi, 19–37. Grand Rapids: Eerdmans, 1988.

Bauckham, R. *God and the Crisis of Freedom: Biblical and Contemporary Perspectives.* Louisville: John Knox Press, 2002.

Binns, J. *Ascetics and Ambassadors of Christ: The Monasteries of Palestine, 314–631.* Oxford: Oxford University Press, 1994.

Boddens Hosang, F. J. E. *Establishing Boundaries: Christian-Jewish Relations in Early Council Texts and the Writings of Church Fathers.* Leiden: Brill, 2010.

Bonner, S. F. *Education in Ancient Rome from the Elder Cato to the Younger Pliny.* Berkeley: University of California Press, 1977.

Bremmer, J. N. "*Christianus sum:* The Early Christian Martyrs and Christ." In *Eulogia: Mélanges offerts à A. A. R. Bastiaensen à l'occasion de son soixante-cinquième anniversaire,* ed. G. J. M. Bartelink, A. Hilhorst, and C. H. Kneepkens, 11–20. Steenbrugge: Abbatia S. Petri, 1991.

Brock, S. "Fire from Heaven: From Abel's Sacrifice to the Eucharist." *StudPatr* 25 (1993): 229–43.

Brodie, T. L. *Luke the Literary Interpreter: Luke-Acts as a Systematic Rewriting and Updating of the Elijah-Elisha Narrative in 1 and 2 Kings.* Diss., University of St. Thomas, 1981.

Bronner, L. *The Stories of Elijah and Elisha as Polemics against Baal Worship.* Leiden: Brill, 1968.

Brooks, E. W., ed. and trans. *John of Ephesus, Lives of the Eastern Saints.* Vol. 2. Turnhout: Brepols, 1924.

Brothwell, D. *Food in Antiquity.* Baltimore: Johns Hopkins University Press, 1998.

Brown, P. "The Diffusion of Manichaeism in the Roman Empire." *JRS* 59 (1969): 92–103.

Burke, P. "*Drances infensus:* A Study in Vergilian Character Portrayal." *TAPA* 108 (1978): 15–20.

Burton, P. *Language in the* Confessions *of Augustine.* Oxford: Oxford University Press, 2007.

Cain, A. "Origen, Jerome, and the *senatus Pharisaeorum.*" *Latomus* 65 (2006): 727–34.

———. *The Letters of Jerome: Asceticism, Biblical Exegesis, and the Construction of Christian Authority in Late Antiquity.* Oxford: Oxford University Press, 2009.

———. "Rethinking Jerome's Portraits of Holy Women." In *Jerome of Stridon: His Life, Writings, and Legacy,* ed. A. Cain and J. Lössl, 47–57. Aldershot: Ashgate, 2009.

———, trans. St. Jerome. *Commentary on Galatians.* FOTC 121. Washington, DC: The Catholic University of America Press, 2010.

———. *Jerome's Epitaph on Paula: A Commentary on the* Epitaphium Sanctae Paulae, *with an Introduction, Text, and Translation.* Oxford: Oxford University Press, 2013.

———. *Jerome and the Monastic Clergy: A Commentary on Letter 52 to Nepotian, with an Introduction, Text, and Translation.* Leiden: Brill, 2013.

———. "Apology and Polemic in Jerome's Prefaces to his Biblical Scholarship." In *Hieronymus als Exeget und Theologe: Der Koheletkommentar,* ed. E. Birnbaum and L. Schwienhorst-Schönberger, 107–28. Leuven: Peeters, 2014.

Cain, A., and N. Lenski, eds. *The Power of Religion in Late Antiquity.* Aldershot: Ashgate Publishing, 2009.

Cain, A., and J. Lössl, eds. *Jerome of Stridon: His Life, Writings and Legacy.* Aldershot: Ashgate, 2009.

Callu, J. P. "Le jardin des supplices au bas-empire." In *Du châtiment dans la cité: Supplices corporels et peine de mort dans le monde antique. Table ronde de Rome (9–11 novembre 1982),* 313–59. Rome: École Française, 1984.

Campen, F. H. M. van. *Latrocinium.* Nijgmegen, 1978.

Campos, J. "El *propositum* monástico en la tradición patrística." In *Miscellanea patristica,* 117–32. Madrid: Monasterio de El Escorial, 1968.

Caner, D. *Wandering, Begging Monks: Spiritual Authority and the Promotion of Monasticism in Late Antiquity.* Berkeley: University of California Press, 2002.

Capelle, B. "*Collecta.*" *RBén* 42 (1930): 197–204.

Capmany, J. "*Miles Christi*" en la espiritualidad de san Cipriano. Barcelona: Casulleras, 1956.

Carp, T. "*Puer senex* in Roman and Medieval Thought." *Latomus* 39 (1980): 736–39.

Casiday, A. "St Aldhelm's Bees (*De virginitate prosa* cc. IV–VI): Some Observations on a Literary Tradition." *ASE* 33 (2004): 1–22.

Chastagnol, A. *Les fastes de la préfecture de Rome au Bas Empire.* Paris: Nouvelles Éditions Latines, 1956.

Chin, C., and C. Schroeder, eds. *Melania: Early Christianity through the Life of One Family.* Oakland: University of California Press, 2017.

Coon, L. *Sacred Fictions: Holy Women and Hagiography in Late Antiquity.* Philadelphia: University of Pennsylvania Press, 1997.

Crouzel, H. "L'imitation et la suite de Dieu et du Christ dans les premiers siècles chrétiens ainsi que leurs sources gréco-romaines et hébraïques." *JbAC* 21 (1978): 7–41.

Dahl, N. A. "Benediction and Congratulation." In *Studies in Ephesians,* N. A. Dahl, 279–314. Tübingen: Mohr Siebeck, 2000.

Daniélou, J. *Sacramentum futuri: Études sur les origines de la typologie biblique.* Paris: Beauchesne, 1950.

Day, J. "God and Leviathan in Isaiah 27:1." *BSac* 155 (1998): 423–36.

Dekkers, E. "Les anciens moines cultivaient-ils la liturgie?" *La Maison-Dieu* 51 (1957): 31–54.

Deliyannis, D. M. "A Biblical Model for Serial Biography: The Book of Kings and the Roman *Liber Pontificalis.*" *RBén* 107 (1997): 15–23.

Dill, D. B. *The Hot Life of Man and Beast.* Springfield, IL: C.C. Thomas Publishing, 1985.

Dunn, G. "Widows and other Women in the Pastoral Ministry of Cyprian of Carthage." *Augustinianum* 45 (2005): 295–307.

Earl, J. W. "Typology and Iconographic Style in Early Medieval Hagiography." *Studies in the Literary Imagination* 8 (1975): 15–46.

Easterling, P., and E. Hall, eds. *Greek and Roman Actors: Aspects of an Ancient Profession.* Cambridge: Cambridge University Press, 2002.

Eggler, J. *Influences and Traditions Underlying the Vision of Daniel 7:2–14.* Göttingen: Vandenhoeck & Ruprecht, 2000.

Elsner, J. "From the Pyramids to Pausanias and Piglet: Monuments, Travel and Writing." In *Art and Text in Ancient Greek Culture,* ed. S. Goldhill and R. Osborne, 224–54. Cambridge: Cambridge University Press, 1994.

Ferguson, E. *Baptism in the Early Church: History, Theology, and Liturgy in the First Five Centuries*. Grand Rapids: Eerdmans, 2009.

Ferrua, A. "*Christianus sum.*" *CivCatt* 84 (1933): 13–26.

Finn, R. *Almsgiving in the Later Roman Empire: Christian Promotion and Practice, 313–450*. Oxford: Oxford University Press, 2006.

Finney, P. *The Invisible God: The Earliest Christians on Art*. Oxford: Oxford University Press, 1994.

Flusin, B. *Miracle et histoire dans l'œuvre de Cyrille de Scythopolis*. Paris: Études Augustiniennes, 1983.

Foreman, B. *Animal Metaphors and the People of Israel in the Book of Jeremiah*. Göttingen: Vandenhoeck & Ruprecht, 2011.

Frank, G. *The Memory of the Eyes: Pilgrims to Living Saints in Christian Late Antiquity*. Berkeley: University of California Press, 2000.

Frayn, J. M. *Subsistence Farming in Roman Italy*. Fontwell: Open Gate Press, 1979.

Frier, B. "Roman Life Expectancy: Ulpian's Evidence." *HSCP* 86 (1982): 213–51.

———. "Roman Life Expectancy: The Pannonian Evidence." *Phoenix* 37 (1983): 328–44.

Frost, P. "Attitudes towards Blacks in the Early Christian Era." *SecCent* 8 (1991): 1–11.

Gaddis, M. *There is No Crime for Those Who Have Christ: Religious Violence in the Christian Roman Empire*. Berkeley: University of California Press, 2005.

Gager, J., ed. *Curse Tablets and Binding Spells from the Ancient World*. Oxford: Oxford University Press, 1992.

Giardina, A. "Banditi e santi: Un aspetto del folklore gallico tra tarda antichità e medioevo." *Athenaeum* 61 (1983): 374–89.

Gijsel, J., and R. Beyers. *Pseudo-Matthaei Textus et Commentarius*. Turnhout: Brepols, 1997.

Goodrich, R. J. *Contextualizing Cassian: Aristocrats, Asceticism, and Reformation in Fifth-Century Gaul*. Oxford: Oxford University Press, 2007.

Goppelt, L. *Typos, die typologische Deutung des Alten Testaments im Neuen*. Gütersloh: Bertelsmann, 1939.

Gorce, D. *Les voyages, l'hospitalité et le port des lettres dans le monde chrétien des IVe et Ve siècles*. Paris: Monastère du Mont-Vierge, 1925.

Grant, R. M. *Miracle and Natural Law in Graeco-Roman and Early Christian Thought*. Amsterdam: Wipf and Stock, 1952.

Greer, R. "Hospitality in the First Five Centuries of the Church." *MonStud* 10 (1974): 29–48.

Griffith, S. "Asceticism in the Church of Syria: The Hermeneutics of Early Syrian Asceticism." In *Asceticism*, ed. V. Wimbush and R. Valantasis, 220–45. New York: Oxford University Press, 1995.

Hanson, R. P. C. *Allegory and Event: A Study of the Sources and Significance of Origen's Interpretation of Scripture*. Oxford: Oxford University Press, 1959.

Henken, E. R. *The Welsh Saints: A Study in Patterned Lives.* Woodbridge: Boydell, 1991.

Hersch, K. *The Roman Wedding: Ritual and Meaning in Antiquity.* Cambridge: Cambridge University Press, 2010.

Hirschfeld, Y. *The Judean Desert Monasteries in the Byzantine Period.* New Haven: Yale University Press, 1992.

Hobgood-Oster, L. *Holy Days and Asses: Animals in the Christian Tradition.* Urbana: University of Illinois Press, 2008.

Hoof, A. J. L. van. "Ancient Robbers: Reflections behind the Facts." *AncSoc* 19 (1988): 105–24.

Hopwood, K. "'All that may become a Man': The Bandit in the Ancient Novel." In *When Men were Men: Masculinity, Power, and Identity in Classical Antiquity,* ed. L. Foxhall and J. Salmon, 195–204. New York: Routledge, 1998.

Horst, P. W. van der. "The Role of Scripture in Cyril of Scythopolis' *Lives of the Monks of Palestine.*" In *The Sabaite Heritage in the Orthodox Church from the Fifth Century to the Present,* ed. J. Patrich, 127–45. Leuven: Peeters, 2001.

Ingenkamp, H. G. "Geschwätzigkeit." *RLAC* 10 (1978): 829–37.

Irudhayasamy, R. J. *A Prophet in the Making: A Christological Study on Lk 4, 16–30 in the Background of the Isaianic Mixed Citation and the Elijah-Elisha References.* Frankfurt am Main: Peter Lang, 2002.

Jasny, N. "The Daily Bread of the Ancient Greeks and Romans." *Osiris* 9 (1950): 227–53.

Jeanes, G. "Baptism Portrayed as Martyrdom in the Early Church." *StLit* 23 (1993): 158–76.

Jeanjean, B. *Saint Jérôme et l'hérésie.* Paris: Institut d'Études Augustiniennes, 1999.

Kech, H. *Hagiographie als christliche Unterhaltungsliteratur: Studien zum Phänomen des Erbaulichen anhand der Mönchsviten des hl. Hieronymus.* Göttingen: Kümmerle, 1977.

Kelhoffer, J. A. *Miracle and Mission: The Authentication of Missionaries and their Message in the Longer Ending of Mark.* Tübingen: Mohr Siebeck, 2000.

Kelly, J. M. *Roman Litigation.* Oxford: Oxford University Press, 1966.

Kelly, J. N. D. *Jerome: His Life, Writings, and Controversies.* London: Hendrickson, 1975.

Keppie, G. *Colonisation and Veteran Settlement in Italy, 47–14 BC.* London: British School at Rome, 1983.

Kleijwegt, M. *Ancient Youth: The Ambiguity of Youth and the Absence of Adolescence in Greco-Roman Society.* Amsterdam: J. C. Gieben, 1991.

Köstenberger, A. J. *A Theology of John's Gospel and Letters.* Grand Rapids: Eerdmans, 2009.

Kötting, B. *Peregrinatio religiosa: Wallfahrten in der Antike und das Pilgerwesen in der alten Kirche.* Münster: De Gruyter, 1950.

Kritzinger, J. P. K. "St. Jerome's Commentary on Daniel 3." *APB* 16 (2005): 54–69.

Krueger, D. "The Old Testament and Monasticism." In *The Old Testament in Byzantium*, ed. P. Magdalino and R. Nelson, 199–221. Washington, DC: Dumbarton Oaks, 2010.

Lampe, G. W. H., and K. J. Woollcombe, eds. *Essays on Typology*. London: SCM Press, 1957.

Leclercq, J. "Martyr." *DACL* 10 (1931): 2425–40.

———. "'*Militare deo*'dans la tradition patristique et monastique." In *Militia Christi e crociata nei secoli XI–XIII. Atti della undecima Settimana internazionale di studio Mendola, 28 agosto–1 settembre 1989*, 3–18. Milan: Vita e Pensiero, 1992.

Lierman, J. *The New Testament Moses*. Tübingen: Mohr Siebeck, 2004.

Lieu, J. M. "The Audience of Apologetics: The Problem of the Martyr Acts." In *Contextualising Early Christian Martyrdom*, ed. J. Engberg, V. H. Eriksen, and A. K. Petersen, 205–23. Frankfurt am Main: Peter Lang, 2011.

Lieu, S. N. C. *Manichaeism in the Later Roman Empire and Medieval China*. Tübingen: Mohr Siebeck, 1985.

Luongo, G. "*Desertor Christi miles*." *Koinonia* 2 (1978): 71–91.

Mähler, M. "Évocations bibliques et hagiographiques dans la vie de saint Benoît par saint Grégoire." *RBén* 83 (1973): 145–84.

Mainardus, O. "The Itinerary of the Holy Family in Egypt." *SOCC* 7 (1962): 1–45.

Malone, E. E. "Martyrdom and Monastic Profession as a Second Baptism." In *Vom christlichen Mysterium*, ed. A. Mayer, J. Quasten, and B. Neunheuser, 115–34. Düsseldorf: Patmos Verlag, 1951.

Malouta, M. "The Terminology of Fatherlessness in Roman Egypt: ἀπάτωρ and χρηματίζων μητρός." In *Proceedings of the 24th International Congress of Papyrology, Helsinki, 1–7 August, 2004*, ed. J. Frösén, T. Purola, and E. Salmenkivi, 615–24. Helsinki, 2007.

Manns, F. "La fuite en Égypte dans l'Évangile apocryphe du Pseudo-Matthieu." *Augustinianum* 23 (1983): 227–35.

Maraval, P. *Lieux saints et pèlerinages d'Orient: Histoire et géographie des origines à la conquête arabe*. Paris: Cerf, 1985.

Marshall, I. H. *The Gospel of Luke*. Grand Rapids: Eerdmans, 1978.

Mauser, U. *Christ in the Wilderness: The Wilderness Theme in the Second Gospel and its Basis in the Biblical Tradition*. London: Wipf and Stock, 1963.

McGuire, E. M. "Yahweh and the Leviathan: An Exegesis of Isaiah 27:1." *RQ* 13 (1970): 165–79.

McHardy, F. "The 'Trial by Water' in Greek Myth and Literature." *LICS* 7 (2008): 1–20.

Meijer, F., and O. van Niff, eds. *Trade, Transport and Society in the Ancient World*. London: Routledge, 1992.

Milburn, R. *Early Christian Art and Architecture.* Berkeley: University of California Press, 1988.

Mohrmann, C. *Die altchristliche Sondersprache in den Sermones des hl. Augustinus.* Nijmegen: Latinitas Christianorum primaeva, 1932.

Muehlberger, E. *Angels in Late Ancient Christianity.* Oxford: Oxford University Press, 2013.

Musurillo, H., ed. and trans. *The Acts of the Christian Martyrs.* Oxford: Oxford University Press, 1972.

Nelson, R. *Joshua: A Commentary.* Louisville: John Knox Press, 1997.

Neri, V. *I Marginali nell' occidente tardoantico.* Bari: Edipuglia, 1998.

Pachoumi, E. "The Erotic and Separation Spells of the Magical Papyri and *Defixiones*." *GRBS* 53 (2013): 294–325.

Pavan, M. "Concordia nel V e VI secolo." *AAAd* 39 (1992): 307–12.

Petersen, J. M. *The Dialogues of Gregory the Great in their Late Antique Cultural Background.* Toronto: Pontifical Institute of Mediaeval Studies, 1984.

Pietersma, A. *The Apocryphon of Jannes and Jambres the Magicians, edited with Introduction, Translation, and Commentary.* Leiden: Brill, 1994.

Poirot, É. *Les prophètes Élie et Élisée dans la littérature chrétienne ancienne.* Turnhout: Brepols, 1998.

Pricoco, S. "*Militia Christi* nelle regole monastiche latine." In *Paideia cristiana: Studi in onore di Mario Naldini,* 547–58. Rome: Gruppo Editoriale Internazionale, 1994.

Ramsey, B., trans. *John Cassian: The Conferences.* New York: Paulist Press, 1997.

Rapp, C. "Old Testament Models for Emperors in Early Byzantium." In *The Old Testament in Byzantium,* ed. P. Magdalino and R. Nelson, 175–98. Washington, DC: Dumbarton Oaks, 2010.

Ricci, M. L. "Topica pagana e topica cristiana negli *Acta martyrum*." *AATC* n.s. 28 (1963–64): 37–122.

Robson, S. *"With the Spirit and Power of Elijah" (Lk 1, 17): The Prophetic-Reforming Spirituality of Bernard of Clairvaux as Evidenced Particularly in His Letters.* Rome: Pontificia Università Gregoriana, 2004.

Roetzel, C. J. *Paul: The Man and the Myth.* Columbia: University of South Carolina Press, 1998.

Rousseau, O. "Saint Benoît et le prophète Élisée." *RMon* 144 (1956): 103–14.

Rush, A. C. *Death and Burial in Christian Antiquity.* Washington, DC: The Catholic University of America Press, 1941.

Savramis, D. *Zur Soziologie des byzantinischen Mönchtums.* Leiden: Brill, 1962.

Sawyer, J. F. A. *The Fifth Gospel: Isaiah in the History of Christianity.* Cambridge: Cambridge University Press, 1996.

Saxer, V. *Bible et hagiographie: Textes et thèmes bibliques dans les actes des martyrs authentiques des premiers siècles.* Bern: Peter Lang, 1986.

Scarpa Bonazza, B., et al. *Iulia Concordia dall'età romana all'età moderna.* Treviso: La Tipografica, 1978.

Scheidel, W. *Death on the Nile: Disease and the Demography of Roman Egypt.* Leiden: Brill, 2001.

Scholz, U. "Drances." *Hermes* 127 (1999): 455–66.

Schürer, M. "Das Reden und Schweigen der Mönche: Zur Wertigkeit des *silentium* im mittelalterlichen Religiosentum." In *Askese und Identität in Spätantike, Mittelalter und Früher Neuzeit,* ed. W. Röcke and J. Weitbrecht, 107–29. Berlin: De Gruyter, 2010.

Schwartz, E., ed. *Kyrillos von Skythopolis.* Leipzig: J. C. Hinrichs Verlag, 1939.

Scobie, A. *More Essays on the Ancient Romance and its Heritage.* Meisenheim am Glan: Verlag A. Hain, 1973.

Serrato Garrido, M. *Ascetismo femenino en Roma.* Cádiz: University of Cádiz, 1993.

Shaw, B. "Bandits in the Roman Empire." *P&P* 105 (1984): 3–52.

Sotinel, C. *Identité civique et Christianisme: Aquilée du IIIe au VIe siècle.* Rome: École Française de Rome, 2005.

Souza, P. de. *Piracy in the Graeco-Roman World.* Cambridge: Cambridge University Press, 1999.

Spinelli, G. "Ascetismo, monachesimo e cenobitismo ad Aquileia nel IV secolo." *AAAd* 22 (1982): 273–300.

Spittler, R. "The Limits of Ecstasy: An Exegesis of 2 Corinthians 12:1–10." In *Current Issues in Biblical and Patristic Interpretation,* ed. G. Hawthorne, 259–66. Grand Rapids: Eerdmans, 1975.

Starr, G. "An Evening with the Flute-girls." *PP* 33 (1978): 401–10.

Stathakopoulos, D. *Famine and Pestilence in the Late Roman and Early Byzantine Empire: A Systematic Survey of Subsistence Crises and Epidemics.* Aldershot: Ashgate, 2004.

Steinhausen, J. "Hieronymus und Laktanz in Trier." *TZ* 20 (1951): 126–54.

Stewart, C. "John Cassian on Unceasing Prayer." *MonStud* 15 (1984): 159–77.

Stockmeier, P. *Theologie und Kult des Kreuzes bei Johannes Chrysostomos.* Trier: Paulinus-Verlag, 1966.

Stramara, D. F. "Double Monasticism in the Greek East, Fourth through Eighth Centuries." *JECS* 6 (1998): 269–312.

Tabor, J. D. *Things Unutterable: Paul's Ascent to Paradise in its Greco-Roman, Judaic, and Early Christian Contexts.* New York: University Press of America, 1986.

Tambroni, F. "La vita economica della Roma degli ultimi re." *Athenaeum* 8 (1930): 299–328, 452–87.

Tanner, N., ed. *Decrees of the Ecumenical Councils.* 2 vols. London: Sheed and Ward, 1990.

Taylor, A. "Just Like a Mother Bee: Reading and Writing *Vitae metricae* around the Year 1000." *Viator* 36 (2005): 119–48.

Thiering, B. E. "The Three and a Half Years of Elijah." *NovTest* 23 (1981): 41–55.

Thomas, D. R. "Elijah on Mount Carmel." *PEQ* 92 (1960): 146–55.

Thompson, C. L. *Taedium vitae in Roman Sepulchral Inscriptions.* Lancaster, UK: Kessinger Publishing, 1912.

Uytfanghe, M. van. "L'empreinte biblique sur la plus ancienne hagiographie occidentale." In *Le monde latin antique et la Bible,* ed. J. Fontaine and C. Pietri, 565–611. Paris: Beauchesne, 1985.

Veen, M. van der. "Food as Embodied Material Culture: Diversity and Change in Plant Food Consumption in Roman Britain." *JRA* 21 (2008): 83–109.

Verheijen, L. "Spiritualité et vie monastique chez S. Augustin: L'utilisation monastique des Actes des Apôtres 4:32–35." In *Jean Chrysostome et Augustin: Actes du colloque de Chantilly 22–24 septembre 1974,* ed. C. Kannengiesser, 93–123. Paris: Beauchesne, 1975.

Vittinghoff, F. "*Christianus sum:* Das "Verbrechen" von Aussenseitern der römischen Gesellschaft." *Historia* 33 (1984): 331–57.

Watts, E. *City and School in Late Antique Athens and Alexandria.* Berkeley, 2006.

Weingarten, S. *The Saint's Saints: Hagiography and Geography in Jerome.* Leiden: Brill, 2005.

Wiles, M. F. *The Divine Apostle.* Cambridge: Cambridge University Press, 1967.

Wilken, R. "The Interpretation of the Baptism of Jesus in the Later Fathers." *StudPatr* 11 (1967): 268–77.

———. *The Church's Bible.* Grand Rapids: Eerdmans, 2007.

Wilkinson, K. "The Elder Melania's Missing Decade." *JLA* 5 (2012): 166–84.

Williams, S., and G. Friell. *Theodosius: The Empire at Bay.* New Haven: Yale University Press, 1998.

Woods, D. "An Unnoticed Official: The *Praepositus Saltus*." *CQ* n.s. 44 (1994): 245–51.

Woods, F. E. *Water and Storm Polemics against Baalism in the Deuteronomic History.* New York: Peter Lang, 1994.

Young, F. "Typology." In *Crossing the Boundaries: Essays in Biblical Interpretation in Honour of Michael D. Goulder,* ed. S. E. Porter et al., 29–50. Leiden: Brill, 1994.

Zeiller, J. *"Paganus": Étude de terminologie historique.* Paris: Éditions de Boccard, 1917.

Zumkeller, A. "*Propositum* in seinem spezifisch christlichen und theologischen Verständnis bei Augustinus." In *Homo spiritalis: Festgabe für Luc Verheijen zu seinem 70. Geburtstag,* ed. C. Mayer and K. Chelius, 295–310. Würzburg: Augustinus-Verlag, 1987.

INTRODUCTION

INTRODUCTION

Rufinus's Life and Writings[1]

Tyrannius Rufinus was born around 345 in Concordia (present-day Concordia Sagittaria), a prosperous town in northeastern Italy just west of Aquileia.[2] Almost nothing is known about his upbringing. One enlightening detail is preserved by Palladius, his good friend later in life, who described him as being "most nobly born" (εὐγενέστατος),[3] from which we may infer that Rufinus's family was well-off.[4] Further evidence of their affluence is that after Rufinus had completed his primary education in his hometown, they sent him to Rome, at around the age of thirteen, to receive a top-flight education in Latin grammar, literature, and rhetoric, which was meant to lay the groundwork for a successful career in a field such as law.[5]

1. Though dated, the standard English-language biography is F.X. Murphy, *Rufinus of Aquileia (345–410): His Life and Works* (Washington, DC: The Catholic University of America Press, 1945). For a succinct outline of the stages of Rufinus's life, see G. Fedalto, "Rufino di Concordia: Elementi di una biografia," *AAAd* 39 (1992): 19–44; see also C.P. Hammond, "The Last Ten Years of Rufinus' Life and the Date of his Move South from Aquileia," *JThS* n.s. 28 (1977): 372–429.

2. Concordia had been founded in 42 BCE as the Roman *colonia* Iulia Concordia, likely as a triumviral or Augustan colony; see L. Keppie, *Colonisation and Veteran Settlement in Italy, 47–14 BC* (London: British School at Rome, 1983), 21, 201. For a history of the town, see B. Scarpa Bonazza et al., *Iulia Concordia dall'età romana all'età moderna* (Treviso: La Tipografica, 1978); M. Pavan, "Concordia nel V e VI secolo," *AAAd* 39 (1992): 307–12.

3. *hist. Laus.* 46.5.

4. On the superlative εὐγενέστατος as a marker of high socio-economic status, see A. Weiss, *Soziale Elite und Christentum. Studien zu ordo-Angehörigen unter den frühen Christen* (Berlin: De Gruyter, 2015), 150–51.

5. Murphy, *Rufinus of Aquileia*, 7–11. The breadth of Rufinus's classical education may be gauged by the classical literary allusions and quotations that

It usually is assumed that here, in the bustling Italian capital, Rufinus befriended Jerome, who was around the same age; having grown up in the remote town of Stridon,[6] he too was sent by his family to Rome for educational purposes.[7] Little could these two adolescents have known at the time that theirs was destined to become one of the most storied friendships— and eventually, bitter rivalries—in the history of the Christian church.[8]

By the late 360s Jerome had moved on to the Gallic city of Trier to take up an entry-level post in the imperial bureaucracy,[9] and Rufinus in the meantime had relocated to Aquileia in his twenties, probably for much the same reason. Aquileia was a thriving port city on the northeastern coast of Italy that served as a terminal for many of the prominent eastern ports, such as Alexandria, Antioch, and Constantinople.[10] Emperors fre-

---

permeate his adult writings. See N. Adkin, "Rufinus Terentianus," *RPL* n.s. 9 (2006): 142–44; idem, "Rufinus Vergilianus," *Orpheus* n.s. 27 (2006): 1–4; idem, "Rufinus Ciceronianus," *RBén* 117 (2007): 5–8; C. Lo Cicero, "Rufino, Basilio e Seneca: Fra aemulatio e arte allusiva," *FAM* 14 (1998): 177–82; idem, "I cristiani e la traduzione letteraria: Il caso di Rufino di Aquileia," in F. Consolino, ed., *Forme letterarie nella produzione latina di IV–V secolo: Con uno sguardo a Bisanzio* (Rome: Herder, 2003), 91–126. On the imperial Roman educational *cursus*, see S. F. Bonner, *Education in Ancient Rome from the Elder Cato to the Younger Pliny* (Berkeley: University of California Press, 1977), 163–327.

6. Stridon was a small and virtually unknown town on the border between the Roman provinces of Dalmatia and Pannonia. For the debate about its precise location, see I. Fodor, "Le lieu d'origine de S. Jérôme: Reconsidération d'une vieille controverse," *RHE* 81 (1986): 498–500.

7. For a brief biography of Jerome, see A. Cain, Introduction to Jerome's *Commentary on Galatians*, trans. A. Cain, FOTC 121 (Washington, DC: The Catholic University of America Press, 2010), 3–14, with references to further bibliography.

8. On their intertwined fates, see Y.-M. Duval, "Rufin d'Aquilée émule de Jérôme de Stridon," in S. Crogiez-Pétrequin, ed., *Dieu(x) et hommes: Histoire et iconographie des sociétés païennes et chrétiennes de l'antiquité à nos jours. Mélanges de Françoise Thelamon* (Rouen: Publications des Universités de Rouen et du Havre, 2005), 163–85; M. Vessey, "Jerome and Rufinus," in F. Young, L. Ayres, and A. Louth, eds., *The Cambridge History of Early Christian Literature* (Cambridge: Cambridge University Press, 2004), 318–27.

9. J. Steinhausen, "Hieronymus und Laktanz in Trier," *TZ* 20 (1951): 126–54.

10. For the history of Aquileia, see C. Sotinel, *Identité civique et Christianisme: Aquilée du IIIe au VIe siècle* (Rome: École Française de Rome, 2005).

quently passed through the city *en route* to eastern destinations and also issued a large number of laws from there, making it one of the centers of the western imperial bureaucracy. Thus this provincial capital presented many employment opportunities to ambitious young careerists from Rufinus's generation.

Aquileia held yet another attraction for Rufinus: at the time it was one of the strongholds in Italy for the rapidly growing Christian ascetic movement.[11] It is impossible to say when or how he first became enamored of the ascetic ideal, but we do know that in 370, at the age of twenty-five, he was baptized. Around the same time he joined like-minded Christians such as the priest Chromatius (the future bishop of Aquileia) and Jerome, with whom he had since reunited, in an informal monastic community.[12] In the early 370s, however, this community dissolved, evidently because of some kind of internal rift.

Around 373 Rufinus, by now having relinquished his secular career, set sail for Alexandria. For the next eight or so years he divided his time between Alexandria, where he studied Scripture under Didymus the Blind,[13] and the renowned monastic establishment at Nitria, which lay sixty miles to the south of Alexandria. During his probably frequent and prolonged stays at Nitria, Rufinus established ties with many of its monks, most notably Macarius of Alexandria,[14] a former confectioner who had moved to Nitria after his baptism in the early 330s and then went on to become one of its most famous residents until his death in 393.

Rufinus cultivated other strategic relations while he was in

---

11. G. Spinelli, "Ascetismo, monachesimo e cenobitismo ad Aquileia nel IV secolo," *AAAd* 22 (1982): 273–300.

12. Cf. *apol. c. Hier.* 1.4 for Rufinus's personal reflection on this experience.

13. Didymus was the last head of the legendary catechetical school at Alexandria; see R. Layton, *Didymus the Blind and his Circle in Late-Antique Alexandria: Virtue and Narrative in Biblical Scholarship* (Urbana: University of Illinois Press, 2004). Despite being blind since the age of four and never learning how to read, Didymus mastered all of the known sciences, had an encyclopedic knowledge of Scripture (Palladius, *hist. Laus.* 4.1–2; Jerome, *vir. ill.* 109), and was a prolific author, composing theological treatises and commentaries on more than a dozen biblical books.

14. Rufinus's friendship with Macarius is mentioned by Jerome (*epist.* 3.2).

northern Egypt. The most valuable of them all, as time would tell, was with Melania the Elder. Born in Spain in 341,[15] Melania boasted a prestigious lineage. She was a member of one of the most distinguished late Roman clans, the *gens Antonia,* and the granddaughter of Antonius Marcellinus, whose impressive résumé included some of the most important political posts of the day: the governorship of Gallia Lugdunensis (313), the proconsulship of Africa (between 333 and 338), the praetorian prefecture of Italy, Illyricum, and Africa (c.340–c.342), and the ordinary consulship (341).[16] Melania married a certain Valerius Maximus, generally accepted as the one who served as Prefect of Rome in 361–62,[17] but in 362 she was widowed at the age of twenty-one, and two of her three children also died within that same year. In 373, by now a fervent devotee of asceticism, she left Rome for Alexandria. Once docked there, she liquidated the considerable movable assets she had brought from Rome and received their equivalent value in gold, and then she traveled with her large entourage to Nitria and spent close to six months visiting with the renowned monks there and in the surrounding desert.[18]

It was probably during her stay in Nitria that the wealthy heiress crossed paths with Rufinus, and the two formed a lasting bond based on their shared passion for monasticism. In 374

15. On all questions of Melanian chronology, see K. Wilkinson, "The Elder Melania's Missing Decade," *JLA* 5 (2012): 166–84. See now also the collection of essays in C. Chin and C. Schroeder, eds., *Melania: Early Christianity through the Life of One Family* (Oakland: University of California Press, 2017).

16. T. D. Barnes, "Proconsuls of Africa, 337–361," *Phoenix* 39 (1985): 144–53 (145); idem, "Praetorian Prefects, 337–361," *ZPE* 94 (1992): 249–60 (255).

17. A. Chastagnol, *Les fastes de la préfecture de Rome au Bas Empire* (Paris: Nouvelles Éditions Latines, 1956), 154–56.

18. Palladius, *hist. Laus.* 46.1–2. Melania, then, was like other aristocratic Christian women in this period who made religious pilgrimages to Egypt to lay eyes on the legendary monks who inhabited its desert regions. See G. Frank, *The Memory of the Eyes: Pilgrims to Living Saints in Christian Late Antiquity* (Berkeley: University of California Press, 2000); N. Hohlwein, "Déplacements et tourisme dans l'Égypte romaine," *Chronique d'Égypte* 15 (1940): 253–78; B. Kötting, *Peregrinatio religiosa: Wallfahrten in der Antike und das Pilgerwesen in der alten Kirche* (Münster: De Gruyter, 1950), 188–210.

she took up residence in Jerusalem, and by 380 or so Rufinus had moved there as well; soon they undertook a major monastic collaboration that was to last nearly two decades. Melania used her vast fortune to fund the construction of a monastic complex on the Mount of Olives, which included a monastery supervised by Rufinus, a convent overseen by herself,[19] and a hostelry for lodging Christian Holy Land pilgrims. By the mid-390s the Olivet establishment had garnered recognition throughout the eastern and western Roman Empire, owing in no small part to Melania's extraordinary patronage of clergy and fellow monastics[20] and to the hospitality that she and Rufinus showed to untold numbers of Christian pilgrims who funneled through Jerusalem on a yearly basis.

In the meantime, in 386, Jerome and his patron Paula as well as her teenaged daughter Eustochium, who recently had left behind their family and home in Rome, settled a few miles to the south in Bethlehem, at the time a tiny agrarian village whose main claim to fame in Christian circles was being the purported birthplace of Christ. Like her much wealthier counterpart Melania, Paula, an ascetically-inclined widow in her late thirties, used part of her inherited senatorial fortune to finance the building of a monastery, convent, and pilgrim hostelry in Bethlehem, which she operated with Jerome.[21]

19. Their monastic complex conformed to the contemporary eastern pattern of what might be termed the "double monastery" (*duplex monasterium* / διπλοῦν μοναστήριον), i.e., a male and a female monastic community that had separate sleeping and living quarters and yet were located within close proximity to each other and were interdependent financially. An example of the "double monastery" phenomenon from a slightly later period is the 80-person monastery and 130-person convent established by Melania the Younger and Pinianus outside Thagaste (Gerontios, *v. Mel.* 22). For the prevalence of double monasticism in the East, see D.F. Stramara, "Double Monasticism in the Greek East, Fourth through Eighth Centuries," *JECS* 6 (1998): 269–312; E. Wipszycka, *Moines et communautés monastiques en Égypte (IVe–VIIIe siècles)* (Warsaw: Journal of Juristic Papyrology, 2009), 568–88; cf. M. Serrato Garrido, *Ascetismo femenino en Roma* (Cádiz: University of Cádiz, 1993), 109–20.

20. Palladius, *hist. Laus.* 46.6; 54.1.

21. Bethlehem was situated near a Roman road that intersected with Jerusalem, and so Christian pilgrims heading to and from Jerusalem on this route would pass right by the village; see P. Maraval, *Lieux saints et pèlerinages*

The two monastic communities in Jerusalem and Bethlehem co-existed peacefully until the outbreak of the Origenist controversy in Palestine.[22] This controversy was precipitated in 393 by Jerome's ecclesiastical ally Epiphanius, bishop of Salamis, accusing Rufinus and his (and Jerome's) diocesan bishop, John of Jerusalem, of being heretics for showing sympathy toward Origen's theology. A series of bitter local conflicts between these factions ensued for the next few years, but tensions for the most part had subsided by 397, only to be reignited at the turn of the fifth century by a pamphlet war between Rufinus and Jerome.

In 397 Rufinus left Palestine, never to return, and for the next decade and a half, until his death in 411, he spent most of his time in Italy—variously in Rome, Aquileia, and the monastery of Pinetum near Terracina between Naples and Rome.[23] It is to this final phase of his life that all of his extant writings belong. As a literary figure, Rufinus was a relative late-bloomer. It was not until 397, when he was in his early fifties, that he evidently made his literary début.[24] From then on he issued a steady stream of both original writings and translations of Greek patristic works. His original writings include his *Apology against Jerome* (401), a commentary on the Apostles' Creed (400),[25] a brief exposition of the patriarchs' blessings (*De benedictionibus patriarcharum*, 408),[26] and the prefaces to his various translations of Greek patristic works.[27]

---

d'Orient: Histoire et géographie des origines à la conquête arabe (Paris: Cerf, 1985), 271–72.

22. See E. A. Clark, *The Origenist Controversy: The Cultural Construction of an Early Christian Debate* (Princeton: Princeton University Press, 1992).

23. Cf. G. Spinelli, "Insediamenti monastici nel territorio dell'antica diocesi di Jesolo," *AAAd* 27 (1985): 147–61 (149).

24. For an overview of his earliest literary productions, see M. Simonetti, "L'attività letteraria di Rufino negli anni della controversia origeniana," *AAAd* 39 (1992): 89–107.

25. M. Villain, "Rufin d'Aquilée, commentateur du Symbole des Apôtres," *RSR* 31 (1944): 129–56.

26. M. Simonetti, "Osservazioni sul *De benedictionibus patriarcharum* di Rufino di Aquileia," *RCCM* 4 (1962): 3–44.

27. See H. Crouzel, "I prologhi di Rufino alle sue traduzioni di Origene," *AAAd* 39 (1992): 109–20.

Rufinus was more prolific as a translator of Greek patristic texts than he was as an original author. His translation portfolio is extensive and encompasses an array of exegetical, theological, monastic, and historiographical writings by a number of different authors.[28] Origen's massive *œuvre* made the most demands on his time and attention.[29] He translated the Alexandrian master's *On First Principles* (398),[30] commentary on Romans (405–6),[31] commentary on the Song of Songs (411),[32] and homilies on Genesis (403–5),[33] Exodus (403–5),[34] Leviticus

28. The dates for Rufinus's works as given above are reproduced, with a few exceptions, from the chronological table found in Hammond, "The Last Ten Years of Rufinus' Life," 428–29, though, as Hammond herself cautions, some of these dates are merely conjectural.

29. For an analysis of Rufinus's Origenist works, see Clark, *The Origenist Controversy*, 159–93.

30. H. Crouzel, "Rufino traduttore del *Peri Archon* di Origene," *AAAd* 31 (1987): 129–39; A. Grappone, *Omelie origeniane nella traduzione di Rufino: Un confronto con i testi greci* (Rome: Institutum Patristicum Augustinianum, 2007); N. Pace, *Ricerche sulla traduzione di Rufino del* De principiis *di Origene* (Florence: La Nuova Italia, 1990).

31. T. Scheck, trans., Origen, *Commentary on the Epistle to the Romans, Books 1–5*, FOTC 103 (Washington, DC: The Catholic University of America Press, 2001); idem, trans., Origen, *Commentary on the Epistle to the Romans, Books 6–10*, FOTC 104 (Washington, DC: The Catholic University of America Press, 2002). Cf. H. Chadwick, "Rufinus and the Tura Papyrus of Origen's Commentary on Romans," *JThS* n.s. 10 (1959): 10–42; C. H. Bammel, "Rufinus' Translation of Origen's *Commentary on Romans* and the Pelagian Controversy," *AAAd* 39 (1992): 131–49; K. D. Hill, "Rufinus as an Interpreter of Origen: Ascetic Affliction in the *Commentarii in Epistulam ad Romanos*," *Augustiniana* 60 (2010): 145–68. Shortly after its appearance in c.406, Rufinus's translation was used by Pelagius as an important doctrinal resource for his own commentary on Romans; see T. Bohlin, *Die Theologie des Pelagius und ihre Genesis* (Uppsala: Lundequist, 1957), 87–103.

32. Origen, *The Song of Songs, Commentary and Homilies*, trans. R. P. Lawson, ACW 26 (New York: Paulist Press, 1957). The Latin translation was left unfinished, having been interrupted by Rufinus's death.

33. Origen, *Homilies on Genesis and Exodus*, trans. R. Heine, FOTC 71 (Washington, DC: The Catholic University of America Press, 1982).

34. Origen, *Homilies on Genesis and Exodus*, trans. R. Heine, FOTC 71. Cf. A. Muraru, "Strategies of Translation in Late Antiquity: Rufinus and the Bilingual Readers of Origen's *Homilia in Exodum* 9," *Adamantius* 17 (2011): 297–302.

(403–5),[35] Joshua (400),[36] Judges (400),[37] Psalms 36–38 (401), and selections of homilies on 1 Samuel and Numbers (408–10). As a part of his larger campaign to promote the study of Origen in the Latin West, Rufinus also translated the *Apology for Origen* (397), which Pamphilus of Caesarea, in collaboration with Eusebius of Caesarea, had composed in Greek between 307 and 310, in order to defend Origen's theological integrity on numerous points by compiling excerpts from across his vast literary corpus.[38]

Rufinus did not confine himself to Origen's works. He also translated nine homilies of Gregory of Nazianzus (398–99).[39] From Basil's corpus he translated several homilies (398–99)[40] and the shorter version of his monastic *Rule* (397).[41] He also

---

35. Origen, *Homilies on Leviticus 1–16*, trans. G.W. Barkley, FOTC 83 (Washington, DC: The Catholic University of America Press, 1990). Cf. P.C. Porta, "L'omelia sul Levitico 5,1: Origene e Rufino a confronto," *Orpheus* 13 (1992): 52–76; C. Noce, "Some Questions about Rufinus' Translation of Origen's *Homiliae in Leviticum*," *StudPatr* 43 (2006): 451–58.

36. Origen, *Homilies on Joshua*, trans. B.J. Bruce, ed. C. White, FOTC 105 (Washington, DC: The Catholic University of America Press, 2002).

37. Origen, *Homilies on Judges*, trans. E.A. Dively Lauro, FOTC 119 (Washington, DC: The Catholic University of America Press, 2010).

38. The Greek original has been lost, and only the first book was translated by Rufinus. For the critical edition with a French translation and commentary, see R. Amacker and É. Junod, eds. and trans., *Pamphile et Eusèbe de Césarée, Apologie pour Origène*, 2 vols. (Paris, 2002). For an English translation, see Pamphilus, *Apology for Origen*, and Rufinus, *On the Falsification of the Books of Origen*, trans. T. Scheck, FOTC 120 (Washington, DC: The Catholic University of America Press, 2010).

39. C. Moreschini, "Rufino traduttore di Gregorio Nazianzeno," *AAAd* 31 (1987): 227–85.

40. C. Lo Cicero, *Tradurre i greci nel IV secolo: Rufino di Aquileia e le omelie di Basilio* (Rome: Herder, 2008); H. Marti, "Rufinus' Translation of St. Basil's Sermon on Fasting," *StudPatr* 16 (1985): 418–22; C. Moreschini, "La traduzione di Rufino dalle *Omelie* di Basilio: Motivi e scopi di una scelta," in C. Moreschini and G. Menestrina, eds., *La traduzione dei testi religiosi* (Brescia: Morcelliana, 1994), 127–47; A. Salvini, "Sulla tecnica di traduzione dal greco in latino nelle *Homiliae Morales* di Basilio-Rufino," *SCO* 46 (1998): 845–89.

41. A.M. Silvas, *The Asketikon of St. Basil the Great* (Oxford: Oxford University Press, 2005); eadem, "Rufinus' Translation Techniques in the *Regula Basili*," *Antichthon* 37 (2003): 71–93; eadem, trans., *The Rule of St. Basil in Latin and English: A Revised Critical Edition* (Collegeville, MN: Liturgical Press, 2013).

made available to western readers in Latin several ascetic works by his spiritual mentor Evagrius of Pontus (403–4).[42] On another literary front, he translated the *Ecclesiastical History* of Eusebius of Caesarea (401–2) and made significant changes to its structure and content, most notably by compressing the ten books of the original work into nine and then adding his own two books covering events from 324 until the death of Theodosius I in 395.[43] Other Greek works he translated are the Pythagorean *Sentences* of Sextus (400),[44] the Pseudo-Clementine *Recognitions* (407),[45] and possibly the *Life* of Gregory Thaumaturgus.[46]

One of the shining jewels in Rufinus's crown as a translator also represents his only foray into the arena of monastic hagiography: the *Historia monachorum in Aegypto* (403–4).[47] This writ-

---

42. Murphy, *Rufinus of Aquileia*, 227.

43. P. Amidon, trans., Rufinus of Aquileia, *History of the Church*, FOTC 133 (Washington, DC: The Catholic University of America Press, 2016). Cf. M. Humphries, "Rufinus's Eusebius: Translation, Continuation, and Edition in the Latin *Ecclesiastical History*," *JECS* 16 (2008): 143–64; J. E. L. Oulton, "Rufinus' Translation of the *Church History* of Eusebius," *JThS* 30 (1929): 150–74; F. Thelamon, *Païens et chrétiens au IVe siècle: L'apport de* l'Histoire ecclésiastique *de Rufin d'Aquilée* (Paris, 1981); C. Torben, *Rufinus of Aquileia and the* Historia Ecclesiastica, *Lib. VIII–IX, of Eusebius* (Copenhagen, 1989).

44. See, e.g., A. Carlini, "Le Sentenze di Sesto nella versione di Rufino. Vel enchiridion si Graece vel anulus si Latine," in G. Fornasir, ed., *Studi forogiuliesi: In onore di Carlo Guido Mor* (Udine: Deputazione di storia patria per il Friuli, 1984), 109–18; F. della Corte, "L'Anulus Sexti di Rufino," *AAAd* 31 (1987): 195–205.

45. Y.-M. Duval, "Le texte latin des *Reconnaissances clémentines*: Rufin, les interpolations et les raisons de sa traduction," in F. Amsler, A. Frey, C. Touati, and R. Girardet, eds., *Nouvelles intrigues pseudo-clémentines* (Prahins: Éditions du Zèbre, 2008), 79–92; C. Moreschini, "Motivi romanzeschi e interessi cristiani nelle *Recognitiones* dello Pseudo Clemente tradotte da Rufino," *Koinonia* 35 (2011): 179–96; B. Neil, "Rufinus' Translation of the *Epistola Clementis ad Iacobum*," *Augustinianum* 43 (2003): 25–39.

46. The Rufinian authorship of this anonymously translated Latin *Life* is argued by S. Mitchell, "The Life and *Lives* of Gregory Thaumaturgus," in J. W. Drijvers and J. W. Watt, eds., *Portraits of Spiritual Authority: Religious Power in Early Christianity, Byzantium and the Christian Orient* (Leiden: Brill, 1999), 99–138.

47. On the dating, see A. de Vogüé, *Histoire littéraire du mouvement monastique dans l'antiquité, 3: Jérôme, Augustin et Rufin au tournant du siècle (391–405)* (Paris: Cerf, 1996), 317–20.

ing, which is the subject of the present volume, was to become
one of his most widely disseminated and influential works in
posterity. And, as we will see later in this Introduction, Rufinus
did not regard it *merely* as a translation but as a self-standing
piece of monastic propaganda.

The Anonymous Greek *Historia monachorum* and Rufinus's Latin *Historia monachorum*

From September 394 to early January 395, seven monks
from Rufinus's monastery on the Mount of Olives journeyed
throughout Egypt and visited many monks and monastic communities from the Thebaid in the south to the delta town of Diolcos in the north. Within months of their return to Jerusalem,
one of them composed in Greek an engaging account of this
trip.[48] He cast it ostensibly as a travelogue which charts, from
the first-person perspective, the various locales and monks they
visited, in the order in which they visited them.[49] He entitled his
work Ἡ κατ᾽ Αἴγυπτον τῶν μοναχῶν ἱστορία,[50] which perhaps is
best translated into English as *Inquiry about the Monks in Egypt.*[51]

---

48. For a comprehensive study of this work, see A. Cain, *The Greek* Historia
monachorum in Aegypto: *Monastic Hagiography in the Late Fourth Century* (Oxford: Oxford University Press, 2016).

49. Although its essential literary form is that of a travelogue, this work in
fact brilliantly combines multiple literary genres (e.g., collective biography,
encomium, *acta martyrum, apophthegmata patrum*) and thus constitutes a hybrid
composition which was truly *sui generis* for its time. See Cain, *The Greek* Historia monachorum, 58–73.

50. The standard critical edition is A.-J. Festugière, ed., *Historia monachorum in Aegypto. Édition critique du texte grec* (Brussels: Société des Bollandistes,
1961). For an English translation, see N. Russell, trans., *The Lives of the Desert
Fathers: The* Historia monachorum in Aegypto, with intro. by B. Ward (Kalamazoo: Cistercian Publications, 1980). All translations from the Greek work in
this volume, however, are my own.

51. Even though the title sometimes is rendered as *History of the Monks of
Egypt,* this translation is potentially misleading because the word ἱστορία in this
case does not have historiographic connotations. As is evident from the form
and content of his narrative, the author did not venture to write anything resembling a linear "history" of contemporary Egyptian monasticism. In its usage
here, the abstract noun ἱστορία refers to the gathering of knowledge through
autopsy and the subsequent writing down of the results of these investigations.

This work is one of the most innovative Christian writings to have been composed during the fourth century CE, and to this day it remains an indispensable primary source for contemporary Egyptian monastic practice and lore. Yet, one of the most curious aspects of this text is that its author chose to release it anonymously.[52] During Late Antiquity and the Middle Ages it was ascribed variously to Bishop Timothy of Alexandria, Palladius, and Jerome, but none of these candidates is even remotely viable: for all intents and purposes the author's identity remains frustratingly irrecoverable.[53] Because we do not have a name by which to call him, I refer to him throughout this volume simply as "Anon." (shorthand for "Anonymous").

A little less than a decade after Anon. had composed the Greek original, Rufinus translated it into Latin and entitled it *Historia monachorum in Aegypto* (*Inquiry about the Monks in Egypt*). By both convention and convenience modern scholars usually refer to the Greek work by the title of Rufinus's translation. In keeping with this custom, I refer henceforth to the Greek original as *GHM* (*Greek Historia monachorum*) and to Rufinus's translation as *LHM* (*Latin Historia monachorum*).

In previous scholarly generations there was contentious debate about the nature of the relationship between the *GHM* and the *LHM*. Erwin Preuschen, the first modern editor of the *GHM*,[54] posited that the *LHM* was the original and the *GHM* its translation. Although Preuschen's theory found favor among many Continental scholars at the time,[55] the Benedictine scholar Cuthbert Butler laid it to rest by definitively demonstrating

52. On the possible reasons for his self-imposed anonymity, see Cain, *The Greek* Historia monachorum, 49–57.

53. The most plausible candidate would appear to be a certain Spaniard named Anatolios, a former *notarius* and monk in Rufinus's monastery; see Cain, *The Greek* Historia monachorum, 48.

54. *Palladius und Rufinus. Ein Beitrag zur Quellenkunde des ältesten Mönchtums* (Giessen: J. Rickersche Buchhandlung, 1897), 1–131.

55. For example, Richard Reitzenstein, the eminent scholar of Hellenistic religion and early Christian gnosticism, accepted Preuschen's view as a point of departure for his monograph *Historia monachorum und Historia Lausiaca. Eine Studie zur Geschichte des Mönchtums und der frühchristlichen Begriffe Gnostiker und Pneumatiker* (Göttingen: Vandenhoeck & Ruprecht, 1916).

the anteriority of the Greek text.[56] Over half a century later, André-Jean Festugière, the second and most recent modern editor of the Greek text, confirmed Butler's conclusions from his own text-critical work.[57] There is now no doubt whatsoever that the *LHM* was translated from the *GHM*. But how does Rufinus's translation compare with Anon.'s Greek original? We may begin by taking a bird's-eye view of the chapter-arrangement of both texts:

GHM	LHM
Prologue	Prologue
1 John of Lycopolis	1 John of Lycopolis
2 Or	2 Or
3 Ammon	3 Ammon
4 Bes	4 Bes
5 Oxyrhynchus	5 Oxyrhynchus
6 Theon	6 Theon
7 Elias	
8 Apollo	7 Apollo
9 Amoun	8 Amoun
10 Copres	9 Copres
Patermuthius	Patermuthius
11 Sourous	10 Sourous
12 Helle	11 Helle
	12 Elias
13 Apelles	
John	
14 Paphnutius	
15 Pityrion	13 Pityrion
16 Eulogius	14 Eulogius
	15 Apelles
	John
	16 Paphnutius
17 Isidore	17 Isidore

56. *The Lausiac History of Palladius: A Critical Discussion together with Notes on Early Egyptian Monachism* (Cambridge: Cambridge University Press, 1898), 257–66.

57. "Le problème littéraire de l'*Historia monachorum*," *Hermes* 83 (1955): 257–84.

18 Sarapion	18 Sarapion
19 Apollonius	19 Apollonius
20 Dioscorus	20 Dioscorus
Nitria	21 Nitria
	22 Kellia
Ammonius	23 Ammonius
Didymus	24 Didymus
Cronides	25 Cronius (Cronides)
	26 Origen
Evagrius	27 Evagrius
21 Macarius of Egypt	28 Macarius of Egypt
22 Amoun (of Nitria)	
23 Macarius of Alexandria	29 Macarius of Alexandria
	30 Amoun (of Nitria)
24 Paul the Simple	31 Paul the Simple
25 Piammonas	32 Piammon (Piammonas)
26 John of Diolcos	33 John of Diolcos
Epilogue	Epilogue

Rufinus, then, generally preserves the same internal structure as Anon., though he does alter the sequence of chapters and adds an entry (chapter 26 on the Nitrian monk Origen) not found in the *GHM*.[58]

Rufinus takes even more liberties with the content of the *GHM* than he does with its structure, translating sense for sense rather than word for word.[59] He also adds to, subtracts

58. In chapter 23 he also mentions Ammonius's three brothers in passing (Eusebius, Dioscorus, Euthymius); none of these three is named in the *GHM*.

59. This was part and parcel of his translation technique in general. See E.C. Brooks, "The Translation Techniques of Rufinus of Aquileia (343–411)," *StudPatr* 17 (1982): 357–64; H.Hoppe, "Rufin als Übersetzer," in A.Gemelli, ed., *Studi dedicati alla memoria di Paolo Ubaldi* (Milan: Vita e pensiero, 1937), 133–50; C. Lo Cicero, "Φρόνημα σαρκός: Tertulliano e Rufino," in M.S. Celentano, ed., *Terpsis: In ricordo di Maria Laetitia Coletti* (Alexandria: Edizioni dell'Orso, 2002), 295–311; M.M. Wagner, *Rufinus the Translator. A Study of his Theory and his Practice as illustrated in his Version of the Apologetica of St. Gregory Nazianzen* (Washington, DC: The Catholic University of America Press, 1945); F. Winkelmann, "Einige Bemerkungen zu den Aussagen des Rufinus von Aquileia und des Hieronymus über ihre Übersetzungstheorie und -methode," in P. Granfield and J. Jungmann, eds., *Kyriakon: Festschrift Johannes Quasten* (Münster: Verlag Aschendorff, 1970), 532–47.

from, and generally retouches Anon.'s prose in numerous ways. For instance, sometimes he omits circumstantial geographical and other details reported in the *GHM*. Anon. states that Abba Or was "the father of hermitages of a thousand brothers" (πατέρα μοναστηρίων ἀδελφῶν χιλίων),[60] but Rufinus drops this numerical specificity and calls him simply "the father of many monasteries" (*multorum monasteriorum pater*).[61] Also, whereas Anon. says that the three monks appointed by Apollo to be his party's guides could speak Greek, Latin, and Coptic,[62] Rufinus lists only Greek and Coptic as their languages of proficiency.[63]

Other Rufinian deviations from the *GHM* concern topographical particulars. Anon. specifies that the blacksmith-turned-ascetic Apelles lived in "the district of Achoris" (ἐν τοῖς μέρεσι τῆς Ἀχωρέως),[64] but Rufinus says only that he lived "in the neighboring region" (*in vicina regione*), which vaguely locates Apelles somewhere in the Thebaid.[65] Likewise, Anon. situates the hermit Elias "in the desert of Antinoë" (ἐν τῇ ἐρήμῳ τῆς Ἀντινόου),[66] but Rufinus defines the area somewhat less precisely as "the territory outlying the city of Antinoë" (*in finibus civitatis Antinoo*).[67]

Rufinus's notice on John of Diolcos, when compared synoptically with Anon.'s, nicely illustrates the license he took as a translator:

GHM 26.1	*LHM* 33.1
We also visited another John in Diolcos, who was the father of hermitages. He, too, was endowed with much grace.[68]	In those parts there was a holy man named John who was completely full of grace. He had such a powerful gift

60. *GHM* 2.1.
61. *LHM* 2.1.
62. *GHM* 8.62.
63. *LHM* 7.12.
64. *GHM* 13.1.
65. *LHM* 15.1.
66. *GHM* 7.1.
67. *LHM* 12.1.
68. Cf. John Cassian, *coll.* 19.2, who mentions "the grace with which [John of Diolcos] was endowed" (*gratiam viri qua erat praeditus*).

He looked like Abraham and had a beard like Aaron's. He had performed many miracles and cures, and was especially successful at healing people afflicted with paralysis and gout.

of offering comfort that a soul, after receiving a few words from him, would be filled with cheer and joy, no matter the dejection or depression that had been oppressing it. God also bestowed upon him a significant gift of healing [the body].

Rufinus modifies the meaning of the Greek text in two striking ways. Anon. specifies that John of Diolcos had the charism of healing paralysis and gout,[69] but Rufinus refers only generically to his "gift of healing" and does not mention any particular afflictions that he was specialized in curing. Even more notably, Rufinus focuses exclusively on John's ability to cure ailments of the mind (and body) but says nothing about his physical appearance, thus dropping Anon.'s physiognomic description of John's face and beard whereby he tries to link the monk typologically to Abraham and Aaron.[70]

Every now and then Rufinus amends the *GHM* by adding an

69. Cf. Sozomen, *hist. eccl.* 6.29.8, who echoes Anon. and reports the same details.

70. How John is supposed to resemble Abraham is unclear, especially because no physical description is given for the patriarch in the Bible. Aaron's beard is mentioned only once in Scripture, in Ps 133(132).2, where the psalmist likens unity among the Israelites to "the precious oil on the head, running down on the beard, on the beard of Aaron." This verse may have inspired Anon. to mention this facial feature, though of course in what respect (length? coloring?) John's beard is imagined to resemble Aaron's is not specified. We need not assume that our narrator is allusively referencing contemporary Christian iconographic traditions about either Aaron or Abraham on the basis of which he would be cueing his readership to visualize John's appearance. The purpose of the comparison, after all, is not to take an accurate verbal snapshot of the monk's face so that he can then be recognized by other pious pilgrims, but rather to depict him, in strictly typological terms, as a holy man of such monumental stature that he channels not one but *two* titans of the biblical past, the one a venerable patriarch and the other the miracle-working first high priest of Israel. This twofold *synkrisis* suggests that John possesses a level of intrinsic sanctity comparable to theirs, and it thereby explains how he came to be endowed by God with healing powers.

explanatory aside for the benefit of his Latin readers. For instance, Anon. recounts that when his party was in the vicinity of Babylon and Memphis, they saw "Joseph's granaries, where he stored grain during biblical times."[71] In his rendering of this passage Rufinus clarifies that some people think that these "granaries," where Joseph stockpiled grain in preparation for seven years of famine,[72] are the pyramids of Giza.[73] In his introductory remarks about the famous monastic settlement at Nitria, Rufinus inserts an etymological sidebar, not present in the Greek, claiming that Nitria received its name from the natron extracted from nearby lakebeds.[74] On the basis of this etymological derivation, which is accepted by modern scholars,[75] and because natron was used as a cleaning agent to purify linen, Rufinus fancifully speculates that God foreordained Nitria to be so named because this would be a place where souls were purified.[76]

Rufinus usually retains the scriptural quotations and allusions found in the *GHM,* but in some cases he replaces them with his own. In one of the anecdotes attributed by Anon. to John of Lycopolis, an unnamed monk is seduced by a demon disguised as a woman, and in the course of succumbing to the temptation he is said to become a "lusty stallion" (θηλυμανὴς ἵπ-πος).[77] This comparison is reminiscent, both verbally and con-

---

71. *GHM* 18.3.

72. Gn 41.47–49.

73. "They say that in that vicinity are the places where Joseph is said to have stockpiled grain, which they also call 'Joseph's storehouses.' Some indeed think they are the pyramids, in which they say grain was gathered back then" (*LHM* 18.2).

74. *LHM* 21.1.

75. See, e.g., R. Bagnall and D. Rathbone, eds., *Egypt from Alexander to the Early Christians* (Los Angeles: Getty Publications, 2004), 110.

76. "This, I surmise, is because divine providence foresaw that in these parts the sins of men would be washed away and erased just as stains are by natron" (*LHM* 21.1). This notion is paralleled, in a more compressed form, in Jerome's famous *Epitaphium* on Paula. When taking stock of Paula's travels in monastic Egypt, Jerome says this about Nitria: "Nitria, in which the filth of the multitudes is daily washed away by the purest natron of virtue"; A. Cain, *Jerome's Epitaph on Paula: A Commentary on the Epitaphium Sanctae Paulae, with an Introduction, Text, and Translation* (Oxford: Oxford University Press, 2013), 63.

77. *GHM* 1.34.

ceptually, of the Lord's condemnation of the wayward Israelites at Jer 5.8: "They became lusty stallions (ἵπποι θηλυμανεῖς), each neighing for his neighbor's wife."[78] In Rufinus's description of the monk—"he became like the horse and mule who have no understanding" (*efficitur sicut equus et mulus, quibus non est intellectus*)—the phraseology from Jeremiah is exchanged for a verbal allusion to Ps 31.9a: "Do not become like the horse and mule, who have no understanding" (*nolite fieri sicut equus et mulus, quibus non est intellectus*). Hence the wayward monk is now likened to not one but two irrational animals.

On a handful of occasions Rufinus also inserts classical literary allusions not present in the *GHM*.[79] There are two examples, both intertexts from Virgil's *Aeneid*, that deserve mention. The first is put into the mouth of John of Lycopolis when he commends the party's diligence for undergoing so much travel-related hardship to visit him:

Virgil, *Aen.* 1.8–11	*LHM* 1.10 (1.2.14)
Musa, mihi causas memora, quo numine laeso ‖ *quidve dolens regina deum tot volvere casus* ‖ *insignem pietate virum, tot adire labores* ‖ *impulerit...*	*Unde plurimum miror intentionem vestri laboris ac studii quod profectus animae vestrae causa tantas superare regiones tantosque labores adire voluistis, cum nos eo usque pigritia desidiaque constringat, ut nec cellulas nostras progredi audeamus.*
Tell me, Muse, the reasons: how galled in her divine pride, and how sore at heart, the queen of the gods forced	I therefore am very much astonished at the resolve underlying your effort and zeal, because you have been

78. This statement continues the sentiment from the previous verse, where the sinful Israelites are rebuked for having "committed adultery and trooped to the houses of whores." On the prophet's use of this equine metaphor, see B. Foreman, *Animal Metaphors and the People of Israel in the Book of Jeremiah* (Göttingen: Vandenhoeck & Ruprecht, 2011), 118–20.

79. Despite the evident lack of classical (Greek) literary references in his text, the anonymous author of the *GHM* was a highly educated man who had received advanced training in classical literature and rhetoric. See A. Cain, *The Greek* Historia monachorum, 92–124.

a man distinguished for his *pietas* to weather so many perils and to undergo so many trials.

willing to traverse such vast lands and to undergo such daunting trials for the advancement of your souls, whereas laziness and idleness have such a grip on us that we do not dare to come out of our cells.

Rufinus adapts Virgil's *tot adire labores,* replacing *tot* with *tantos* to emphasize the qualitative rather than the quantitative aspect of the party's travel ordeals. John of Lycopolis and his cohort of Egyptian monks, then, are cast implicitly as Christian Aeneases,[80] though rather ironically so, inasmuch as they undertake their journey willingly (*voluistis*), whereas Aeneas's travels are thrust upon him by a vengeful goddess (*impulerit*).

Rufinus invokes Virgil also in the story about Apollo's tense encounter with the thuggish leader of a faction of pagan villagers who had made war against fellow villagers who were Christians. This man, the instigator of the war, opposed Apollo's attempts to broker a truce between the two rival groups, and so the monk cursed him, and soon thereafter he died and his corpse was devoured by wild animals. Rufinus labels him as "the leader of the pagans and the reason for that conflict" (*inter gentiles quasi caput et causa belli illius*).[81] In doing so he borrows the epithet that Drances,[82] the leader of the Latin emissaries to Aeneas and the rival of Turnus, applies to Turnus in his speech before the Latin council: "Latium's source and reason for these woes" (*Latio caput horum et causa malorum*). Thus Rufinus typologically likens Apollo's unnamed opponent to Turnus, both of whom not coincidentally meet with an ignominious death at the hands of their respective arch-enemies (Apollo and Aeneas).

---

80. Cf. Jerome's implicit casting of Paula as a feminized Christian Aeneas who made her own "epic" journey from Rome to the Holy Land; see Cain, *Jerome's Epitaph on Paula,* 204.

81. *LHM* 7.8. See p. 115n37 below.

82. On Virgil's portrayal of Drances, see P. Burke, "*Drances infensus:* A Study in Vergilian Character Portrayal," *Transactions of the American Philological Association* 108 (1978): 15–20; U. Scholz, "Drances," *Hermes* 127 (1999): 455–66.

The New Prophets and Apostles

In the previous section we surveyed some of the ways in which Rufinus altered the content of the *GHM*. But despite the many, often subtle, differences between the two texts, major thematic continuities run throughout both of them. Perhaps most significantly, Rufinus, following Anon.'s lead, uses a sophisticated system of typological figuration to heroize the Egyptian monks as the latter-day successors to the biblical prophets and apostles. This in fact is a cardinal structuring principle of their respective writings.

In its inner-biblical Christian sense, typology refers to Old Testament people, events, and things prefiguring or foreshadowing New Testament realities.[83] This imitative mode of discourse had been used by the authors of the New Testament,[84] and it subsequently was adopted by postbiblical Christian authors of martyrological literature[85] and hagiographic *Lives*,[86]

83. See J. Daniélou, *Sacramentum futuri: Études sur les origines de la typologie biblique* (Paris: Beauchesne, 1950); R.P.C. Hanson, *Allegory and Event: A Study of the Sources and Significance of Origen's Interpretation of Scripture* (Oxford: Oxford University Press, 1959); G.W.H. Lampe and K.J. Woollcombe, eds., *Essays on Typology* (London: SCM Press, 1957); F. Young, "Typology," in S.E. Porter et al., eds., *Crossing the Boundaries: Essays in Biblical Interpretation in Honour of Michael D. Goulder* (Leiden: Brill, 1994), 29–50.

84. See, e.g., T.L. Brodie, *Luke the Literary Interpreter: Luke-Acts as a Systematic Rewriting and Updating of the Elijah-Elisha Narrative in 1 and 2 Kings* (diss., University of St. Thomas, 1981); L. Goppelt, *Typos, die typologische Deutung des Alten Testaments im Neuen* (Gütersloh: Bertelsmann, 1939); R.J. Irudhayasamy, *A Prophet in the Making: A Christological Study on Lk 4, 16–30 in the Background of the Isaianic Mixed Citation and the Elijah-Elisha References* (Frankfurt am Main: Peter Lang, 2002); J. Lierman, *The New Testament Moses* (Tübingen: Mohr Siebeck, 2004).

85. See V. Saxer, *Bible et hagiographie: Textes et thèmes bibliques dans les actes des martyrs authentiques des premiers siècles* (Bern: Peter Lang, 1986).

86. For the use of typological reference from the Bible in early Christian hagiography, especially in *Lives*, see, e.g., L. Coon, *Sacred Fictions: Holy Women and Hagiography in Late Antiquity* (Philadelphia: University of Pennsylvania Press, 1997), 1–27; D.M. Deliyannis, "A Biblical Model for Serial Biography: The Book of Kings and the Roman *Liber Pontificalis*," *RBén* 107 (1997): 15–23; J.W. Earl, "Typology and Iconographic Style in Early Medieval Hagiography," *Studies in the Literary Imagination* 8 (1975): 15–46; J.M. Petersen, *The Dialogues of Gregory the Great in their Late Antique Cultural Background* (Toronto: Pontifical

who made their subjects conform to pre-fabricated paradigms of personal holiness (and thaumaturgy) that were derived from the Bible, such that they were "saints" insofar as they bore a likeness to the great figures of sacred history, including Elijah,[87] Elisha,[88] and Christ.[89]

The vast majority of instances of typological figuration in the *HM* fall under the heading of what we may call indirect reference, in which the comparison to a biblical personality remains implicit and is not overtly spelled out. This imitative mode is subtle and requires some hermeneutical effort from pious readers, because it presupposes their ready familiarity with the text of the Bible and prompts them to perceive the biblical affinities latent in the narrative and then, on the basis of these recognized correspondences, to "read" the hagiographic subject in the light of the scriptural paradigm(s) being evoked.

A holy person's ability to endure intense heat safely, whether emanating from open flames[90] or some other source, is a commonplace of early martyrological literature[91] and late antique

---

Institute of Mediaeval Studies, 1984), 25–55; M. van Uytfanghe, "L'empreinte biblique sur la plus ancienne hagiographie occidentale," in J. Fontaine and C. Pietri, eds., *Le monde latin antique et la Bible* (Paris: Beauchesne, 1985), 565–611.

87. See M. Mähler, "Évocations bibliques et hagiographiques dans la vie de saint Benoît par saint Grégoire," *RBén* 83 (1973): 145–84; É. Poirot, *Les prophètes Élie et Élisée dans la littérature chrétienne ancienne* (Turnhout: Brepols, 1998). On the tendency to cite Elijah in early medieval and medieval hagiography as a type of the prophet-reformer monk, see S. Robson, *"With the Spirit and Power of Elijah" (Lk 1, 17): The Prophetic-Reforming Spirituality of Bernard of Clairvaux as Evidenced Particularly in His Letters* (Rome: Pontificia Università Gregoriana, 2004), 18, 99n110.

88. See O. Rousseau, "Saint Benoît et le prophète Élisée," *RMon* 144 (1956): 103–14; S. Weingarten, *The Saint's Saints: Hagiography and Geography in Jerome* (Leiden: Brill, 2005), 174–75.

89. See H. Crouzel, "L'imitation et la suite de Dieu et du Christ dans les premiers siècles chrétiens ainsi que leurs sources gréco-romaines et hébraïques," *JbAC* 21 (1978): 7–41; H. Kech, *Hagiographie als christliche Unterhaltungsliteratur: Studien zum Phänomen des Erbaulichen anhand der Mönchsviten des hl. Hieronymus* (Göttingen: Kümmerle, 1977), 74–89.

90. Cf. the unusual miracle recorded by Gregory of Tours (*lib. mirac. Mart.* 3.42): fire could not even harm or destroy St. Martin's written *Vita*.

91. The most famous example concerns Polycarp. The fire that was supposed

hagiography.[92] There are several such examples in the *LHM*, but two in particular are worth a close look because they exemplify how Rufinus uses typological figuration to depict the protagonists of these stories implicitly as quasi-biblical figures.

Apollonius was a deacon famed for his holiness and miracle-working. During the reign of the emperor Maximian he was arrested for professing the Christian faith and thrown into prison,[93] where he was visited by a flute-player named Philemon, who, along with some of his fellow pagans, came to taunt the monk as a charlatan and blasphemer. Apollonius blessed Philemon, who was so pierced by compunction that he became a professing Christian. Both men appeared together before a judge and were subjected to various kinds of torture when they refused to recant their faith. When all else failed, the judge ordered that the two men be burned alive in front of all the people. The pyre was lit, and as the flames blazed around him, Apollonius cried out to God in the words of the psalmist: "'Do not deliver to the wild beasts, Lord, the souls that give praise to you,'[94] but reveal yourself clearly to us." The prayer was answered, and "a cloud soaked with dew (*nubes repleta rore*) enveloped the men and extinguished the flames of the fire."[95]

to burn him alive encircled his body but did not touch his skin; see H. Musurillo, ed. and trans., *The Acts of the Christian Martyrs* (Oxford: Oxford University Press, 1972), 15.

92. According to Cyril of Scythopolis (*v. Sab.* pp. 89–90 Schwartz), as a boy Sabas retrieved some clothes and emerged unscathed from a walk-in oven that was hotly burning. A variation on this theme, in which the body itself is not impervious to heat but rather is shielded from the effects of heat by some external force, is also found in Cyril of Scythopolis's *Life* of Sabas (p. 109 Schwartz): one of the brothers in Sabas's laura was protected from the desert's blazing sun by a moist cloud that enveloped him, and Cyril likens this to the pillar of cloud that guided the Israelites after they had escaped from Egypt (Ex 13.21). In the *Life of Pachomius* (*SBo* 14; *G¹* 8) a proud monk is able to walk on hot coals without his feet being burned, but Apa Palamon attributes this to demonic rather than to divine intervention. For miracles of preservation from fire in Gregory the Great's *Dialogi*, see 1.6; 3.18. Miraculous insulation from fire is not a privilege of men alone. According to one martyrological tradition, St. Agnes was condemned to death by fire but was decapitated after she had proved invulnerable to the flames (PL 17:818–19).

93. *LHM* 19.1 (*GHM* 19.2).
94. Ps 73.19 LXX.
95. *LHM* 19.3 (*GHM* 19.8).

This episode conjures up the biblical story about Shadrach, Meschach, and Abednego, the three young men from the kingdom of Judah who refused to bow before the massive golden statue erected by Nebuchadnezzar and who consequently were locked in a blazing furnace yet remained unharmed. Apollonius and Philemon, like their biblical forebears, undergo a trial by fire when they are unwilling to betray their personal religious convictions, and both sets of men are kept from being burned by a divinely manufactured cooling agent that is described as being dewlike: the angel of the Lord makes the interior of the furnace feel as though a dewy breeze (*ventum roris flantem*) were whistling through,[96] and a cloud soaked with dew extinguishes the flames that threaten to engulf Apollonius and Philemon.

Both events, and the fortitude of the saintly sufferers, elicit comparably positive reactions from previously unsympathetic onlookers, even from the very men who consigned them to a fiery fate. Nebuchadnezzar is astounded (*obstupuit*) that the three young men sing hymns and praise God while inside the furnace,[97] and when they emerge unscathed he exclaims: "Blessed be the God of Shadrach, Meschach, Abednego... who gave their bodies to the fire so that they might not serve or worship any god except their God."[98] Similarly, the judge and the crowd of people who witness the attempted execution of Apollonius and Philemon are duly astonished (*obstupefacti*) at the miracle transpiring before their very eyes, and they all spontaneously affirm both the existence and the might of the God worshiped by the persecuted: "Only the God of the Christians is great and one." So then, Rufinus "reads"—and prompts his readers to do likewise—the *passio* of Apollonius and Philemon as a Christianized recapitulation of the experience of Shadrach, Meschach, and Abednego.[99] He could be reasonably assured that this typolog-

96. Dn 3.50 Vulg.

97. Dn 3.91 Vulg.

98. Dn 3.95 Vulg.

99. For a patristic Christological reading of the fiery furnace episode, see J.P.K. Kritzinger, "St. Jerome's Commentary on Daniel 3," *APB* 16 (2005): 54–69.

ical "reading" would resonate with his contemporary monastic readers inasmuch as this biblical episode had been popularly depicted in Christian iconography since the second century[100] and the song of the three Hebrew youths was being chanted during morning prayer by eastern monks in the fourth century.[101]

Another story about miraculous preservation from fire was told by the ninety-year-old monk Copres, who lived near Hermopolis in the Thebaid. Copres told of an encounter he once had with a certain Manichaean who was trying to proselytize the local populace. He publicly debated with him but failed to convince the townspeople of the man's error, and so he resorted to an extraordinary measure, declaring to the crowd of onlookers:

"Light a huge fire in the middle of the street, and let us both walk into the flames. Whichever of us is not burned by it, rest assured that his is the true faith." Once I had said this, the common folk were satisfied, and a huge fire was lit. Then I grabbed him and started dragging him with me toward the fire. He said: "Not this way! Each of us should enter the fire individually. But you must go first because you are the one who proposed this." Signing myself with the Cross in Christ's name, I walked in. The flames actually began to part and disperse this way and that and to go out of their way to avoid contact with me. I stood in the midst of the fire for almost half an hour, and, by the Lord's name, I was not harmed in any respect whatsoever. The people looking on cheered in great amazement and praised God. They started to pressure the Manichaean to enter the fire, but he resisted and backed away. Then the crowds seized him and hurled him into the midst of the fire, and the flames, immediately engulfing and searing him, left him burned on half of his body. The people drove him out of the city in shame, crying out and saying: "Let the deceiver be burned alive!" But as for me, they took me with them and escorted me to the church as they praised the Lord.[102]

100. P. Finney, *The Invisible God: The Earliest Christians on Art* (Oxford: Oxford University Press, 1994), 83–84.

101. D. Krueger, "The Old Testament and Monasticism," in P. Magdalino and R. Nelson, eds., *The Old Testament in Byzantium* (Washington, DC: Dumbarton Oaks, 2010), 199–221 (209); cf. M.-H. Rassart-Debergh, "Les trois hébreux dans la fournaise en Égypte et en Nubie chrétiennes," *Rivista degli studi orientali* 58 (1987): 141–51.

102. *LHM* 9.7 (*GHM* 10.30–32).

Copres's encounter with the unnamed Manichaean is reminiscent of Elijah's confrontation of the 450 prophets of Baal on Mount Carmel.[103] Elijah is incensed that the Israelites cannot decide whether they want to follow Yahweh or Baal, and he wants to give them compelling proof that Yahweh alone deserves to be worshiped.[104] Two altars are built, one for each deity, and freshly slain bulls are laid thereupon; whichever god sends fire to consume the sacrifice is the true God. Copres, too, is the one to propose the ordeal by fire because the locals remain indecisive about the truth of orthodox Christianity even after he has publicly refuted the Manichaean. Both Elijah and Copres succeed in demonstrating that God is on their side in winning over the people: the Israelites fall on their faces and proclaim that Yahweh is the one true God,[105] and Copres's audience shout their approval and escort him, in a victory procession, to the church.[106]

The two stories diverge on a number of important points. For instance, Elijah calls down fire from heaven, but in the *LHM* the fire is started by the locals, not God. Elijah allows his opponents to go first, and as they invoke Baal in vain for several hours, he all the while mocks their god's silence.[107] In the *LHM* the order of events is reversed to underscore Copres's bravery and his foe's cowardice: the Manichaean agrees to step into the fire only after Copres has done so, yet after Copres has come out unharmed, he cowers and has to be thrust into the

103. 1 Kgs 18.17–40.

104. 1 Kgs 18.21. As argued by L. Bronner, *The Stories of Elijah and Elisha as Polemics against Baal Worship* (Leiden: Brill, 1968), the Elijah-Elisha cycles originally were composed as attacks on Canaanite mythology and Baal worship; see also J. R. Battenfield, "YHWH's Refutation of the Baal Myth through the Actions of Elijah and Elisha," in A. Gileadi, ed., *Israel's Apostasy and Restoration: Essays in Honor of Roland K. Harrison* (Grand Rapids: Eerdmans, 1988), 19–37; F. E. Woods, *Water and Storm Polemics against Baalism in the Deuteronomic History* (New York: Peter Lang, 1994), 95–121.

105. 1 Kgs 18.39. Cf. D. R. Thomas, "Elijah on Mount Carmel," *PEQ* 92 (1960): 146–55.

106. The separation of truth from falsehood by fire is a motif in Syrian Christianity; see S. Brock, "Fire from Heaven: From Abel's Sacrifice to the Eucharist," *StudPatr* 25 (1993): 229–43.

107. 1 Kgs 18.25–27.

flames by the onlookers. Another key difference between the two stories is their respective endings. By Elijah's order, all of the disgraced prophets of Baal are taken to the Wadi Kishon and executed.[108] The Manichaean escapes with his life, however, and Copres ostensibly does not encourage the crowd to do him further harm beyond what the fire itself has already done. Finally, there is the matter of numbers: a lone Elijah faces 450 prophets of Baal and 400 prophets of Asherah,[109] but in the *LHM* the confrontation is one-on-one. On this basis alone Copres's miracle seems to pale in comparison, by a very wide margin, with Elijah's. Nevertheless, one could argue that Copres's exploit actually is exponentially more impressive with respect to what really is at stake: what is exposed to open flames is not slaughtered bulls but the flesh of living human beings, a fact of which we are reminded by the Manichaean being "burned on half of his body" and thus nearly losing his life.

In any event, Copres's miracle, as it is presented in the text— "The flames actually began to part and disperse this way and that and to go out of their way to avoid contact with me. I stood in the midst of the fire for almost half an hour, and, by the Lord's name, I was not harmed in any respect whatsoever"— may well simultaneously draw inspiration, albeit more remotely than from the incident on Mount Carmel, from other Old Testament miracles. In being preserved through the fire, Copres, like Apollonius and Philemon, may recall Shadrach, Meschach, and Abednego, and the parting of the flames themselves may be reminiscent of Moses's parting of the Red Sea[110] or of Elisha's parting of the Jordan[111] allowing safe passage on dry land and preservation from a natural force that is potentially destructive to humans.

The two stories just examined (of Copres and of Apollonius and Philemon) draw inspiration from Old Testament models. Others in the *LHM*, however, adapt elements from *both* Testaments simultaneously. Such intertestamental reference is not

---

108. 1 Kgs 18.40.
109. 1 Kgs 18.19.
110. Ex 14.21–22.
111. 2 Kgs 2.14.

only more sophisticated, from an intertextual perspective, than
its intratestamental counterpart, but it also is more potent as
a device of typological narrative because it conveys the sub-
liminal message that the outstanding Egyptian monks actual-
ize in their lives the fullness of God's grace as revealed across
the entire spectrum of the Bible. A prime illustration of how
Rufinus uses intertestamental typology to portray a monk as
enacting the dual roles of (Old Testament) prophet and (New
Testament) apostle simultaneously is the following account of a
miracle of abundance performed by Apollo:

Once there arose a famine in the Thebaid. The inhabitants of that
territory, aware that the monks who served the Lord with Apollo often
were fed through the grace of the Lord even when they did not have
any food, all went together with their wives and children to ask him
for food and a blessing. Without hesitating at all, he brought out provisions stored up for the brothers' use and distributed these liberally
to each person. In fact, when only three baskets of bread remained,
even though the famine was still decimating the populace, he ordered
that the only baskets left, which were supposed to provide the monks
with food for one day, be brought out. In the hearing of all the people
whom the famine had forced to come together, he raised his hands to
God and said: "Is the hand of the Lord not strong enough to multiply
these? For the Holy Spirit says: 'The bread in these baskets will not
run out until all of us are satisfied with new returns.'"[112] As a great
many who had been present at that time confirmed, for four straight
months bread never once stopped being dished out of the baskets,
and there was not at any time the possibility of a shortage. They asserted that on another occasion Apollo had done the same with grain
and oil. It is related that the devil, irritated by these miracles, said to
him: "Are you Elijah or one of the other prophets or apostles, that
you have presumed to do these things?"[113] He replied: "Why do you
say that? Were not the prophets and apostles men who bequeathed to
us both their faith and grace? Or was God present then, but now he
is absent? God can do anything, and what he can do, he can do at any
time.[114] So then, if God is good, why are you evil?" As I said earlier, we
learned by faithful testimony from the elder holy monks that these
deeds had been performed through Apollo. Although their account
ought to be taken as trustworthy, what we ourselves beheld with our

112. Cf. 1 Kgs 17.14.
113. This contumelious question echoes the response of Christ's disciples
when he asked them who people believed him to be: "And they told him, 'John
the Baptist; and others say, Elijah; and others one of the prophets'" (Mk 8.28).
114. Cf. Lk 1.37.

own eyes nevertheless has given more credence to matters. For we saw baskets full of bread loaves being carried to empty tables, and when the tables were covered with loaves, which were consumed to the point of complete satiety, the baskets nonetheless were full when they were gathered up again.[115]

Perhaps the most readily apparent biblical model for this increase miracle is Christ's feeding of the hungry multitudes who had gathered in the countryside to hear him teach: the five thousand with five loaves of bread and two fish,[116] and the four thousand with seven loaves of bread and a few small fish.[117] There are indeed a number of notable points of convergence shared by the biblical accounts and the narrative of Apollo's feat. Like Christ, the Egyptian monk is motivated by compassion for a starving throng of men, women, and children. Both thaumaturgists, confident in their faith, provide their respective crowds with enough bread[118] for their sustenance.

Yet Apollo's miracle is but a dim and imperfect reflection of the Christic prototype upon whose prestige it is not allowed to encroach. For one thing, the victuals multiplied by Apollo are measured in basketfuls of loaves of bread, while those increased by Christ are measured in individual loaves; in other words, Jesus began with less bread to feed thousands of people. Secondly, Rufinus modestly declines from assigning any round numerical figure to the famished crowd; he opts simply for the ambiguous "the inhabitants of that territory." The only figure he furnishes is five hundred—the population of Apollo's monastery[119]—which is an unimpressive fraction of the number of the four thousand and the five thousand reported by the Gospel writers to have been fed by Christ.

This story draws some of its vital elements also from the biblical account of an increase miracle attributed to Elijah.[120] At

---

115. *LHM* 7.9.

116. Mt 14.15–21; Mk 6.35–44; Lk 9.12–17; Jn 6.5–14.

117. Mt 15.32–39; Mk 8.1–9. Both miracles are referred to at Mt 16.8–10.

118. On bread as a staple of the ancient Mediterranean diet, see, e.g., N. Jasny, "The Daily Bread of the Ancient Greeks and Romans," *Osiris* 9 (1950): 227–53.

119. *LHM* 7.1 (*GHM* 8.2).

120. 1 Kgs 17.10–16. Cf. the notice at 2 Kgs 4.42–44 about Elisha's feeding

the beginning of a three-and-a-half-year[121] drought that he had predicted, the prophet hid himself by the brook Cherith (east of the Jordan), from which he drank and where ravens twice daily brought him bread and meat.[122] But after the brook had dried up he was commanded by the Lord to go to Zarephath, where he would stay with a widow and be fed by her. She had just enough flour and oil to make some bread for herself and her son, but Elijah, invoking the God of Israel, declared: "Thus says the Lord: 'The jar of flour will not be consumed, and the jug of oil will not be empty, until the day that the Lord sends rain upon the earth.'"[123] This passage is evoked by Apollo: "For the Holy Spirit says: 'The bread in these baskets will not run out until all of us are satisfied with new returns.'" Apollo's miracle mirrors Elijah's in other significant ways: both are prompted by the circumstances of famine, and both multiply oil and other ingredients necessary for bread-making until the famine comes to an end, over three years in Elijah's case and four months in Apollo's case.

The typological connection made between Apollo's miracle and its Old Testament archetype is cemented by words put into the mouth of no less than Satan himself: "Are you Elijah or one of the other prophets or apostles, that you have presumed to do these things?" This question echoes the response of Christ's disciples when he asked them who people believed him to be: "And they told him, 'John the Baptist; and others say, Elijah; and others one of the prophets.'"[124] Satan's taunt thus further contributes to an already colorful intertextual mosaic, but even more importantly it is inserted into the narrative to affirm the validity of the miracle: this acknowledgment that it did indeed occur gains inestimable weight inasmuch as it comes from the arch-enemy of Christians. Apollo by no means shrinks from the challenge and in fact uses it as an occasion to argue that with

---

of 100 people in a time of famine on twenty loaves of barley and fresh ears of grain.

121. On the duration, see B. E. Thiering, "The Three and a Half Years of Elijah," *NovTest* 23 (1981): 41–55.

122. 1 Kgs 17.1–7.

123. 1 Kgs 17.14.

124. Mk 8.28, as mentioned above in note 113.

respect to his wonder-working capabilities he belongs to the same elite spiritual lineage as the Old Testament prophets and New Testament apostles.

In Rufinus's view, the Egyptian monks are neither inferior nor superior to their biblical predecessors. His overarching concern is to stress not distinctions between them but common ground: the monks are on an equal footing with the prophets and apostles inasmuch as they all draw from the same divine source of grace.[125] Indeed, the premise underlying his typological approach is that there is an unbroken continuity between the sacred history of the Bible and the ever-evolving "sacred history" of contemporary Egypt. In this respect he is very much a product of the Christian ideology of his own times. Theologians in Late Antiquity generally believed that the Old Testament had been fulfilled only partially by Christ's first coming and also that the promises made by God in Scripture remained valid for all of his people (that is, Christians) until Christ's second coming.

This open-ended conception of biblical time empowered hagiographic authors such as Rufinus to make ostensibly legitimate claims that their subjects fulfilled the words of Scripture, especially verses of potentially momentous prophetic import.[126] The most salient examples from the *LHM* are found in chapter 7 on Apollo, the charismatic monastic leader for whom Rufinus had enormous esteem for purportedly ridding his territory completely of paganism.[127] Commenting on the multitudes of holy monks who had congregated around Apollo, he says

125. This conventional idea is expressed also by Athanasius (*v. Ant.* 84.1), the anonymous authors of two of the *Lives* of Pachomius (*SBo* 45; *G*[1] 45), Besa (*v. Shen.* 2, 20), and Theodoret (*hist. rel.*, prol. 10). By contrast, the (probably Montanist) redactor of the *Passio Perpetuae et Felicitatis* (1.3) advocates the superiority of latter-day outpourings of the Spirit to what occurred in biblical times: "Let those then who would restrict the power of the one Spirit to times and seasons look to this: the more recent events should be considered the greater, being later than those of old, and this is a consequence of the extraordinary graces promised for the last stage of time."

126. See C. Rapp, "Old Testament Models for Emperors in Early Byzantium," in Magdalino and Nelson, eds., *Old Testament,* 175–98 (179–80).

127. *LHM* 7.6.

that they realized in their own lives the "words of Scripture": "The thirsty desert rejoiced, and its many children were spotted in the wilderness."[128] Rufinus acknowledges that although this prophecy originally had been made about the church, "it nevertheless has been fulfilled historically in the deserts of Egypt."[129] He elaborates:

For where in the cities do such great multitudes come to salvation that are as vast as those the deserts of Egypt have produced? The multitudes of monks in the deserts are almost as vast as the number of people in the cities. Hence it seems to me that a saying of the Apostle has been fulfilled in them: "Where sin abounds, grace abounds that much more."[130]

Further on, Rufinus tells of the conversion of a brigand chief who previously had opposed Apollo but later became a monk, having amended his life as if he had been changed from a wolf into an innocent lamb.[131] Picking up on his analogy of the wolf-turned-lamb, he says: "The prophecy of Isaiah found complete fulfillment in him: 'Wolves will feed with lambs, and the lion and ox will eat together.'"[132] As an aside, Rufinus proceeds to note that he saw there also "some men of Ethiopian extraction" practicing asceticism alongside Apollo's monks, and he ties their presence there to a scriptural prophecy: "Ethiopia will stretch out her hands to God."[133]

So then, just as the Old Testament prefigured the New Testament and its Christian realities, so the Bible in its totality prefigures the Egyptian monks. What their biblical forebears had been for their own generations, the monks were for theirs: the purest conduits of divine grace on earth. Humanity relies on them (as we will see in the following section), and indeed "the world stands firm on account of their just actions."[134] God provides for all of their needs and honors every single one of their

---

128. *LHM* 7.5; cf. Is 35.1; 54.1.
129. *LHM* 7.5.
130. *LHM* 7.5.
131. *LHM* 7.7.
132. *LHM* 7.7; cf. Is 65.25.
133. *LHM* 7.7; cf. Ps 67.32 LXX.
134. *LHM* Prol. § 9.

prayer requests,[135] and he invests them with miracle-working prowess, thus empowering them in their mission as his ambassadors to the world at large. Like the biblical prophets and apostles, they play an integral role in the unfolding of salvation history, both modeling in their own lives what perfect communion with God is supposed to be and acting as apostolic emissaries to bring the message of faith to the masses.[136]

The Egyptian Monks as Redeemers

The Egyptian monks perform miracles that defy the laws of physics. They walk across water,[137] teleport themselves,[138] multiply loaves of bread,[139] are impervious to intense heat,[140] cause the sun to stand still,[141] and awake the dead.[142] These are not the only ways in which they exhibit their divinely bestowed restorative authority over the physical world. In the narrative they are cast implicitly as new Adams who have achieved the communion with God that man had enjoyed prior to the Fall, and by virtue of this they have returned a sense of equilibrium to the cosmos that humanity had lost through Original Sin. The basic principle is vividly illustrated by an anecdote about a certain Abba Paul, monk in the Thebaid who used to take various kinds of snakes in his hands and cut them through the middle. Some fellow monks, awestruck by this, asked him how he had obtained such a powerful grace. He replied: "If someone has obtained purity, everything is in submission to him, as it was

135. *LHM* Prol. § 8, etc.

136. This accords with Rufinus's understanding (and literary portrayal) of both monks and orthodox bishops in his *LHM* as well as in his translation and continuation of Eusebius's *Ecclesiastical History*. See F. Thelamon, "Apôtres et prophètes de notre temps: Les évêques et les moines présentés comme apôtres et prophètes contemporains dans l'*Histoire Ecclésiastique* de Rufin," *AAAd* 39 (1992): 171–94; cf. F. Thelamon, "Rufin historien de son temps," *AAAd* 31 (1987): 41–59.

137. *LHM* 9.5; 16.4.

138. *LHM* 9.5.

139. *LHM* 7.9.

140. *LHM* 15.1; 19.3.

141. *LHM* 9.4.

142. *LHM* 9.3; 28.2.

to Adam, when he was in Paradise before he transgressed the commandment."[143]

The holy men featured in the *LHM* restored cosmic harmony partly by reinstating the utopian horticultural conditions of prelapsarian Eden. By making lush vegetation spring up in parched sand,[144] they reversed the Original Curse, according to which the earth would bring forth nothing but thorns and thistles to Adam and all of his descendants.[145] Abba Or was one such miracle-farmer: after settling in a non-arable part of the desert, he planted groves of fruit trees and green shrubbery and made them thrive.[146] Another monk, Copres, blessed sand brought to him by some local peasant farmers, and after they sprinkled it on their land, it immediately became fertile; subsequently he blessed his own land and made a garden full of fruit trees grow out of the sand.[147]

The monks also exercised complete dominion over even the deadliest wildlife and therefore recaptured Adam's prelapsarian sovereignty over every living thing.[148] Abba Theon would keep company at night with antelopes, wild asses, gazelles, and

---

143. *AP* Paul 1; cf. Cyril of Scythopolis, *v. Euth.* p. 23 Schwartz.

144. Cf. Orosius, *hist. adv. pag.* 7.33.2, on how the dry climate and sterile topsoil of the Egyptian desert made this region of the world uninhabitable for all but the monks who were brave enough to colonize it.

145. Gn 3.18.

146. *LHM* 2.1.

147. *LHM* 11.4.

148. Gn 1.26, 28. Saintly ascetics becoming new Adams by taming dangerous wildlife comprise a literary *topos* of late antique and medieval monastic hagiography. See D. Alexander, *Saints and Animals in the Middle Ages* (Woodbridge: Boydell, 2008), 30–34; R. Bauckham, *God and the Crisis of Freedom: Biblical and Contemporary Perspectives* (Louisville: John Knox Press, 2002), 128–77; D. Burton-Christie, *The Word in the Desert: Scripture and the Quest for Holiness in Early Christian Monasticism* (New York: Oxford University Press, 1993), 231–33; E. R. Henken, *The Welsh Saints: A Study in Patterned Lives* (Woodbridge: Boydell, 1991), 80–96; L. Hobgood-Oster, *Holy Days and Asses: Animals in the Christian Tradition* (Urbana: University of Illinois Press, 2008), 63–80; A. Voytenko, "Paradise Regained or Paradise Lost: The Coptic (Sahidic) Life of St. Onnophrius and Egyptian Monasticism at the End of the Fourth Century," in *Actes du huitième congrès international d'études coptes,* II (Leuven: Peeters, 2007), 635–44.

other desert animals.[149] Amoun ordered two large serpents to stand guard outside his hermitage to ward off thieves.[150] Abba Helle commanded an ass grazing in the wild to carry a load for him,[151] and on another occasion he tamed a notoriously ferocious crocodile and made it carry him across a river.[152] If serpents, crocodiles, scorpions, and other beasts acted aggressively toward humans and threatened innocent lives, the monks subjugated and even killed them. Abba Bes banished both a hippopotamus and a crocodile that were harassing the local farmers.[153] The Nitrian monk Didymus smashed scorpions and horned vipers with his bare feet.[154] Amoun confronted a serpent that was wreaking havoc on people in the countryside and murdering their livestock. As soon as he rebuked it in Christ's name, it vomited venom together with its breath and died right then and there.[155]

The Egyptian monks exerted their redemptive influence in the human sphere as well. On the one hand, all of them lived both culturally and geographically on the periphery of human civilization, but on the other hand, virtually all of them remained actively engaged, in a variety of capacities, in the everyday lives of men, women, and children who ran the socioeconomic gamut.[156] On the less prestigious end of the spectrum there were Coptic peasant farmers,[157] the faceless urban

149. *LHM* 6.3.
150. *LHM* 8.2.
151. *LHM* 11.2.
152. Ibid.
153. *LHM* 4.2.
154. *LHM* 24.1.
155. *LHM* 8.3.

156. A comparable variety of social interaction may be observed in the case of Shenoute, who had dealings with people from all walks of life and ideological persuasions, from pagan philosophers to Christian dignitaries. See H. Behlmer, "Visitors to Shenoute's Monastery," in D. Frankfurter, ed., *Pilgrimage and Holy Space in Late Antique Egypt* (Leiden: Brill, 1998), 341–71. On the Egyptian desert monks' interactions with the laity and clergy, see G. Gould, "Lay Christians, Bishops, and Clergy in the *Apophthegmata patrum*," *StudPatr* 25 (1993): 396–404.

157. *LHM* 9.6; 11.4.

poor,[158] and marginalized figures such as flute-players.[159] On the other end we find affluent merchants,[160] rich rural land-owners,[161] military generals,[162] tribunes[163] (and their wives),[164] senatorial aristocrats,[165] and even the emperor himself.[166] In other words, the reach of the monks' spiritual authority is portrayed in the narrative as being universal.

Rural Coptic subsistence farmers surface rather often in the *LHM* as beneficiaries of the monks' miracles.[167] Because they relied on a steady crop each year to feed their families and to make a living, they worried about perennial threats to the agricultural vitality of their land.[168] One threat came in the form of pests such as mice, rats, locusts, birds, and worms.[169] In the *LHM* some peasants who owned a plot of land next to Copres's hermitage had their entire crop destroyed one year by a worm, and they asked him to pray for their harvest. He blessed some sand, which they then sowed together with their seeds to produce a plentiful, pest-resistant crop.[170] Other types of pests, such as snakes and crocodiles, posed a less direct threat to the crops themselves but nonetheless terrorized the local populace and killed their livestock. As we saw earlier, after the monks had been begged to intercede, they either banished or killed the beasts.

An even greater worry for Coptic farmers than pest man-

158. *LHM* 18.1.
159. *LHM* 16.1–2; 19.1.
160. *LHM* 16.5–6.
161. *LHM* 16.3–4.
162. *LHM* 1.3.
163. *LHM* 1.4; 29.5.
164. *LHM* 1.4.
165. *LHM* 1.7.
166. *LHM* 1.2.
167. Their constant presence is a function of the fact that they were the monks' closest neighbors, geographically speaking.
168. Cf. J. M. Frayn, *Subsistence Farming in Roman Italy* (Fontwell: Open Gate Press, 1979).
169. See D. Stathakopoulos, *Famine and Pestilence in the Late Roman and Early Byzantine Empire: A Systematic Survey of Subsistence Crises and Epidemics* (Aldershot: Ashgate, 2004), 41–46.
170. *LHM* 11.4, as mentioned above on p. 34.

agement was the unpredictability of the water level of the Nile. In antiquity the Nile would flood each year between July and October, depending on the timing of the annual torrential rainfall in the Ethiopian highlands, which was the source of its inundation. This flooding was essential to agriculture because the overflowed waters irrigated the soil and also deposited silt, which acted as a fertilizer. If the flood came too late, sowing and harvesting were delayed,[171] and if it came too little, the area of cultivation was reduced and the crop yield suffered. Throughout Egyptian history, there developed an increasingly institutionalized Nile cult in which priests and villagers would perform rites annually to incur the divine river's favor.[172] As monasticism flourished in the fourth-century Egyptian countryside, Christian holy men emerged who, according to the hagiographic literary sources, usurped the authority of the priests of the Nile cult by making accurate predictions about the river's inundation and also by guaranteeing it would happen through their special appeal to God.[173] In the *LHM* two different monks assume this kind of prerogative. John of Lycopolis predicted for local peasant farmers not only when the Nile would flood each year but also precisely how the river's level would impact their harvest.[174] Apollo used a stunning miracle to interrupt a local Nile procession and to effect the mass conversion of the worshipers to Christianity,[175] the implication being that he abolished one localized manifestation of the "national" Nile cult.

If crop failure did occur and famine ensued, the monks

171. I. Arnon, *Crop Production in Dry Regions, Volume I: Background and Principles* (London: Leonard Hill, 1972), 120.

172. On the development and ritualistic aspects of the Nile cult, see D. Bonneau, *La crue du Nil, divinité égyptienne, à travers mille ans d'histoire* (Paris: Klincksieck, 1964), 393–98; Bonneau, "Les fêtes de la crue du Nil: Problèmes de lieux, de dates et d'organisation," *RdE* 23 (1971): 49–65; D. Frankfurter, *Religion in Roman Egypt: Assimilation and Resistance* (Princeton: Princeton University Press, 1998), 42–46.

173. On the post-third-century transformation of the Nile cult under Christian influence more generally, see Bonneau, *La crue du Nil*, 421–39; A. Hermann, "Der Nil und die Christen," *JbAC* 2 (1959): 30–69.

174. *LHM* 1.6.

175. *LHM* 7.5.

stepped in to prevent widespread starvation. During one famine in the Thebaid, Apollo, in a self-conscious imitation of Christ, multiplied three baskets of bread daily for four months in order to feed famished peasants who implored him for help.[176] The monks did not always have to resort to thaumaturgy in order to fill the bellies of the masses. Sarapion's community of ten thousand monks pooled their grain harvest each season and used it to feed the poor in nearby Arsinoë and more distantly in Alexandria.[177]

The monks helped people from all walks of life come to terms with the vicissitudes of everyday living not only by alleviating their physical pain and suffering, but also by assuaging their concerns about the future. The infant mortality rate was high in Roman Egypt,[178] as it was in other parts of the late Empire,[179] and so enormous uncertainties surrounded the beginning of the life-cycle; yet the monks used their prophetic powers to give confident assurances not only that births would be free of complications but also that infants would safely reach adulthood.[180]

Likewise, on account of inclement weather, piracy, and highway robbery, travel by land and sea notoriously was fraught with life-threatening perils.[181] To allay anxieties about these risk factors, the monks assured travelers that their journeys would be safe.[182] Their prophecies sometimes had regional and even empire-wide significance. For instance, John of Lycopolis predicted the emperor Theodosius's victorious battles over bar-

176. *LHM* 7.9, as related above on p. 29.

177. *LHM* 18.1.

178. In Roman Egypt about one-third of all children died before their first birthday, and more than half died by the age of five; see R. Bagnall, *Egypt in Late Antiquity* (Princeton: Princeton University Press, 1995), 182.

179. The rate may have been as high as 30%–40% in the first year of life; see B. Frier, "Roman Life Expectancy: Ulpian's Evidence," *HSCP* 86 (1982): 213–51; Frier, "Roman Life Expectancy: The Pannonian Evidence," *Phoenix* 37 (1983): 328–44.

180. *LHM* 1.5.

181. See, e.g., F. Meijer and O. van Niff, eds., *Trade, Transport and Society in the Ancient World* (London: Routledge, 1992), 168–72; P. de Souza, *Piracy in the Graeco-Roman World* (Cambridge: Cambridge University Press, 1999), 225–40.

182. *LHM* 1.4–6.

barian armies.[183] He also accurately predicted that Theodosius would die of natural causes.[184]

Because sickness and disease were prevalent among all social classes in the late Roman world,[185] and because the medical science of the day lacked the resources to treat the more serious ailments effectively, the Christian holy man was able to step in and provide hope (or at least the appearance of hope) where there otherwise was none. The Egyptian monks accordingly cured cataracts,[186] fever,[187] rabies,[188] and other unspecified maladies.[189] But they are portrayed as healers not just of the body but even more importantly as healers of the soul. Like the biblical prophets and apostles to whom they are compared in the narrative, they occupy center stage in the unfolding drama of salvation history as the cosmic mediators between God and fallen humanity, as the divinely appointed human agents through whom eternal redemption is brought to the ephemeral world of their time.

The *LHM* at times reads like a "Book of Conversions." It documents several mass conversions of pagans—by Copres,[190] Patermuthius,[191] Apollonius,[192] and Apollo.[193] There also are recorded numerous conversions of individuals, from debauched flute-players[194] to a high-ranking military official[195] and a wealthy

183. *LHM* 1.2.
184. *LHM* 1.26. Cf. Theodoret, *hist. rel.* 2.14, on how the Syrian ascetic Julian foretold the death of the emperor Julian.
185. For the evidence concerning Roman Egypt in particular, see, e.g., W. Scheidel, *Death on the Nile: Disease and the Demography of Roman Egypt* (Leiden: Brill, 2001); P. van Minnen, "P.Oxy. LXVI 4527 and the Antonine Plague in the Fayyum," *ZPE* 135 (2001): 175–77.
186. *LHM* 1.7.
187. *LHM* 1.8.
188. *LHM* 30.2; 31.5.
189. *LHM* 1.4; 6.1; 9.1.
190. *LHM* 9.7.
191. *LHM* 9.4.
192. *LHM* 19.3–4.
193. *LHM* 7.6, 8.
194. *LHM* 19.1.
195. *LHM* 29.5.

merchant,[196] and in virtually every case the conversion entails
not simply an embrace of creedal Christianity but even more so
a wholesale adoption of the monastic lifestsyle. The most compelling conversions involve a marginalized segment of the lower classes: robbers.[197] In the Roman world robbers represented
the epitome of bloodthirstiness,[198] rapacity,[199] sneakiness,[200] and
all-around lawlessness.[201] As such, they were ideal converts to a
religion that emphasizes honesty, generosity, and love for one's
neighbor.[202] This stereotypical perception of them explains why
the conversion of robbers eventually would become one of the
saint's standard accomplishments cited in hagiographic literature.[203] Rufinus gives this motif prominence in his narrative because the extreme nature of the robber's sinner-to-saint transformation emphasizes how the monks are such pure conduits of

196. *LHM* 16.5.

197. *LHM* 6.2; 7.7; 8.2; 9.1, 8; 16.2. On their marginalized status in Roman society, see V. Neri, *I Marginali nell' occidente tardoantico* (Bari: Edipuglia,
1998), 289–418.

198. Cf. Apuleius, *met.* 8.1.

199. Cf. Cyprian, *zel. et liv.* 7; Heliodorus, *Aeth.* 1.3.3; Gregory of Nazianzus,
orat. 14.6; Jerome, *epist.* 52.7.

200. Cf. John Cassian, *coll.* 7.16.

201. See A. J. L. van Hoof, "Ancient Robbers: Reflections behind the Facts,"
AncSoc 19 (1988): 105–24; B. Shaw, "Bandits in the Roman Empire," *P&P* 105
(1984): 3–52.

202. By contrast with the robbers in the *LHM* who become spiritual success
stories, the ones who appear in ancient novels typically meet a bad end; see K.
Hopwood, "'All that may become a Man': The Bandit in the Ancient Novel," in
L. Foxhall and J. Salmon, eds., *When Men were Men: Masculinity, Power, and Iden-
tity in Classical Antiquity* (New York: Routledge, 1998), 195–204; A. Scobie, *More
Essays on the Ancient Romance and its Heritage* (Meisenheim am Glan: Verlag A.
Hain, 1973), 19–34.

203. On the recurrence of the *topos* of the *brigand repenti* in hagiographic
literature, see A. Giardina, "Banditi e santi: Un aspetto del folklore gallico tra
tarda antichità e medioevo," *Athenaeum* 61 (1983): 374–89; F. H. M. van Camp-
en, *Latrocinium* (Nijgmegen, 1978), Appendix 2; J. Wortley, *"De latrone converso:*
The Tale of the Converted Robber," *Byzantion* 66 (1996): 19–43. For some late
antique examples, see Eusebius, *hist. eccl.* 3.23; Jerome, *v. Hilar.* 6.1–4; Sulpicius Severus, *v. Mart.* 5.4–6; Cyril of Scythopolis, *v. Sab.* p. 119 Schwartz. The
conversion of sinners to monks is a *Leitmotiv* of late antique monastic literature in general; see, e.g., B. Ward, *Harlots of the Desert: A Study of Repentance in
Early Monastic Sources* (Kalamazoo: Cistercian Publications, 1987), 1–9.

divine grace that God is able through them to soften even the
hardest of hearts.

Evagrius of Pontus and his
Teachings in the *LHM*

In the Prologue (§ 12) to the *GHM*, Anon. asserts that the
aim of his writing is to edify his pious readers and to provide a
catalyst for their advancement in the ascetic life.[204] Throughout
the work he takes a two-pronged approach to this edification:
he sets up the Egyptian monks as Christ-like exemplars who are
to be imitated by his readership, and he presents them as divinely inspired teachers, preserving their teachings as a chres-
tomathy of discourses, anecdotes, and aphorisms, all of which
they ostensibly relay in their own voice.[205] Now, as he frequently
reminds his readers, during his Egyptian travels he had heard
from his monastic hosts an indefinitely large number of spiritual discourses and sayings that did not make the final cut of the
GHM.[206] Since he had so much potential narrative material at
his disposal, he must have exercised considerable editorial discretion to arrive at the precious small remnant he personally
deemed most useful to his readers.

I have demonstrated elsewhere that the monks' teachings
have conspicuously strong affinities to those of the famed ascetic theologian Evagrius of Pontus (345–99),[207] as the monks

204. "Because I have derived much help from [the monks], I have undertaken this work to provide the perfect (τῶν τελείων) with a stimulus to emula-
tion (ζῆλον) and a reminder (ὑπόμνησιν), and beginners in the ascetic life (τῶν
ἀρχομένων ἀσκεῖν) with edification (οἰκοδομήν) and guidance (ὠφέλειαν)."
205. Cain, *The Greek* Historia monachorum, 214–44.
206. See, e.g., *GHM* 12.16; 13.12; 15.2; 21.1; Epil. §1.
207. The principal ancient sources for Evagrius's life are the church histori-
ans Socrates (*hist. eccl.* 4.23) and Sozomen (*hist. eccl.* 6.30) and his disciple Palladius, both the Greek version of the *Lausiac History* (ch. 38) and the Coptic version, which contains additional material; on this latter, see G. Bunge and A. de
Vogüé, eds., *Quatre ermites égyptiens d'après les fragments coptes de* l'Histoire Lausiaque (Bégrolles-en-Mauges: Abbaye de Bellefontaine, 1994); T. Vivian, "Coptic
Palladiana II: The Life of Evagrius (*Lausiac History* 38)," *CCR* 21 (2000): 8–23.
On Evagrius's life and thought, see Antoine Guillaumont's magisterial monograph *Un philosophe au désert: Évagre le Pontique* (Paris: J. Vrin, 2004).

both collectively and individually invite readers to view crucial aspects of spiritual reality through the same prism that
Evagrius offers to the readers of his writings.[208] In particular,
several of the monks featured in the *GHM*—including its two
headlining "stars" John of Lycopolis and Apollo of Bawit—are
fashioned into vocal advocates of the core principles of Evagrian ascetic mysticism, which include the sharp distinction
between the active and the contemplative monastic life,[209] the
theory and practice of pure prayer,[210] the monastic ideal of im-

---

208. Cain, *The Greek* Historia monachorum, 245–59. For scholarly discussions of Evagrius's ascetic theory, see K. Corrigan, *Evagrius and Gregory: Mind,
Soul and Body in the 4th Century* (Farnham: Ashgate, 2009); R.E. Sinkewicz,
trans., *Evagrius of Pontus: The Greek Ascetic Corpus* (Oxford: Oxford University
Press, 2003), xxi–xl. The finer points of Evagrian theology have recently been
analyzed by A. Casiday, *Reconstructing the Theology of Evagrius Ponticus* (Cambridge: Cambridge University Press, 2013); see also Clark, *Origenist Controversy*,
43–84.

209. In Evagrius's hierarchy of spiritual progress, the monk who lives the
"active life" (βίος πρακτικός) advances in personal holiness while practicing
the monastic social virtues (e.g., almsgiving and hospitality), but with spiritual
maturity he eventually moves on to the "gnostic life" (βίος γνωστικός), or "contemplative life" (βίος θεωρητικός), in which, having left behind the mundane,
he directs his attention to contemplation (θεωρία) and the acquisition of mystical knowledge (γνῶσις), first of the cosmos in both its visible and invisible
dimensions and then of the Holy Trinity.

210. I.e., prayer in which the mind is undisturbed by the passions (πάθη)
and harmful thoughts (λογισμοί). The Evagrian doctrine of pure prayer (κα-
θαρὰ προσευχή) was, for its time, an innovative concept lying at the very heart
of Evagrius's mystical theology. See G. Bunge, "The Spiritual Prayer: On the
Trinitarian Mysticism of Evagrius of Pontus," *MonStud* 17 (1987): 191–208;
idem, *Das Geistgebet: Studien zum Traktat* De oratione *des Evagrios Pontikos* (Cologne: De Gruyter, 1987); idem, "La Montagne intelligible: De la contemplation indirecte à la connaissance immédiate de Dieu dans le traité *De oratione*
d'Évagre le Pontique," *StudMon* 42 (2000): 7–26; L. Dysinger, *Psalmody and
Prayer in the Writings of Evagrius Ponticus* (Oxford: Oxford University Press,
2005); Guillaumont, *Un philosophe*, 298–306; I. Hausherr, *Les leçons d'un contemplatif: Le traité de l'Oraison d'Évagre le Pontique* (Paris: Beauchesne, 1960);
D. Ousley, *Evagrius' Theology of Prayer and the Spiritual Life* (diss., Univ. of Chicago, 1979). On the far-reaching posthumous influence of Evagrius's doctrine
of pure prayer, see B. Bitton-Ashkelony, "The Limit of the Mind (ΝΟΥΣ):
Pure Prayer according to Evagrius Ponticus and Isaac of Nineveh," *ZAC* 15
(2011): 291–321.

passibility (ἀπάθεια),[211] and the demonic inspiration of impure thoughts.[212]

In translating the GHM into Latin, Rufinus not only retained the pro-Evagrian material present in the Greek original, but he also made his own substantive additions to it. His favoritism in this regard is readily visible from a synoptic comparison of Anon.'s notice on Evagrius and his own:

GHM 20.15	LHM 27.1
We also saw Evagrius, a wise and erudite man, who was gifted at discerning thoughts, having acquired this skill through experience. He often went down to Alexandria and would reduce the pagan philosophers to silence. He admonished the brothers who were with us not to gorge themselves on water: "For the demons," he said, "habitually congregate in well-watered	We also visited there a man named Evagrius, who was extremely wise and wonderful in every way. Among other spiritual virtues, he was bestowed with such a great gift of discerning spirits and of "purifying thoughts" (as the Apostle says) that none other of the fathers is believed to have attained such profound knowledge of lofty spiritual matters. Although he was

211. I.e., the condition in which the monk experiences perfect emotional and intellectual stability because he has learned to keep the passions in check. Even though Evagrius was by no means the only fourth-century eastern Christian thinker to advocate *apatheia* as an ethical norm, he nevertheless was the only one to make this concept a centerpiece of his system of thought. See J. Driscoll, *Steps to Spiritual Perfection: Studies on Spiritual Progress in Evagrius Ponticus* (New York: Paulist Press, 2005), 76–93; J. Driscoll, "*Apatheia* and Purity of Heart in Evagrius Ponticus," in H. A. Luckman and L. Kulzer, eds., *Purity of Heart in Early Ascetic and Monastic Literature: Essays in Honor of Juana Raasch* (Collegeville: Liturgical Press, 1999), 141–59; B. Maier, "*Apatheia* bei den Stoikern und *Akedia* bei Evagrios Pontikos: Ein Ideal und die Kehrseite seiner Realität," *OC* 78 (1994): 230–49. R. Somos, "Origen, Evagrius Ponticus, and the Ideal of Impassibility," in W. A. Bienert and U. Kühneweg, eds., *Origeniana septima* (Leuven: Peeters, 1999), 365–73, argues (against the current majority opinion) that Evagrius derived his doctrine of impassibility from Origen.

212. See Guillaumont, *Un philosophe*, 242–53; C. Stewart, "Evagrius Ponticus and the Eight Generic *Logismoi*," in R. Newhauser, ed., *In the Garden of Evil: The Vices and Culture in the Middle Ages* (Toronto: Pontifical Institute of Medieval Studies, 2005), 3–34.

places." He gave us many other discourses about the ascetic life, thereby strengthening our souls.

granted great understanding through personal trials involving the matters themselves and most of all through the grace of God, nevertheless this also happened to him: he was instructed for a long period of time by the blessed Macarius, who, as all are aware, was extremely famous for having God's grace and working miracles and for being distinguished in virtuousness. This Evagrius practiced unbelievable abstinence, yet above all he would admonish any brothers who happened to be engaged in an exercise to subdue the body or to repel from the body the imagined forms brought on by demons, not to drink a large amount when consuming water. For he would say that if the body is inundated with water, it gives rise to more powerful imagined forms and provides more robust dwelling-places for demons. With the utmost judiciousness he taught many other things about abstinence. Moreover, he himself not only drank water very sparingly, but he also abstained entirely from bread.

Rufinus has considerably amplified his Greek precursor. Omitting any mention of Evagrius's prowess as a Christian apologist,[213] which Anon. duly touts,[214] he is concerned solely with firming up Evagrius's credentials as an unrivaled authority on ascetic theory and practice. His "great understanding," which made him superior to even the most venerable desert monks of his cohort ("the fathers"), had a divine origin and was cultivated through the trial and error of daily struggle. In eremitic spirituality, vast personal experience with the monastic life was absolutely foundational to any and all claims a would-be teacher might make to spiritual authority,[215] and so in citing Evagrius's experience in the ascetic life Rufinus is attempting to validate his authority along recognizable lines. He authenticates Evagrius's credibility by invoking another conventional component of the eremitic *cursus honorum,* namely the need for a novice monk to serve as an apprentice under a seasoned elder monk (*abba*) from whom he was to learn the ropes of the monastic life.[216] Before acquiring his own disciples (that is, the

213. Palladius (*hist. Laus.* 38.11) mentions Evagrius's encounters with heretics but none with pagan philosophers (cf. Antony's debates with pagan philosophers at Athanasius, *v. Ant.* 72–80); on Evagrius's participation in the intellectual culture of Alexandria, see A.D. Rich, *Discernment in the Desert Fathers: Διάκρισις in the Life and Thought of Early Egyptian Monasticism* (Waynesboro: Paternoster, 2007), 12–15; E. Watts, *City and School in Late Antique Athens and Alexandria* (Berkeley: University of California Press, 2006), 184–86. Casiday, *Reconstructing the Theology,* 81–82, suggests, as a literary parallel to this passage, Athanasius's report in the *Life of Antony* (69.2) of Antony going to Alexandria to denounce Arius's supporters publicly.

214. Anon. furnishes this intriguing bit of information presumably to support one of the leitmotifs of the *GHM,* namely the desert monks' decisive triumph over paganism in all its forms; see Cain, *The Greek* Historia monachorum, 183–88.

215. A. Cain, *The Letters of Jerome: Asceticism, Biblical Exegesis, and the Construction of Christian Authority in Late Antiquity* (Oxford: Oxford University Press, 2009), 30–42, 144–67; R.J. Goodrich, *Contextualizing Cassian: Aristocrats, Asceticism, and Reformation in Fifth-Century Gaul* (Oxford: Oxford University Press, 2007), 32–116. On ascetic experience as a form of practical wisdom, see Athanasius, *v. Ant.* 39.1; Gregory of Nazianzus, *orat.* 16.20.

216. See G. Gould, *The Desert Fathers on Monastic Community* (Oxford: Oxford University Press, 1993), 26–87; A. Louf, "Spiritual Fatherhood in the Literature of the Desert," in J.R. Sommerfeldt, ed., *Abba: Guides to Wholeness and Holiness East and West* (Kalamazoo: Cistercian Publications, 1982), 37–63.

"brothers" mentioned above), Evagrius had interned under Macarius the Great.[217] Rufinus does not just name Macarius, but he also trumpets some of his accomplishments to imply that Evagrius inherited his master's prophetic greatness.[218]

In order to capitalize further on Evagrius's ties to Macarius, Rufinus, after concluding his entry on Evagrius, proceeds with a chapter in which he profiles Macarius's miracles. One of these miracle stories differs significantly from the version found in the Greek:

GHM 21.17	*LHM* 28.3
A certain evildoer had changed a girl consecrated to virginity into a mare through certain magic arts. Her parents brought her to him [Macarius] and asked if he would be willing to pray and change her into a woman. So, having locked her up by herself for seven days, while her parents remained close by, he devoted himself to prayer in another cell. Entering with her parents on the seventh day, he anointed her all over with oil. He bent his knees and prayed with them and after getting back up they found her changed into a girl.	The virgin daughter of a certain father from a nearby town looked to people as if she had been turned into a horse through the illusions of magic, such that she was thought to be a mare and not a girl. They brought her to Macarius. After he had inquired of her parents about what they wanted, they said: "This mare that your eyes see was a virgin girl and our daughter, but wicked men used evil arts to turn her into the animal you see. We therefore ask you to pray to the Lord and change her into what she was." But he said: "This one you point out—I see her as a girl who has nothing animal-like about her.

217. Evagrius became Macarius's disciple upon moving to Kellia in 385. See G. Bunge, "Évagre le Pontique et les deux Macaires," *Irénikon* 56 (1983): 215–27, 323–60.

218. For added effect, Rufinus follows the entry on Evagrius immediately with accounts of some of Macarius's thaumaturgical exploits.

Rather, what you are referring
to is not in her body but in the
eyes of onlookers, for these
are demons' illusions (*fantasi-
ae*), not how things truly are."
After bringing her into his
cell along with her parents, he
bent his knees and began to
pray to the Lord, and at the
same time he encouraged the
parents to join him in entreating the Lord. Afterward
he anointed her with oil in
the Lord's name, removed all
the visual deceptiveness, and
made her appear as a virgin
to all, as indeed she used to
appear to herself.

Rufinus has modified his source in several ways, but for our
purposes here his most substantive alteration concerns the nature of the virgin's affliction: in the Greek she is turned into
a mare (presumably by means of a curse spell),[219] but in the
Latin she never becomes an *actual* mare and is only *perceived*
to be one by others. On one level Rufinus may be making a
conscious concession to contemporary western readers who
might find the idea of an actual bodily metamorphosis to be
too fantastical (that is, the stuff of mythology or of novels),[220]
and this incredulity obviously would undercut Macarius's authority as a thaumaturge. But there is another, more pressing
reason why Rufinus rewrites Anon.'s version of the story, and

219. On the wide variety of curse spells cast in the ancient world, see M.
Meyer, ed., *Ancient Christian Magic: Coptic Texts of Ritual Power* (San Francisco,
1994), 183–256. On women in particular as victims of curse spells in late Roman Egypt, see E. Pachoumi, "The Erotic and Separation Spells of the Magical Papyri and *Defixiones*," *GRBS* 53 (2013): 294–325.

220. E.g., Apuleius's *Metamorphoses*, in which the protagonist Lucius is
changed into an ass at the beginning of the novel but transformed back into a
human in the final book.

that is to superimpose a distinctly Evagrian template onto it. For one thing, he casts Macarius essentially as the consummate Evagrian "gnostic" monk who has reached such a high level of discernment, and acquired such intimate knowledge of creation in its visible and invisible dimensions, that he sees things for what they truly are. Whereas everyone with whom the girl comes into contact is fooled by the optical illusion and is horrified that she has turned into an animal, Macarius, in direct speech invented by Rufinus to make the point more forceful, identifies it as a demonic ruse and even uses the Evagrian catchword *fantasia* (φαντασία) to describe the phenomenon.

Rufinus occasionally augments a monk's discourse to infuse even more of an Evagrian element than is already present in the Greek. An excellent example is the following passage from his account of John of Lycopolis's discourse on pure prayer (*LHM* 1.3):

It is the monk's chief occupation to offer pure prayer to God while having nothing blameworthy on his conscience.... If we stand before God with a pure heart and are free from all the vices and passions I enumerated earlier, we will be able (insofar as this is possible) even to see God and to direct the eye of our heart toward him while praying—to see him who is invisible with the mind, not with the body, and with the perception gained through knowledge, not with the flesh's faculty of sight. For let no one suppose that he can gaze upon the very essence of God in and of itself, such that in his heart he would devise for himself some appearance or image akin to some corporeal image. In God there is no form, no limitation, but only perception and thought. Although he certainly can be perceived and can arouse the mind's feeling, he nevertheless cannot be apprehended, described, or captured in words. It is therefore necessary to approach God with all reverence and fear and to focus the gaze of our mind on him so that the human mind—everything whatsoever it can conceive of that is splendid, bright, effulgent, and majestic—may always realize that he is above all these things. As I have said, this is the case if the mind is pure and not enslaved to any base encumbrances of a depraved will. Therefore, those who are seen to renounce the world and follow God are duty-bound to devote their utmost attention to this, just as it is written: "Be still and know that I am God" [Ps 45.11 LXX]. If he knows God (insofar as it is possible for a human being to know him), then he will acquire knowledge of the remaining things that exist and will apprehend the mysteries of God. The purer his mind is, the more God reveals to him and shows him his secret counsels.

This passage, virtually none of which is reproduced from the Greek,[221] is a grab-bag of cardinal Evagrian teachings on ascetic mysticism and epistemology. Pure prayer is the foundation of the monk's life and can only become possible once he has achieved impassibility, and it also is the meditative means by which he acquires progressive knowledge of God and the cosmos (that is, "the remaining things that exist"). Yet, while God is "perception and thought" (*sensus et mens* = αἴσθησις καὶ ἔννοια),[222] the finite mind is incapable of fully knowing him in his infinitude. The praying mind therefore must approach him humbly and reverently and resist the temptation to imagine him in reductive anthropomorphic terms, for he is a purely immaterial being without form or shape.[223]

In their respective works both Anon. and especially Rufinus not only extol the figure of Evagrius of Pontus but also give a highly favorable, not to mention rather prolific, representation of the very teachings that stand at the center of his ascetic mysticism and indeed help to define this "system" of spirituality as peculiarly Evagrian. This phenomenon becomes explainable once we view it against the backdrop of Evagrius's close, long-standing ties to Rufinus's monastery on the Mount of Olives, where Anon. and his six traveling companions were living as monks at the time of their Egyptian excursion in 394–95.

Evagrius evidently met Rufinus for the first time in 381.[224] For the previous few years he had been in Constantinople serving as a deacon under Gregory of Nazianzus and then briefly under Gregory's successor, Nectarius. After leaving Constanti-

221. Cf. P. Tóth, "Lost in Translation: An Evagrian Term in the Different Versions of the *Historia monachorum in Aegypto*," in G. Heidl and R. Somos, eds., *Origeniana, IX* (Leuven: Peeters, 2009), 613–21; idem, "Honey on the Brim of the Poison [*sic*] Cup: Translation and Propaganda in Rufinus' Latin Version of the *Historia monachorum in Aegypto*," in J. Glucker and C. Burnett, eds., *Greek into Latin from Antiquity until the Nineteenth Century* (London: Routledge, 2012), 117–29.

222. Evagrius, *Chapters on Prayer* 4. On God as "mind" or "thought" in Evagrius, see J. Konstantinovsky, *Evagrius Ponticus: The Making of a Gnostic* (Aldershot: Ashgate, 2009), 53–54.

223. See Evagrius, *Chapters on Prayer* 67–75, 114–18, 120.

224. For a detailed reconstruction of Evagrius's biography, see Guillaumont, *Un philosophe*, 25–64.

nople Evagrius headed for Jerusalem, presumably to become a monk, for at that time Jerusalem was known as not only a destination for religious pilgrims but also a nerve center for Christian monasticism. Evagrius ended up staying for approximately two years at the monastic complex recently established on the Mount of Olives by Rufinus and Melania the Elder. This was a formative period in his spiritual development: it was there that he resolved to become a monk, and in fact it was from Rufinus's hands that he received the monastic habit.

By 383 Evagrius had become intent upon experiencing first-hand the monasticism of the Egyptian desert, and so he moved on to the famed monastic settlement at Nitria, probably at the suggestion of Melania, who had personal connections to some of its resident celebrities. After two years in Nitria, he relocated to the quieter atmosphere of nearby Kellia and lived there until his death in 399, though according to his Coptic *Life* he returned briefly to Rufinus's monastery in Palestine when Bishop Theophilus of Alexandria tried to ordain him bishop of Thmuis against his will.[225]

During his time in Egypt Evagrius maintained close ties with Rufinus and Melania through regular correspondence. The eminent Evagrian scholar Gabriel Bunge,[226] in his German translation of Evagrius's extant epistolary corpus,[227] identifies six letters he definitely wrote to Rufinus and Melania,[228] and nine others he probably wrote to them.[229] The most famous among the group of six is an item traditionally known as the *Great Letter to Melania* (though it may have been written to Rufinus), in which Evagrius gives an epitome of his theological

225. E. Amélineau, *De Historia Lausiaca quaenam sit huius ad monachorum Aegyptiorum historiam scribendam utilitas* (Paris: Leroux, 1887), 115; cf. Socrates, *hist. eccl.* 4.23.

226. For an overview of his significant contributions to our understanding of Evagrius's mystical theology and asceticism, see A. Casiday, "Gabriel Bunge and the Study of Evagrius Ponticus: Review Article," *SVTQ* 48 (2004): 249–98.

227. *Evagrios Pontikos: Briefe aus der Wüste* (Trier: Beuroner Kunstverlag, 1986). For the critical edition of Evagrius's letters, see W. Frankenberg, ed., *Evagrius Ponticus* (Berlin: Weidmann, 1912).

228. *Letters* 22; 31; 32; 35; 36; 37.

229. *Letters* 1; 5; 7; 8; 10; 19; 40; 44; 49.

system.[230] From all of these letters we see Evagrius emerge as a spiritual mentor to both Melania's and Rufinus's respective monastic communities. He enacted this same advisory role in other literary contexts. For instance, he composed his short treatise *Exhortation to a Virgin* most likely as a primitive monastic rule for Melania's convent;[231] he addressed his *To Monks in Monasteries and Communities* to Rufinus's community in Jerusalem;[232] and his treatise *Chapters on Prayer*, in which he elaborates on the theoretical and practical dimensions of "pure prayer," was dedicated probably to Rufinus.[233]

Rufinus was not the only monk in the monastery on the Mount of Olives who was a devotee of Evagrian spirituality. Bunge convincingly argues that one of Evagrius's surviving letters (*Letter* 25) was addressed to a Spaniard named Anatolios, a former senior imperial official (*notarius*) who by the early 380s had renounced his public position and taken up residence in Rufinus's monastery.[234] Bunge posits reasonably that Evagrius first met Anatolios when he stayed at this monastery between 381 and 383.[235] In his letter, written from Kellia at least a decade after this possible first meeting, Evagrius enunciated what by then had become familiar themes of his ascetic mysticism when he exhorted Anatolios to graduate from the "active" life to the

---

230. This work survived beyond antiquity in Syriac; for a critical edition of the Syriac text and a French translation, see G. Vitestam, ed., *La seconde partie du traité qui passe sous le nom de La Grande Lettre d'Évagre le Pontique à Mélanie l'Ancienne* (Lund: CWK Gleerup, 1964). For a German translation, see Bunge, *Briefe*, 303–29, and for an English translation, see M. Parmentier, "Evagrius of Pontus' *Letter to Melania*," in E. Ferguson, ed., *Forms of Devotion: Conversion, Worship, Spirituality, and Asceticism* (New York: Routledge, 1999), 272–309 (278–91).

231. S. Elm, "The *Sententiae ad Virginem* by Evagrius Ponticus and the Problem of the Early Monastic Rules," *Augustinianum* 30 (1990): 393–404; Elm, "Evagrius Ponticus' *Sententiae ad Virginem*," *DOP* 45 (1991): 265–95.

232. Guillaumont, *Un philosophe*, 110.

233. J.E. Bamberger, trans., *Evagrius Ponticus: The Praktikos, Chapters on Prayer* (Kalamazoo: Cistercian Publications, 1981), 51; Guillaumont, *Un philosophe*, 128; Sinkewicz, *Evagrius of Pontus*, 184.

234. See O. Zöckler, *Evagrius Pontikus: Seine Stellung in der altchristlichen Literatur- und Dogmengeschichte* (Munich: Beck, 1893), 25–26 n. 37.

235. Bunge, *Briefe*, 35.

"contemplative" life,[236] to stay on guard against evil λογισμοί,[237] to strive to attain ἀπάθεια, and to practice pure prayer.[238] This extant letter represents the tip of the iceberg of their communication and of Evagrius's mentoring of Anatolios: at Anatolios's request, Evagrius dedicated to him his great trilogy of *Praktikos, Kephalaia gnostika,* and *Gnostikos.*[239]

So, then, from his cell in rural Egypt Evagrius maintained a strong virtual presence in Rufinus's monastery in Jerusalem from the mid-380s through the 390s, and his theoretical writings found an eager readership there in two confirmed cases (Anatolios and Rufinus). It is safe to assume that the rest of the monks in that monastery had also been exposed, probably to a great extent, to the principles of Evagrian spirituality.[240] After all, their abbot was a vocal proponent of these principles and actively encouraged this interest among his monks, even to the point of regularly sending groups of them to visit Evagrius in Egypt so that they could interact with him in person.[241] Indeed, this encouragement very well may have been one of the impetuses for Anon.'s trip to Egypt in 394–95.

Rufinus tried to spread Evagrius's teachings on a broader scale as well by making some of his writings available to western readers through his own Latin translations.[242] His efforts were successful enough by 415 that Jerome, in a letter written that same year to a certain Ctesiphon,[243] was able to lament: "A great many people read [Evagrius's] books in Greek throughout the East and in Latin in the West thanks to his disciple Rufinus, who translates them."[244] Prior to his departure for Italy

236. *Letter* 25.5 (Bunge, *Briefe,* 237).
237. *Letter* 25.4 (Bunge, *Briefe,* 237).
238. *Letter* 25.6 (Bunge, *Briefe,* 237–38).
239. Bunge, *Briefe,* 34.
240. Clark, *Origenist Controversy,* 190.
241. See Evagrius, *Letter* 37.1 (Bunge, *Briefe,* 250).
242. Murphy, *Rufinus of Aquileia,* 227.

243. Ctesiphon's precise identity is unknown, but it has been conjectured that he was one of Pelagius's wealthy lay supporters; see J. N. D. Kelly, *Jerome: His Life, Writings, and Controversies* (London: Hendrickson, 1975), 314.

244. *Huius libros per orientem Graecos et interpretante discipulo eius Rufino Latinos plerique in occidente lectitant* (*epist.* 133.3).

in 397, Rufinus had transformed his monastery in Jerusalem into a hub for disseminating Evagrius's writings at home and abroad,[245] and he employed his monks, who occupied themselves in their cells with copying texts,[246] as the front-line workers in this cottage industry. After he had returned to Italy, and especially after Evagrius's death in 399, Rufinus continued to act as a self-appointed publicist and apologist for Evagrius and his teachings. This sense of purpose, I submit, was one of the main driving forces behind his Latin translation of the *GHM* around 403, which (as we have seen) not only retains the pro-Evagrian material already present in the Greek original but also substantially adds to it.

Going one step further, I propose also that Rufinus conceived the *LHM* to be, on one level, a creative platform for popularizing the foundational principles of Evagrian ascetic theory, to make these accessible in a streamlined form to a far broader readership than would normally be predisposed to study Evagrius's corpus of theoretical treatises. The weighty authority of the great Egyptian monks themselves, which Rufinus carefully constructs throughout the *LHM*, only lends allure and intrinsic legitimacy to the teachings being conveyed. Hence he touts the spiritual credentials of the main "Evagrian" teachers in his monastic portrait-gallery. Apollo is widely regarded by his fellow monks and countrymen as a "prophet" and "apostle."[247] Pityrion is a noted exorcist as well as Antony's monastic successor and the heir to his spiritual graces.[248] John of Lycopolis "had made so much progress in purifying his mind that he not only received from the Lord the knowledge of things in the here-and-now, but he also was deemed worthy of the knowledge of things to come."[249] This description is not found in the *GHM* but is an addition whereby Rufinus explains the origin of John's clairvoyance in terms conspicuously reminiscent of Evagrius's conceptualization of spiritual progress:

245. Guillaumont, *Un philosophe*, 171.
246. See Rufinus, *apol. c. Hier.* 2.11.
247. *LHM* 7.3.
248. *LHM* 13.1.
249. *LHM* 1.2.

John's acquisition of two tiers of divinely acquired "knowledge" was predicated upon sufficient mental purification.

In invoking these and other illustrious monks in the *LHM* as standard-bearers of Evagrian monastic ideology, Rufinus also may well have had apologetic designs. Evagrius would later be condemned, along with Origen and Didymus, at the Second Council of Constantinople in 553.[250] Even in his own lifetime and shortly thereafter, some of his monastic teachings were met with derision and disapproval.[251] His doctrine of *apatheia* in particular was a polemical lightning-rod: Jerome famously mocked it, claiming that true impassibility would make a human being either a stone or God;[252] and John Cassian, a disciple of Evagrius, translated the term ἀπάθεια with the more positive-sounding phrase *puritas cordis* ("purity of heart") so as to avoid certain negative connotations that the Greek term had acquired through Evagrius's usage of it.[253] If Rufinus had a sense of the controversial nature of this and other Evagrian teachings, he might have hoped that the sterling reputation of Egypt's monastic luminaries would provide some protective insulation for these ideas and enhance their credibility among the skeptical segments of his readership.

Rufinus's stated objective in composing the *LHM* was to es-

---

250. Although Evagrius is not named explicitly in the Council's fifteen anathemas, there is general agreement that he was an intended target (Konstantinovsky, *Evagrius Ponticus*, 20). The Council's condemnations were later ratified by the Third Council of Constantinople (680–81), the Second Council of Nicea (787), and the Fourth Council of Constantinople (869); see N. Tanner, ed., *Decrees of the Ecumenical Councils*, 2 vols. (London: Sheed and Ward, 1990), 1.125, 135, 161.

251. For other contemporary opposition to Evagrius's anthropology and theology, see Clark, *Origenist Controversy*, 105–21, and on his troubled *Nachleben* more generally, see Casiday, *Reconstructing the Theology*, 46–71.

252. Jerome, *epist.* 133.3; cf. S. Driver, *John Cassian and the Reading of Egyptian Monastic Culture* (London: Routledge, 2002), 53–58; A. Guillaumont, *Les 'Képhalaia Gnostica' d'Évagre le Pontique et l'histoire de l'origénisme chez les grecs et chez les syriens* (Paris: Éditions de Seuil, 1962), 79–80; B. Jeanjean, *Saint Jérôme et l'hérésie* (Paris: Institut d'Études Augustiniennes, 1999), 395–96.

253. B. Ramsey, trans., *John Cassian: The Conferences* (New York: Paulist Press, 1997), 19. On Cassian's understanding of this concept, see further A. Casiday, "*Apatheia* and Sexuality in the Thought of Augustine and Cassian," *SVTQ* 45 (2001): 359–94.

tablish the lives and teachings of the Egyptian monks as the touchstone of authentic ascetic spirituality for his pious readers. Thus he declares in the Prologue (§ 12):

Because it was granted to me by God's favor both to see them and to be a witness to their way of life, I will now attempt to elaborate on particular things that the Lord has brought back to my remembrance, so that people who have not seen them in person, in learning about their deeds and gathering information about the perfect life from reading, may be incited to emulate their holy deeds and to seek the prize of perfect patience.

He then proceeds immediately to open the chapter on John of Lycopolis by emphasizing John's supreme exemplarity in a passage that, like the one just quoted from the Prologue, is not found in the Greek but is his own personal addition.[254] Rufinus, then, was like all other authors of hagiographic literature, such as Jerome, who, in his letters and other works, idealized as "saints" the women in his circle who personally endorsed his controversial ascetic and scholarly special interests and thereby legitimized these pursuits.[255] To this list of authors I propose now to add Rufinus, whose monastic hagiography, I have argued, had a narrowly focused propagandistic thrust, and that was to promulgate covertly the central principles of Evagrian monastic ideology.[256]

About This Translation

Nearly three decades ago, Giulio Trettel published an Italian translation of the *LHM*.[257] It is based, however, upon the

254. "So, then, let us take John first as truly being the foundation of our work, as the model of all the virtues, for indeed he all by himself is more than capable of inspiring pious minds devoted to God to reach the pinnacle of the virtues, and of spurring them on to the lofty heights of perfection" (*LHM* 1.1).

255. Cain, *Letters of Jerome*, 68–98; idem, "Rethinking Jerome's Portraits of Holy Women," in A. Cain and J. Lössl, eds., *Jerome of Stridon: His Life, Writings, and Legacy* (Aldershot: Ashgate, 2009), 47–57; Cain, *Jerome's Epitaph on Paula*, 23.

256. I say "covertly" because he chose to allow these principles to be voiced not by the character of Evagrius but by other characters in the *LHM* who are given far more prominence in the narrative.

257. *Rufino di Concordia, Storia di monaci. Traduzione, introduzione e note* (Rome: Città nuova editrice, 1991).

deficient and severely outdated (1615) Latin text of Heribert Rosweyde, which is printed in the Patrologia Latina.[258] What is worse, Trettel's rendering of Rufinus's Latin is frequently suspect, and at times it amounts to little more than an infelicitous paraphrase. Hence the longstanding need for a new translation, especially one that can serve as a reliable point of reference for English-language scholarship on this important but under-studied Rufinian writing.

The present volume accordingly presents the first English translation of Rufinus's *LHM*. I have based my translation on Eva Schulz-Flügel's critical edition.[259] I have retained her chapter-numbering sequence but have adopted a more reader-friendly system of section-divisions within each chapter.

258. PL 21:387–462.

259. *Tyrannius Rufinus, Historia monachorum sive De vita sanctorum patrum* (Berlin: De Gruyter, 1990). For a lengthy review of this edition, see C. Bammel, "Problems of the *Historia monachorum*," *JThS* n.s. 47 (1996): 92–104.

INQUIRY
ABOUT THE MONKS
IN EGYPT

PROLOGUE

LESSED BE GOD,[1] "who desires everyone to be saved and to come to the knowledge of the truth,"[2] and who guided our journey to Egypt and showed us great and extraordinary things,[3] the memory of which it will be beneficial to preserve for posterity, so that these things not only may be a source of salvation for us, but also may form the basis of a salvific narrative that is eminently suitable for teaching holiness and that opens up, to those keen on making the journey towards virtue, a robust path paved by the deeds of those who came before us in the faith.

(2) Even though I am rather ill-equipped to write about such

---

1. Lat. *Benedictus deus*. Rufinus opens the prologue with a standard benediction found in the Psalms (LXX numbering: 17.47; 65.20; 67.19, 36) and occasionally in the NT (2 Cor 1.3; Eph 1.3; 1 Pt 1.3; cf. Rom 9.5; 2 Cor 11.31); on biblical blessing formulae, see N.A. Dahl, "Benediction and Congratulation," in N.A. Dahl, *Studies in Ephesians* (Tübingen: Mohr Siebeck, 2000), 279–314.

2. 1 Tm 2.4.

3. After opening the preface with a biblical benediction formula and a quotation from Paul, Rufinus continues to set a strong biblicizing tone for the work by alluding to Moses's reminder to the Israelites about how God delivered them from captivity in Egypt and in the process made a spectacular show of his own power and might: "The Lord brought us out of Egypt with a mighty hand and an outstretched arm, with great deeds of terror, with signs and wonders" (Dt 26.8). Thus Rufinus implicitly configures the pilgrimage as a reverse exodus and plays on the biblical stereotype of the "desert" as the place of God's mighty acts; on this stereotype, see U. Mauser, *Christ in the Wilderness: The Wilderness Theme in the Second Gospel and its Basis in the Biblical Tradition* (London: Wipf and Stock, 1963), 14. God had brought the Israelites out of Egypt and on to Mount Sinai, where he revealed himself to them and gave them the Law. Now he has escorted the band of seven Jerusalemite monks from the biblical Promised Land to Egypt to witness "great and extraordinary things."

weighty matters, and even though it does not seem appropriate for those who are lowly and insignificant to become authors and to write about sublime virtues in an ordinary style,[4] nevertheless, because the charity of the brothers who live on the holy Mount of Olives frequently urges me to describe the Egyptian monks' way of life, spiritual virtues, cultivation of piety, and the firmness of the ascetic discipline I personally witnessed in them, I shall proceed, entrusting myself (as one who needs assistance) to the prayers of those who commission this and not seeking praise for the composition but hoping that readers will be edified by the narration of stories, as each person, inspired by the examples of the feats, is called upon to bristle at the world's enticements and to cultivate stillness and the practice of monastic holiness.

(3) For I have seen—I assuredly have seen—the treasure of Christ hidden in human vessels.[5] After I had found this treasure, I did not want to conceal it as a spiteful person would do but rather to make it known and to share it as if it had been discovered for the benefit of many. I am confident that the more people who will be enriched by it, the more that treasure will come into my possession, for I will become richer because the salvation of others will have been secured by my diligent efforts. (4) Therefore, at the outset of my narrative I beg for the grace of our Lord Jesus Christ to be with me, for it is by his might that all these practices of holiness are sustained among the monks in Egypt.

(5) I saw among these monks many fathers who live on earth yet lead a heavenly life as well as new prophets raised up for the cultivation of spiritual virtues and for prophesying.[6] As a testament to their worthiness, they have the power to work signs and

---

4. Lat. *humili sermone* = "ordinary style," i.e., a prose style lacking pretentious rhetorical refinement. Rufinus's self-depreciation is conventional and not a little ironic: the entire paragraph (§ 2 above) consists of one long, continuous sentence full of syntactical complexity and rhetorical conceits (I have preserved the elaborate periodicity in translation). Lactantius opens his *De opificio dei* in the same vein, decrying his ineloquence (*rudibus paene verbis*) and lack of talent (*ingenii mediocritas*), all the while writing in elegant prose.

5. Cf. 2 Cor 4.7; Col 2.3.

6. Cf. Dt 18.18.

wonders, and rightly so: for why should those who desire nothing earthly and nothing fleshly not receive heavenly authority? (6) In fact, I also saw some of them who were so unencumbered by every malicious thought and feeling of mistrust that they were unaware of there being anything evil still happening in the world. So great was the sense of tranquility within them, and such an intense feeling of goodwill had blossomed within them, that it deservedly has been said about them: "Those who love your name have much peace."[7] (7) They live scattered throughout the desert and separated by cells, yet they are bound together by love. They are divided from one another by their dwellings, such that no sound or accidental meeting or any idle word disturbs the repose of their silence and the concentration of their minds in pursuit of divine things.

(8) As a result, each one stays in his residence with focused determination and awaits the coming of the good father, Christ, as a soldier standing at attention in the army camp awaits the appearance of the emperor, or as faithful servants hold out for their master to bestow upon them freedom and tokens of favor. All of them entertain no concern over food, clothing, or any such things. For they know that "the pagans think about all these things," as it is written,[8] yet they themselves "seek righteousness and the kingdom of God, and all these are added to them,"[9] according to the Savior's promise. Furthermore, if most of them happen to be lacking in any bodily provisions, they turn not to human sources of help but to God and, asking him as they would ask a father, obtain what they asked for.

(9) So mighty is the faith within them, in fact, that it is capable of ordering mountains to be moved from their place.[10] This also is how by their prayers some of them have stopped the

---

7. Cf. Ps 118.165. Psalm numbering in this volume is from the LXX.

8. Mt 6.32.

9. Mt 6.33. In other hagiographic texts, too, saints are said to embody Christ's promise in this verse; see Athanasius, *v. Ant.* 45.7; *AP* John the Eunuch 1; Paphnutius, *narr. On.* 16; Theodoret, *hist. rel.* 15.6; Cyril of Scythopolis, *v. Sab.* p. 159 Schwartz.

10. Cf. Mt 17.20, a verse quoted elsewhere in monastic hagiography to explain the divine origin of monks' wonder-working powers (Athanasius, *v. Ant.* 83.2; Jerome, *v. Hilar.* 29.5).

flooding of the Nile when it threatens neighboring areas, and how they have crossed the deep parts of its river-bed on foot, and how they have slain its wild animals, and how they have performed countless more signs which had been done in ancient times by the prophets and apostles. Hence, there should be no doubt that the world stands firm on account of their just actions.[11] (10) It is truly remarkable, since every excellent thing is uncommon,[12] that among them both of the following conditions are met in an equal degree: they are vast in number and unparalleled in their virtues.

(11) Some live on the outskirts of cities, others in the countryside, but most, including the most eminent ones, are scattered throughout the desert like a heavenly army girded for battle and on alert in the military tents, always ready to heed the call of their king. Fighting with the weapons of prayer and protected from the enemy's onslaughts by the shield of faith,[13] they are on a quest to attain the kingdom of heaven. Their character is pristine, and they are free from care, gentle, peaceful, and bound together by the chains of a brotherhood, as it were. They engage in a herculean struggle and contests in order to best one another in the virtues.[14] For each one strives

11. Cf. *Epistle to Diognetus* 6.7: "Christians are confined in the world as in a prison, yet they are the preservers of the world." Both the anonymous author of the *GHM* and Rufinus attach cosmic significance to the lives and ministries of the Egyptian monks by insisting that the very fate of the universe lies in their capable hands. See A. Cain, *The Greek* Historia monachorum in Aegypto: *Monastic Hagiography in the Late Fourth Century* (Oxford: Oxford University Press, 2016), 195–213.

12. *Sed illud valde mirum est, cum semper optima quaeque rara sint.* Rufinus here is not reproducing anything found in the Greek version. His phraseology may have been inspired by Cicero, *fin. bon. et mal.* 2.81: *In ipsa virtute optimum quidque rarissimum est.*

13. Cf. Eph 6.16.

14. A healthy sense of spiritual rivalry was integral to the ascetic Christian ethos (cf. Athanasius, *v. Ant.* 4.3, on how Antony did not want to be bested in virtue by any contemporary monk; see also Palladius, *hist. Laus.* 18.1). This is why it became standard in late antique and medieval hagiographic literature to portray holy men (and women) striving to outdo one another in self-discipline; see J. Wortley, "The Spirit of Rivalry in Early Christian Monachism," *GRBS* 33 (1992): 383–404. The *locus classicus* of this literary commonplace is the opening sentence of the prologue to the *Life of Antony:* "You have

to be found more compassionate, more humble, kinder, and more patient than his neighbor. If any is wiser than the rest, he acts towards all as if he is average and insignificant, so that, in accordance with the Lord's commandment, he may appear the least of all and the servant of all.[15]

(12) Because it was granted to me by God's favor both to see them and to be a witness to their way of life, I will now attempt to elaborate on particular things that the Lord has brought back to my remembrance, so that people who have not seen them in person, in learning about their deeds and gathering information about the perfect life from reading, may be incited to emulate their holy deeds and to seek the prize of perfect patience.

---

entered upon a noble rivalry with the monks in Egypt by your determination either to equal or surpass them in your training in the way of virtue."

15. Cf. Mk 9.34.

CHAPTER 1
JOHN OF LYCOPOLIS

O, THEN, LET us take John first as truly being the foundation of our work, as the model of all the virtues, for indeed he all by himself is more than capable of inspiring pious minds devoted to God to reach the pinnacle of the virtues, and of spurring them on to the lofty heights of perfection.[1]

When we visited him, he was living on the cliff of a steep mountain in the Thebaid in the desert adjacent to the city of Lyco.[2] The way up to him was arduous, and the entrance to his hermitage was closed off and locked, such that nobody entered it from his fortieth to his ninetieth year, the age he was when we saw him. He would make himself visible to visitors from a window, and through it he would give them either a word from God to edify them or answers to encourage them.[3] No woman,

---

1. This paragraph is missing from the *GHM*. It is Rufinus's addition and is meant to pick up immediately on the theme of the Egyptian monks' exemplarity, which was just elaborated on at the conclusion of the Prologue. For a similar sentiment, this one regarding the holy exemplarity of Paphnutius, see John Cassian, *coll.* 18.15: "In his early youth he already gave these signs of his future character, and even in his boyish years he sketched the lines of the perfection that was to grow up in mature age. If we want to attain to his height of virtue, we must lay the same foundation."

2. For an overview of the primary sources about John of Lycopolis, see M. Sheridan, "John of Lycopolis," in G. Gabra and H. Takla, eds., *Christianity and Monasticism in Middle Egypt* (Cairo: The American University in Cairo Press, 2015), 123–32.

3. These "answers" (*responsa*), referred to again in §2 below, are prophetic replies to queries of various kinds that visitors would make of him. Cf. *hist. Laus.* 35.4–11, where Palladius records a conversation he had with John while sitting outside his window.

however, ever went there or even entered his field of vision,[4] and men only did so rarely and at specific times.

(2) He allowed a guesthouse to be built outside for visitors from far-off places to stay for short stretches.[5] He remained inside alone, devoting his time only to God, and neither day nor night would he stop conversing with God and praying, but always with complete purity of mind he would seek after the divine and that which is beyond every mortal mind. For the more he cut himself off from human concerns and interactions, the nearer and closer God was to him. In a word, he had made so much progress in purifying his mind that he not only received from the Lord the knowledge of things in the here-and-now, but he also was deemed worthy of the knowledge of things to come. For the Lord conferred on him an evident gift of prophecy, such that he foretold the future not only for any people from his own city and province who happened to make inquiries, but also he often foretold for the emperor Theodosius either the outcome of a war in which he was about to engage,[6] or how he would prevail over enemy leaders,[7] and also that he was about to endure invasions by barbarians.[8]

(3) Once the Ethiopians attacked a Roman military depot around Syene,[9] a city in the Thebaid on the border of Ethio-

4. According to Palladius (*hist. Laus.* 35.13), John of Lycopolis once told him: "I have been in this cell for forty years and have never looked on a woman's face."

5. Rufinus says that this guesthouse (*cella hospitalis*) was physically unattached to John's abode. Palladius (*hist. Laus.* 35.1) describes John's home as consisting of three different cells, one for sleeping, one for working and eating, and one for praying, but he does not specifically mention any guest quarters.

6. Cf. Augustine, *cur. mort. ger.* 21.

7. A reference to Theodosius's executions of the usurpers Magnus Maximus (388) and Eugenius (394). Palladius (*hist. Laus.* 35.2), and elsewhere Rufinus (*eccl. hist.* 11.32) and Augustine (*civ. dei* 5.26), cite the same prophecy by John, but they mention Maximus and Eugenius by name.

8. An allusion to Theodosius's military campaigns against the Goths starting in 379 and culminating in a peace treaty signed in 382.

9. Syene was one of the main strategic military outposts in Roman Egypt; see J. G. Keenan, "Evidence for the Byzantine Army in the Syene Papyri," *BASP* 27 (1990): 139–50.

pian territory. After they had carried out several massacres of our troops and made off with booty, the Roman commander of the province came to John and expressed trepidation about engaging with them because the number of his soldiers was very small, while the enemy was a vast multitude. Designating a specific day, John said: "Go with confidence, for on the day that I have named, you will annihilate the enemy, you will seize the spoils, and you will reclaim the booty." After this had come to pass, John also foretold that the commander would be cherished and welcomed by the emperor. This gift for prophesying manifested itself in him in such a way that he ascribed it more to the merits of his petitioners rather than to his own merits. For he said that things were foretold by the Lord not for his sake but for the sake of those who heard the prophecies.[10]

(4) The Lord also wrought another great miracle through him. A certain tribune on his way to take up his military command came to John and begged permission for his wife also to visit, for he said that she had braved many perils for the singular purpose of seeing his face. John then avowed that it had never been his custom to visit with women,[11] especially since he had taken up life in the hermitage on that cliff. The tribune, however, continued to beg and asserted that she most certainly would die from terrible sadness unless she saw him. He kept making the same request over and over again and affirmed that John would be the cause of his wife's death and that she would find damnation where she had hoped for salvation.

Taking into account the tribune's faith and persistence, the old man said: "Go. Your wife will see me tonight. She will not come here, however, but will remain in her own home and in her own bed." Upon hearing these words the man left, ponder-

10. Cf. Athanasius, *v. Ant.* 62.2, where Antony is said to have encouraged beneficiaries of his miracles to marvel not at him but rather at the Lord's grace at work in him.

11. John was far from being the only male ascetic who refused to have contact with women; cf. Anon., *v. Pach. G*[1] 43; John Cassian, *inst.* 11.18; Theodoret, *hist. rel.* 3.22, 26.21; John Moschus, *prat. spir.* 217. On the frequently voiced patristic prohibition against monks associating with women, see A. Cain, *Jerome and the Monastic Clergy: A Commentary on Letter 52 to Nepotian, with an Introduction, Text, and Translation* (Leiden: Brill, 2013), 135–37.

ing in his heart the ambiguity of the response. When he had related it to his wife, the woman likewise was no less perplexed by the obscurity of the message. But as soon as it came time to sleep, the man of God appeared in a vision.[12] He stood by the woman's side and said: "Your faith is great, woman,[13] and so I have come to fulfill your desire. I nevertheless admonish you not to long to see the physical face of God's servants but to contemplate in spirit their deeds and achievements. For it is the spirit that gives life, while the flesh counts for nothing.[14] I am not a righteous man or a prophet,[15] as you suppose, yet on account of your faith I have interceded with the Lord on your behalf and he has granted you healing of all the maladies you suffer in your body. Therefore, from now on both you and your husband will be healthy and your household will be blessed.[16] But both of you remember the blessing bestowed on you by God. Always fear the Lord and do not ask for more than is owed to you for your just deserts. Therefore, let it be enough for you to see me in your dream; do not ask for more."[17] When she awoke, the woman detailed to her husband what she saw and heard, and she also described the man's manner of dress, his face, and all of his distinguishing features. Amazed at this, her husband returned and gave thanks to the man of God, and after receiving a blessing from him, he departed in peace.[18]

(5) On another occasion a certain military officer visited him.[19] His pregnant wife, whom he had left at home, gave birth on the very day he visited John and was in danger of los-

---

12. James of Edessa also is said to have appeared to people in their dreams and healed them of their illnesses (Brooks, *John of Ephesus*, 578).

13. Mt 15.28 (Jesus's words commending the faith of the Canaanite woman whose daughter was demon-possessed).

14. Jn 6.63.

15. Cf. Athanasius, *v. Ant.* 48.2, where Antony similarly rebuffs a military officer who asks him to heal his demon-possessed daughter.

16. Cf. Acts 11.14.

17. Cf. Lk 3.14.

18. Augustine tells a shortened version of this story in *cur. mort. ger.* 21.

19. Lat. *praepositus militum*. In the late Roman army, *praepositi* were officers put in temporary charge of their own troop, often a troop of soldiers in transit to and from a battle.

ing her life.[20] The holy man of God said: "If you recognized the gift of God[21] and that a son was born to you today, you would give thanks to the Lord. But realize that the boy's mother almost died. Nevertheless, the Lord will be with her and you will find her healthy. Hurry, then, and go back, and you will find a seven-day-old boy, and you will name him John.[22] Let him be brought up in your home without him coming into contact with any worldly influence for seven years. Once the seven years are over, hand him over to monks to be reared on holy and heavenly lessons."

(6) Many people from his own province and from abroad visited him, and when the circumstances demanded it, he would reveal the secrets of their hearts. If they happened to have committed any sin in secret, he would reproach them sternly in private and exhort them to repent and change their lives. He also foretold whether the Nile River would have an abundance or scarcity of water.[23] Likewise, if some judgment or chastisement from God happened to be looming as a consequence of human sin, he would forewarn about it and indicate the reason why the punishment was being levied.

(7) John also would perform bodily healings and cures on those who sought them, yet he did so in such a way as to avoid all showiness about it. For he did not allow the sick to be brought to him, but he would distribute oil he had blessed so that those who were anointed with it might be cured of what-

---

20. Lat. *periclitabatur*. In medical Latin *periclitari* (= verbal form of *periculum*) means to be so ill that one is in danger of death, and Rufinus is accessing this clinical sense of the term in order to dramatize his narrative and vividly capture the reality that, during his time (and indeed all throughout Roman antiquity), mortality rates for pregnant women were extremely high due to any number of complications that could occur not just during pregnancy but also in the course of childbirth.

21. Cf. Jn 4.10.

22. Cf. Lk 1.13.

23. According to Shenoute's biographer, this monk, and he alone, wielded this prophetic power; see L. S. B. MacCoull, "*Stud. Pal.* XV 250ab: A Monophysite Trishagion for the Nile Flood," *JThS* n.s. 40 (1989): 129–35 (130–32). From the present passage, however, we gather that John of Lycopolis also was a reputed prophet in this regard.

ever infirmity afflicted them.[24] One time the wife of a certain senator[25] went blind, and she begged her husband to take her to the man of God. When her husband replied that John had a policy against visiting with women, she asked only that he tell him why she was infirm and beg John to pray for her. After her husband had sent a delegation to him,[26] John prayed and blessed some oil and sent it to her. Starting then, and for the next three days, she put it on her eyes and received back her sight and gave thanks to God.

In summary, his feats are numerous, and it would take too long to describe them in detail. Therefore, putting aside for now what we learned from hearing, let us come to what we witnessed with our own eyes.

(8) There were seven of us fellow travelers who went to see him.[27] After we had greeted him and he had welcomed us with immense jubilation, he addressed each of us obligingly once we requested a prayer as well as a blessing. For it is the custom in Egypt that brothers[28] be united with one another through

24. On the Egyptian monastic practice of anointing the sick or demon-possessed, see Palladius, *hist. Laus.* 18.22.

25. This probably was not a Roman senator visiting from abroad. A number of Egyptian cities had their own senates (e.g., Alexandria, Naucratis, Ptolemais Hermiou, Oxyrhynchus, Hermopolis Magna), and this senator likely belonged to one of these local legislative bodies.

26. The *GHM* makes no mention of any such delegation (*legatio*). Rufinus makes this minor addition in order to emphasize the senator's socio-economic prestige and thus to enhance John's credibility as the healer of people from the upper echelon of society.

27. This was not the only monastic party known to have traveled in a caravan of seven: Abba Pistus was one of seven anchorites who went to see Abba Sisoes at Clysma (*AP* Pistus 1), and Abba Sisoes and Macarius the Great, when they were living at Scetis, went with five other monks to bring in the harvest (*AP* Macarius the Great 7). On the early monastic custom of traveling outside the monastery in groups of at least two, see M. Dietz, *Wandering Monks, Virgins, and Pilgrims: Ascetic Travel in the Mediterranean World, A.D. 300–800* (University Park: Penn State University Press, 2005), 97–99.

28. Lat. *fratres*. In patristic Latin, *frater* has a degree of lexical flexibility in that it is able to refer generically to a fellow Christian or, in its more technical sense, to a monk, as it does here. See A. Cain, *Jerome's Epitaph on Paula: A Commentary on the* Epitaphium Sanctae Paulae, *with an Introduction, Text, and Translation* (Oxford: Oxford University Press, 2013), 209.

prayer as soon as they arrive. He asked if any among us was a clergyman.[29] We all answered in the negative, but he gazed at each of us and discerned that there was one among us who was of clerical rank but wanted to keep it a secret. He in fact was a deacon, but even his fellow travelers, except for one who was his confidant, were unaware of this. Knowing that he was about to lay eyes on so many eminent men, out of humility he wanted to conceal the honor of his ecclesiastical order so that he might be regarded as inferior in rank to these men, to whom he judged himself far inferior with regard to his merits. Saintly John looked at him and, even though he was younger than the rest of the group, pointed at him and said: "This man is a deacon." Although he still tried to deny it, John embraced him and kissed his hand and said: "My son, do not deny the grace of God,[30] do not commit evil for the sake of good, and do not lie for the sake of humility. To be sure, a lie is to be avoided at all costs, whether it seems to be told for an evil or even good cause, because every lie comes from the Evil One, not from God, as the Savior says."[31] Upon hearing this, he was silent and calmly accepted John's mild rebuke.

When he had finished offering prayer to the Lord, one of our brothers who was severely ill with the tertian fever entreated the man of God to heal him. John said to him: "You are hoping to cast off a thing necessary for you, for, as bodies are washed of filth by natron or other such cleansers, so also are souls purified by infirmities and other such chastisements." After he taught us much about these matters in his style of mystical teaching, John blessed oil and gave it to him. Once anoint-

---

29. Lat. *clericus*. The substantive *clericus* (from κληρικός) for "clergyman" had been used already by Cyprian in the third century and was standard usage by the late fourth century. It broadly refers to any ordained minister of the church (as opposed to a layman). See Cain, *Jerome and the Monastic Clergy*, 63–64.

30. Cf. 1 Tm 4.15.

31. An allusion to Mt 5.37: "Let your word be 'Yes, Yes' or 'No, No'; anything more than this comes from the Evil One." See also Jn 8.44: "You belong to your father, the devil, and you want to carry out your father's desires. He was a murderer from the beginning, not holding to the truth, for there is no truth in him. When he lies, he speaks his native language, for he is a liar and the father of lies."

ed, the sick brother immediately vomited a big portion of bile. Completely regaining his health, he returned to the guest quarters on his own two feet.

(9) Afterward John ordered that the duties of kindness and hospitality be performed for us and that our bodily needs be taken care of,[32] and he was attentive to us but unmindful of his own needs. For by that point, owing to continual discipline and constant practice, he was unable to eat except at night, and only a tiny bit of food at that. His body was weak and gaunt on account of his abstinence [from food]. The hair on his head and his beard, as if the result of a serious illness, was sparse and thin, because his food was not enough to nourish him and there was no abundance of water to use [for cooking].[33] For even when he was ninety years old (I mentioned his age earlier), he made sure that he consumed no cooked food.[34]

To return to what I was saying, after we had returned from being shown hospitality, he bid us to sit down by him and then at last inquired about whence and why we came there. He welcomed us graciously and with complete joy, as if we were his own children,[35] and we told him that we came from Jerusalem to see him for the benefit and strengthening of our souls, so that we could witness with our eyes what word of mouth had brought to our ears. For what the eye has seen is more likely to stick firmly in the memory than what the ear has heard.[36]

---

32. Evidently there were some local monks on hand whom John instructed to provide his visitors with a meal and perhaps other refreshments.

33. Cf. Palladius, *hist. Laus.* 18.29, where the same is said of Macarius.

34. Uncooked food (usually vegetables) was the standard fare of Egyptian desert monks (see, e.g., Palladius, *hist. Laus.* 11.4; 18.1). The same was true of many Syrian monks in Late Antiquity (see, e.g., Theodoret, *hist. rel.* 1.2; 3.21; 17.6; 21.11).

35. This image of paternal affection, along with the reciprocal feeling by the adoring "children," is deployed also by Gregory of Nazianzus, who addressed his congregation at Constantinople as his dear children whom he had not lately seen (*orat.* 24.2).

36. Rufinus plays on the commonplace ancient belief that sight is a more trustworthy form of sensory perception than hearing. For other expressions of this notion, see Lucretius, *rer. nat.* 5.99–104; Livy, *a.u.c.* 6.26.5; Seneca, *epist.* 6.5; Philo, *ebr.* 82; Lucian, *dom.* 20; Cyril of Jerusalem, *myst.* 1.1; Theodoret, *hist. rel.*, prol. 1.

(10) Then blessed John, with the warmest look on his face and almost grinning out of an overflow of joy, addressed us: "I am absolutely astonished, sweetest children, that you have undertaken the burden of such an intense journey even though you are able to see nothing in us which is worthy of this honor. For we are humble and insignificant men who possess nothing in ourselves which ought either to be sought out or to be wondered at. Nevertheless, even if there *were* something in us, as you believe, it is not of the sort you read about in the biblical prophets of God and the apostles, now is it? They assuredly are read from the lectern in all the churches of God so that each person may have at home what he ought to imitate rather than seek out men in faraway foreign places as models of life. I therefore am very much astonished at the resolve underlying your effort and zeal, because you have been willing to traverse such vast lands and to undergo such daunting trials for the advancement of your souls,[37] whereas laziness and idleness have such a grip on us that we do not dare to come out of our cells.[38] Nevertheless, since you suppose that there is something in us from which you ought to derive profit, you must realize first and foremost that the very fact of your visiting us, and expending so much effort in doing so, should not lead to any boasting, in that none of you should care more about exalting himself and boasting because he has seen men who are known by others only by word of mouth, than you care about advancing in spiritual virtue.[39]

(11) "Boasting is a serious vice and very perilous because it casts souls down even from the loftiest height of perfection,[40]

---

37. Similarly, Athanasius (*v. Ant.* 62.1) says that none of Antony's visitors considered the arduous journey to see him too onerous because each one realized that he would profit from interacting with the great ascetic.

38. Cf. Virgil, *Aen.* 1.8–11.

39. Cf. John Cassian, *coll.* 24.2, where Abba Abraham rebukes Cassian's party for putting more time and effort into their pilgrimage to see the Egyptian monks than into their self-mortification. Cf. also Evagrius, *Eul.* 15, on how novice monks should not simply speak glowingly about the accomplishments of great monks but actually imitate their virtues.

40. Warnings about excessive boasting in ascetics are echoed throughout patristic literature; see, e.g., Gregory of Nazianzus, *orat.* 2.14; John Chrysostom, *hom. in Hebr.* 7.3 (PG 63:64); *AP* Antony 37; Julian Pomerius, *v. cont.* 1.9.2.

and for that reason I want you to be on guard against it at all costs. This evil has a twofold nature. It befalls some in the very earliest stages of their monastic life when they have either achieved some small feat of abstinence or have kept aside some small amount of money for the poor. Although they ought to regard it as casting away what was holding them back, they think and behave as if they are superior to those to whom they have given something. There is another type of boasting: when someone approaching the summit of virtue attributes all not to God but to his own effort and zeal and loses the glory that comes from God while he seeks it from men.

"Therefore, little children, let us run from the vice of boasting in every form so that we do not accidentally fall into the trap the devil has set. Furthermore, we must be especially watchful over our hearts[41] and thoughts. For we must ensure that no lust, no depraved inclination, no vain desire, and nothing that is not of God takes root in our hearts. For from these kinds of roots there constantly sprout up random and futile thoughts which are so troublesome that they neither cease while we are praying nor are ashamed when we stand in God's presence and offer prayers for our salvation. Rather, they kidnap our mind and hold it hostage, and although we appear to be standing physically in prayer,[42] we roam about in our minds and thoughts and are carried off in sundry directions.

(12) "So, if there is anyone who supposes that he has renounced the world and the devil's works, the renunciation is not enough if it merely involves relinquishing material possessions, property, and the rest of the world's affairs, unless he also has renounced his own vices and has cast aside futile and vain inclinations.[43] For these are the things that the Apostle[44]

---

41. Lat. *cor,* "heart," the seat of the emotions.

42. Standing was a common posture for prayer in early Christianity, and standing for prolonged periods for prayer also is a widely attested practice in Egyptian monastic culture.

43. Cf. Athanasius, *v. Ant.* 17.1–7.

44. The epithet "the Apostle" (Lat. *apostolus*), which conventionally was applied to Paul by Greek and Latin patristic writers, is but one manifestation of the exalted status he enjoyed in later centuries as the first Christian theologian and as the most recognizable apostolic face of the Gospel; see C.J. Roetzel,

calls 'vain and harmful desires that plunge men into ruin.'[45] This, then, is what it means truly to renounce the devil and his works. The devil creeps into our heart through the occasion of any vice and opening afforded by a depraved inclination because vices originate with him just as virtues originate with God. So, if there are vices in our heart, when their prince the devil arrives, they offer a place to him, as their originator, and they welcome him as if they are welcoming him to what belongs to him. Hearts like this are never able to have peace, never a sense of calm, because they are always thrown into confusion, always in a state of alarm: now they are weighed down by empty happiness, another time by injurious sadness. For they have a malevolent occupant within, to whom they have opened the door through their passions and vices.[46]

"At the other end of the spectrum is the mind that truly has renounced the world, that has uprooted and torn from itself every vice and has allowed the devil no point of entry. It restrains anger, suppresses rage, avoids deceit, abhors envy, and has no tolerance not only for slander but also for even thinking ill or harboring suspicions about its neighbor; it instead regards its brother's joys as being its own and reckons his sadness as its own. This mind, then, is attentive to these and other like things, and it opens up a place in itself for the Holy Spirit. When he enters and illuminates it, there always spring up 'joy, happiness, love, patience, longsuffering, goodness, and all the fruits of the Spirit.'[47] This is what the Lord was speaking about in the Gospel: 'A good tree cannot produce bad fruit, and a bad tree cannot produce good fruit, for a tree is known by its fruit.'[48]

(13) "There are some who ostensibly have renounced the world but have no concern for purity of heart, for excising vices and passions from their soul, or for building their charac-

---

Paul: The Man and the Myth (Columbia: University of South Carolina Press, 1998), 152–77; M. F. Wiles, The Divine Apostle (Cambridge: Cambridge University Press, 1967), 14–25.

45. 1 Tm 6.9.
46. Cf. Athanasius, v. Ant. 36.1–2.
47. Gal 5.22.
48. Cf. Mt 7.17–20; 12.33.

ter. They are eager only to see such-and-such holy fathers and
to hear such-and-such words from them, which they tell others about so that they may boast about having been taught by
this or that father. If they have happened to learn some tidbit
of knowledge anywhere either by hearing or by reading, they
immediately want to become teachers and to teach not what
they have put into action, but what they have heard and seen.[49]
Looking down on everyone else, they aspire to the priesthood
and try to ingratiate themselves with the clergy, not realizing
that a lesser condemnation awaits someone who abounds in
virtues and yet does not dare to teach others, than someone
who is gripped by vices and passions and teaches others about
virtues.

"Now, little children, I am not saying that the clerical life
or the priesthood should be avoided at all costs, nor by the
same token am I saying that it should be sought out at all costs.
But effort should be made to expel vices and cultivate spiritual virtues. Moreover, it must be left to God's judgment whom
he wants (and if he wants) to recruit for the ministry or priesthood. 'For it is not he who commends himself that is approved,
but he whom the Lord commends.'[50] It is the monk's chief
occupation to offer pure prayer to God while having nothing
blameworthy on his conscience, just as the Lord said in the
Gospel: 'When you stand for prayer, forgive your brothers from
your heart if you have something against them. For unless you
forgive your brothers, your Father will not forgive you. But if
you forgive your brothers, your Father who is in heaven will forgive you.'[51]

(14) "So, as I said earlier, if we stand before God with a pure
heart and are free from all the vices and passions I enumerated
earlier, we will be able (insofar as this is possible) even to see
God and to direct the eye of our heart toward him while praying—to see him who is invisible with the mind, not with the
body, and with the perception gained through knowledge, not
with the flesh's faculty of sight. For let no one suppose that he

49. Cf. John Cassian, *coll.* 24.13, 16.
50. 2 Cor 10.18.
51. Mk 11.25; Mt 6.14.

can gaze upon the very essence of God in and of itself, such that in his heart he would devise for himself some appearance or image akin to some corporeal image. In God there is no form, no limitation, but only perception and thought. Although he certainly can be perceived and can arouse the mind's feeling, he nevertheless cannot be apprehended, described, or captured in words.

"It is therefore necessary to approach God with all reverence and fear and to focus the gaze of our mind on him so that the human mind—everything whatsoever it can conceive of that is splendid, bright, effulgent, and majestic—may always realize that he is above all these things. As I have said, this is the case if the mind is pure and not enslaved to any base encumbrances of a depraved will. Therefore, those who are seen to renounce the world and follow God are duty-bound to devote their utmost attention to this, just as it is written: 'Be still and know that I am God.'[52] If he knows God (insofar as it is possible for a human being to know him), then he will acquire knowledge of the remaining things that exist[53] and will apprehend the mysteries of God. The purer his mind is, the more God reveals to him and shows him his secret counsels. For he then becomes a friend of God[54] like those about whom the Savior spoke: 'I no longer call you servants but friends.'[55] Anything whatsoever he asks of God, God gives it to him as if to a dear friend. The angelic principalities and all the divine servants also love him as a friend of God and fulfill his requests. He is one whom 'neither death nor life, nor angels, nor principalities, nor powers, nor

52. Ps 46.10.

53. *Reliquorum quae sunt scientiam capiet.* Rufinus, adding wording not found in the *GHM*, is alluding to Wisdom of Solomon 7.17a (*ipse enim mihi dedit horum quae sunt scientiam veram* = "For it is he who gave me unerring knowledge of what exists"). This statement introduces a list of all the branches of learning over which Pseudo-Solomon says God (*ipse*) gave him a firm command, such as zoology, astronomy, climatology, physics, and medicine (Wis 7.17–22a). Both John and Pseudo-Solomon speak of the divinely facilitated acquisition of universal knowledge, but in Wisdom it is of the physical universe and runs the gamut of human learning, whereas in the *LHM* this knowledge has more of an esoteric and mystical flavor.

54. Cf. Athanasius, *v. Ant.* 4.4.

55. Jn 15.15.

any other creature separates from the love of God which is in Christ Jesus.'[56]

(15) "Therefore, dearest ones, since you have chosen to please God and to advance in your love of him, work hard to distance yourselves from every form of boasting, every spiritual vice, and all bodily allurements. Now, do not suppose that the only bodily allurements are the ones in which men of the world indulge themselves. The ascetic should look at whatever he enjoys lustfully as being an allurement, even if that thing is a common item and one customarily used by ascetics. Even if water itself or bread is consumed lustfully—that is, to satisfy not the body's needs but inner desire—even this act is considered the vice of allurement for an ascetic.

"For in every situation the soul must become accustomed to being without vice. This is why the Lord, when he wanted to teach the soul that it must resist its own desires and longings, said: 'Enter through the narrow gate because the way that leads to death is wide and broad, whereas the way that leads to life is narrow and tight.'[57] So, then, the soul's way is wide when it has satisfied any of its own desires, but its way is narrow when it fights against its own longings. A secluded dwelling and a solitary lifestyle are very beneficial for reaching this goal because when brothers visit and a crowd of people comes and goes, the reins of asceticism and poverty are relaxed for periods of time. Through occasions such as these, one little by little gets used to and enjoys allurements, and thus sometimes even men who have already reached perfection become ensnared. This, in short, is why David said: 'Behold, I have flown far away, and I lived in the desert. I was waiting on him to save me from a weak spirit and the storm.'[58] Along these lines, I will recount for you what happened lately to a certain one of our brothers so that you may have examples before you to keep you on your guard.

---

56. Rom 8.38–39. Antony used this same verse-block to rebuke demons who harassed him in his cell (Athanasius, *v. Ant.* 9.2). For citations of it in other hagiographic literature, see Palladius, *hist. Laus.* 54.2; Callinicus, *v. Hyp.* 24.60.

57. Mt 7.13–14.

58. Ps 54.8–9.

(16) "There was a certain man who lived by us in a cave in the neighboring desert and practiced asceticism impeccably.[59] He earned his daily bread by the work of his hands[60] and persevered in his prayers day and night and was distinguished for having all the spiritual virtues. He became puffed up, however, by invigorating successes and began to trust in his own achievements and to attribute all his progress to himself, not to God. The Tempter, noticing his inner presumption, at once drew near and prepared his traps. One day, towards evening, he conjured up the image of a beautiful woman wandering through the desert. As though worn out from too much physical exertion, she came to the entrance of the monk's cave and pretended that she was exhausted and about to keel over. She hurled herself forward and, falling at the man's knees, begged him to take pity on her. She said: 'The night has caught me in a bad way, lurking in the desert. Let me get some rest in a corner of your cell so that I do not happen to fall prey to the animals of the night.'

"He welcomed her inside initially under the pretext of showing pity and asked why she had been roaming through the desert. She made up a plausible-sounding reason, all the while weaving the venom of flattery and the poison of enticement throughout the whole fabric of her story. First she made herself seem pitiful, then, deserving of shelter. She swayed the man's emotions by the elegance and sweetness of her speech, and through seductive passion she enticed him to fall for her. From then on, there was a combination of increasingly flirtatious conversation, jokes, and laughter. Her wanton hand reached out for his chin and beard in a gesture of admiration, and then she gently stroked and caressed the front and back of his neck. What more is there to say? She finally made the soldier of Christ[61] her captive. For right away he began to lose his inner

59. On the tendency of monks to dwell in caves, see Paphnutius, *narr. On.* 2, 3, 9, 14; *AP* Ammonas 7, Bessarion 4, Elias 8, Cassian 8; Mark the Deacon, *v. Porph.* 4; Cyril of Scythopolis, *v. Euth.* p. 24; *v. Sab.* p. 94 Schwartz; George of Sykeon, *v. Theod. Syk.* 19.

60. Cf. 1 Tm 3.6.

61. In late antique and medieval Christian literature it is customary for ascetics to be referred to as "soldiers of Christ." See J. Capmany, *"Miles Christi"*

composure and to be tossed about by billows of lust, completely forgetting his past endeavors as well as his pious vocation and ascetic way of life.[62] He compromised with the concupiscence in his heart and in his inmost thoughts he made a pact with deceitful pleasure.

(17) "The foolhardy man moved his loins toward her and 'became like the horse and mule who have no understanding.'[63] As he was initiating his licentious embraces, she let out the shrillest shriek with her dreadful voice. Because she was a tenuous shadow, she slipped through his hands as he was clutching for her. As he was groping the empty air with the disgraceful motions of his body, she abandoned him in a barrage of abusive taunting.[64] Then a throng of demons that had gath-

---

en la espiritualidad de san Cipriano (Barcelona: Casulleras, 1956); J. Leclercq, "Militare deo dans la tradition patristique et monastique," in Militia Christi e crociata nei secoli XI–XIII (Milan: Vita e Pensiero, 1992), 3–18; G. Luongo, "Desertor Christi miles," Koinonia 2 (1978): 71–91; S. Pricoco, "Militia Christi nelle regole monastiche latine," in Paideia cristiana: Studi in onore di M. Naldini (Rome: Gruppo Editoriale Internazionale, 1994), 547–58.

62. I have rendered Rufinus's propositum here as "ascetic way of life." Beginning in the fourth century CE, this word acquired a new sense in Latin: it could mean the resolve to live the monastic life or, in a more technical sense, the monastic life itself; see J. Campos, "El propositum monástico en la tradición patrística," in Miscellanea patristica (Madrid: Monasterio de El Escorial, 1968), 117–32; A. Zumkeller, "Propositum in seinem spezifisch christlichen und theologischen Verständnis bei Augustinus," in C. Mayer and K. Chelius, eds., "Homo spiritalis": Festgabe für Luc Verheijen zu seinem 70. Geburtstag (Würzburg: Augustinus-Verlag, 1987), 295–310.

63. Ps 31.9. The anonymous author of the GHM (1.34) instead likens the wayward monk to a "lusty stallion," borrowing phraseology from Jer 5.8 ("They became lusty stallions, each neighing for his neighbor's wife"). See Introduction, pp. 18–19.

64. In hagiographic literature the devil and his demons often are portrayed as making sneaky and abrupt exits such as this one, and the swift exit usually is described in terms of disappearing smoke. Thus Athanasius says that when the devil is rebuffed by Antony, he "vanishes like smoke before a fire" (v. Ant. 11.5; cf. Ps 67.3 LXX). Having been rebuked by St. Martin of Tours on one occasion, the devil immediately vanished like smoke (statim ut fumus evanuit) (Sulpicius Severus, v. Mart. 24.8). Likewise, when a demon disguised himself as St. Martin and appeared to a man named Landulf, Landulf, testing him, told him to make the sign of the cross, whereupon the demon became frightened and vanished like smoke (tamquam fumus evanuit) (Gregory

ered in the air to witness this spectacle made a deafening noise with their viterupative jeering and said: 'You who were lifting yourself all the way up to heaven, how have you been plunged all the way down to hell? Learn from this that he who exalts himself will be humbled.'[65]

"Then he became like a madman and could not cope with the shame of his self-deception: he was deceived more grievously by himself than he had been deceived by the demons.[66] Although he should have revived himself, undertaken the contest anew, and erased the sin of his former pride through the tears of his repentance and the practice of humility, he became hopeless, and, as the Apostle says, 'he gave himself over to every sensuality and impurity.'[67] For he returned to worldly living, having fallen prey to demons. He fled from the sight of all the saints so that nobody could bring him back from the brink through salvific admonitions. If indeed he had wanted to restore himself to his former life of asceticism, he would undoubtedly have regained both his position and state of grace.

(18) "Listen now to what happened to another man who was tempted in a similar way yet who was not overwhelmed by a similar outcome of the temptation. In the city nearest to here he led the most disreputable of lifestyles by every sort of crime, becoming notorious for his shameful behavior. At one point, owing to God's compassion, he was struck by compunction and was repentant. He closed himself up inside a tomb[68] and

---

of Tours, *lib. mir. Mart.* 2.18.4). For more examples, see Anon., v. *Pach. SBo* 113; Besa, *v. Shen.* 73; Anon., *v. Sym. Styl. iun.* 39, 125.

65. Cf. Lk 14.11.

66. Similarly, in the *Life of Pachomius* (*SBo* 14; G^1 8) the story is told of how a demon disguises himself as a beautiful woman and visits the cell of a conceited monk. Alleging that she is fleeing a creditor, she begs him to allow her to stay the night. He lets her in and becomes inflamed with lust, only to realize regretfully afterward that this all was a diabolical trick.

67. Eph 4.19.

68. Starting evidently in the late third century, some Christian ascetics, especially in Egypt, took up residence in tombs and lived out their monastic lives there. The archetypal example is Antony (Athanasius, *v. Ant.* 8–10); cf. D.J. Kyrtatas, "Living in Tombs: The Secret of an Early Christian Mystical Experience," in C.H. Bull, L. Lied, and J.D. Turner, eds., *Mystery and Secrecy in the Nag Hammadi Collection and Other Ancient Literature: Ideas and Practices*

washed away the filth of his former crimes with outpourings of tears. He fell prostrate on his face day and night and did not dare even to raise his eyes heavenward nor to utter a word or mention God's name. Rather, he continued in only his groans and tears, and, like a living corpse, he would let out visceral bellowing and wailing as if from the depths of hell.

"After one week had passed and he was still in this situation, demons came to him at night crying out in the tomb: 'What are you doing, wretched and shameful fellow? After you got your fill of immorality and debauchery, now you approach us as morally pure and pious? After you spent all your time on crimes and no longer have the energy for perpetrating misdeeds, now you want to be seen as a Christian and as chaste and repentant? As if you, mired in wickedness as you are, could occupy any other position than the one you should occupy with us! You are one of us; you can no longer be anything else. Come back to us! Come back, so that you do not miss out on the time you have left for basking in pleasure! We are readying ample allurements; we are readying voluptuous whores[69] and all the kinds of things that revitalize the flower of your beloved youth. Why are you wearing yourself out with empty and futile tortures? Why are you delivering yourself to judgment before the appointed time? After all, what else are you going to suffer in hell besides what you are bringing on yourself now? If punishment delights you, wait a little while and you will find it prepared. But now, in the meantime, enjoy what gifts we have to offer, which you always regarded as sweet and pleasurable.'

(Leiden: Brill, 2012), 245–57. This act of self-burial (as it were) represented a symbolic death that was supposed to bring them to a holier life through their self-mortification and one-on-one battles with the demons who inhabited the tombs. This practice had become relatively popular in Egypt by the late sixth century, to the extent that a sizeable number of Christian ascetics had transformed ancient necropoleis into monasteries; see E. R. O'Connell, "Transforming Monumental Landscapes in Late Antique Egypt: Monastic Dwellings in Legal Documents from Western Thebes," *JECS* 15.2 (2007): 239–73.

69. Lat. *scorta*. The two most common words in Latin for "prostitute" are *meretrix* and *scortum*, the latter being in many cases the slightly more pejorative of the two terms; see J. N. Adams, "Words for 'Prostitute' in Latin," *RhM* 126 (1983): 321–58 (321–27). I accordingly have rendered Rufinus's *scorta* here as "whores."

(19) "As they upbraided him with these and other such statements, he lay perfectly still and did not so much as lend an ear to them or respond with a single word. They kept repeating the same statements and even more awful ones, yet he still was not bothered in the least. The demons became furious when they saw their words being snubbed and advanced to assault him with scourges, leaving him beaten and half-dead from the many blows. Even despite so much intense torture, he could not so much as be budged from where he had lain prostrate to pray. The next day some members of his family, who had been looking for him only out of concern for his well-being, found him in deplorable shape from the horrific punishments. After questioning him and learning what had happened, they asked that he allow himself to be taken back home so that he could convalesce. He refused and stayed in the same spot. But then on the following night, the demons came for him again and tormented him with more savage beatings. Yet even under these circumstances he did not want to budge from the spot, saying that it is preferable to undergo death than to obey demons any longer.

"Nevertheless, on the third night a throng of demons converged and rushed at him mercilessly and assaulted him with every imaginable punishment and torture. Although his body had already been worn out by the beatings, his spirit nevertheless held out until the end and withstood the demons' authority. When the impious demons realized this, they cried out in a loud voice: 'You have won! You have won!'[70] Then, as if chased off by some power from heaven, they tripped over themselves as they fled and no longer directed at him any of their cunning deceit or treachery. He made so much progress in spiritual virtues and became so decorated in good works and filled with the fullness of divine grace that this entire region looked at

---

70. *Vicisti, inquiunt, vicisti.* The *GHM* has: ἐνίκησας, ἐνίκησας, ἐνίκησας ("You have won, you have won, you have won"). The anonymous author, like Rufinus, employs the figure of *epizeuxis,* the deliberate repetition of the same word in immediate succession for emphasis or emotive excitement, though Rufinus economizes by reducing the tricolon to a bicolon and thereby somewhat lessens the rhetorical effect present in the Greek.

him as if he had descended from heaven and believed that he
was one of the angels. Almost all of them, simultaneously and
with one mouth, said: 'This is the change brought about by the
right hand of the Most High!'[71]

(20) "How many people who already had despaired of themselves returned to the hope of salvation as a result of his example and took the initiative to better themselves—something of
which they had despaired beforehand? How many people, out
of admiration for him, were snatched out of the very hell of
sin and restored to a disposition towards virtue? Indeed, after
he had undergone such a profound transformation, all things
seemed possible to all people. For not only were a change in
character and cultivation of virtue evident in him, but also a
great deal of God's grace was bestowed on him. To be sure, the
signs and miracles performed by him attest to how much favor
he had with God. Thus, humility and conversion furnish the
substance of all that is good,[72] but pride and despair are the
cause of ruin and death.

"A secluded way of life and dwelling in the inner desert are
greatly advantageous for avoiding the perils of spiritual laps-
es,[73] seeking out God's grace, and acquiring a more intimate
knowledge of the Godhead. In my judgment, you teach this

---

71. Ps 76.11 LXX.

72. From the earliest days of Christianity humility was considered a cardinal virtue: Christ made it the centerpiece of his own ethical teaching (see,
e.g., Mt 10.27; Lk 18.14; Jn 13.14), and Paul in turn held up Christ as its supreme embodiment (Phil 2.3–11). The primacy of humility among the Christian virtues is acknowledged by many patristic authors (see, e.g., Jerome, *epist.*
46.10; Pelagius, *epist. ad Celant.* 20.1; John Cassian, *coll.* 15.7). The extremely
high regard in which it was held in Egyptian and other monastic circles is
concisely captured by a maxim attributed to Abba Or: "Humility is the crown
of the monk" (*AP* Or 9). On the central importance of humility to the theory
and *praxis* of Egyptian desert monasticism, see D. Burton-Christie, *The Word in
the Desert: Scripture and the Quest for Holiness in Early Christian Monasticism* (New
York: Oxford University Press, 1993), 236–60; S. Driver, *John Cassian and the
Reading of Egyptian Monastic Culture* (London: Routledge, 2002), 82–84.

73. Cf. Evagrius, *Foundations* 6, who counsels monks to avoid living in or
even entering cities if at all possible in order to avoid distractions to their cultivation of spiritual stillness (ἡσυχία); see R. Sinkewicz, *Evagrius of Pontus: The
Greek Ascetic Corpus* (Oxford: Oxford University Press, 2003), 7.

principle less in words than in actual deeds and examples. There was a certain monk who inhabited this desert but lived in a more remote area than the rest of the monks. For many years he persevered in asceticism. As time passed and he had come to the cusp of old age, he was decked out in every ornament of virtue and ennobled by the grandeur of uncompromised chastity. Since he assiduously served God in his prayers and hymnody, the Lord remunerated him as a veteran soldier. For, while still being in a human body, he performed the duties of the incorporeal life in imitation of the angels, and the Lord deemed it worthwhile to provide heavenly food in the desert for a man who waited for the heavenly king during long vigils.

(21) "God wanted to reward his faithful way of life even in this world and made solicitude about his daily provisions a matter of concern for his own providence. Since the needs of nature had required the intake of food, he entered his cave and found bread on the table which was wondrously delectable and dazzling white in color. After eating it, he gave thanks to God's surpassing greatness and returned to his hymns and prayers. Many revelations and many premonitions about future events even came to him from God.

"Having attained such great successes as these, he began to boast about his own merits and regarded the gift of heavenly kindness as a debt owed to himself. As a result, a tiny bit of spiritual complacency immediately crept into him, and it was so tiny that he could not detect it. Then a more serious form of indolence sprang up, such that he became lazier with his hymns, rose more reluctantly for prayer, and did not recite the Psalms with the same attentiveness as before. In fact, when any glimmer of his usual effort was shown, his soul was in a hurry to rest as if it had been worn out from over-exertion, because his mind had become depraved[74] and tumbled down from loftier heights to the nether regions, and his thoughts were dragging him through round after round of headlong falls. For already in his heart there lay hidden a foul and abominable thought, but nevertheless his ascetic routine trumped it. Just as a ripple of water still carries a boat by the initial propulsion of the oars

74. Cf. Rom 1.28.

even when the rowing stops, so his former training was drawing the man back to his customary responsibilities. This is why to all appearances he was still standing firm in place.

"In the evening, after praying, he looked for food and came to the spot where he had gotten used to being fed and found bread on the table as usual. Once he had eaten, he did not care about any of the things that occupied his heart's attention, nor was he fully aware of the extent of the injury caused by the change he had undergone. He did not realize that he would fall little by little since he was being dismissive of the least significant matters.[75]

(22) "In the meantime, he was being goaded on by an already formidable fire of lust: aflame with foul sexual desire, he was thrust back into the world. Even still, on that day he restrained himself and performed by rote his customary activities of hymnody and prayer. When he went in to eat, he did in fact find bread on the table, but it was a little darker in color. He was astonished and became sad, for he understood the import of this portent. He nevertheless ate and was satisfied. On the third day he began to be tormented by attacks that were three times worse. For his thoughts had been infiltrated by the image of a woman who seemed as if she were right there with him and lying beside him, and to his own perception he was embracing her and had her in submission for sexual purposes. The next day he went out to perform his usual duties of psalmody and prayer, yet he stood with wandering eyes and an enslaved mind. In the evening he went in as usual to look for food, and he did indeed find bread on the table, but it was very dark-colored and very stale and looked as if mice or dogs had nibbled all over it. As he looked on, he wailed and poured out tears—however, they were not from his heart and were not plentiful enough to extinguish the flame of so great a fire.

"In any event, he ate, though not as much as he wanted nor the kind of food to which he was accustomed. In the meantime, his thoughts surrounded him on all sides like a barbarian army and launched a withering onslaught on him, dragging him back to the world bound and enslaved. So he got up and start-

75. Cf. Sir 19.1.

ed to make his way through the desert at night and head to the city. But when it was daytime, the city was still a long way off. As he was being baked by the skyrocketing temperature and was being worn out in the desert, he began surveying the land all around him to see if there was a monastery nearby, and when he caught sight of the cell of some brothers, he headed in that direction to seek shelter with them.

"As soon as the servants of God became aware that he was near, they ran up to him. Welcoming him as if he were an angel of God, they greeted him, washed his feet, invited him to prayer, set the table with food and performed all the duties of brotherly love according to the divine commandment. Once he was fed and got a little rest, they begged for an edifying word and requested salutary exhortation from him as a matter of course, as if he were a very seasoned and distinguished spiritual father. They also interrogated him about how to avoid the devil's traps and how to repel and cast off lascivious thoughts he may level at the mind.

(23) "At that point, as he was forced to give exhortations to the brothers, to teach them the way of salvation, and to deliver a discourse about the treachery the demons perpetrate on God's servants, he did indeed give them full and sufficient instruction, yet he kindled the prods of compunction against himself and reflected inwardly and said: 'How do I admonish others and am myself deceived? How do I correct others when I do not change myself? Act accordingly, wretch: do first what you teach others to do.'[76] After he was bringing reproaches like these against himself and realized that he had lost his own footing in a pitiful way, he bade farewell to the brothers and at once ventured into the desert at a breakneck pace. He returned to the cave he had left, prostrated himself before God in prayer, and said: 'If the Lord had not come to my aid, my soul would soon have dwelt in hell,'[77] and: 'I was almost in ut-

76. The principle that an ascetic's deeds should mirror his profession of belief, and (correspondingly) that a figure of spiritual authority loses credibility if he fails to practice what he preaches, is voiced widely in patristic literature. For references to the primary sources, see Cain, *Jerome and the Monastic Clergy*, 174–76.

77. Ps 93.17.

ter ruin,[78] and they almost put an end to me on earth.'[79] In this man truly was fulfilled the Scripture that says: 'A brother helping a brother is like a strong fortified city.'[80]

"Thereafter he spent the rest of his life in lamentation and tears, realizing that he had lost the gift of the heavenly table that had been given to him by God. To be sure, he began to eat his bread in the hard work and sweat of his face.[81] He shut himself up inside the cave. Lying in sackcloth and ash and lamenting and weeping for a long time, he persevered in his prayers until an angel of God appeared beside him and said: 'The Lord has accepted your repentance and is again favorable towards you. But be careful not to be deceived again out of pride. The brothers you yourself taught will come to you bringing blessings, which you should not decline to accept. Eat with them and give thanks to God.'

(24) "I have told you these things, my children, so that you may know how much strength is in humility and how destruction follows on the heels of pride. This is why our Savior taught us the first Beatitude about humility: 'Blessed are the poor in spirit, for theirs is the kingdom of heaven.'[82] Also, taking to heart examples such as these, you should be more on your guard so that you are not led astray by the demons in the recesses of your thoughts. This is why a certain custom is observed among monks: if anyone visits them—man or woman, old or young, acquaintance or not—the first priority is to pray and invoke the Lord's name, because if any demonic phantasm is at hand, it will take flight the moment a prayer is uttered.

"If the demons plant some suggestion in your thoughts about how you ought to be praised or extolled, do not give in to them, but rather humble yourselves that much the more in the Lord's sight and consider yourselves as nothing when they plant some suggestion in you about pursuing praise. For example, the demons often have led even me astray at night and have pre-

78. Prv 5.14.
79. Ps 118.87.
80. Prv 18.19.
81. Cf. Gn 3.19.
82. Mt 5.3.

vented me from praying and sleeping, implanting fantasies in my emotions and thoughts throughout the whole night. In the morning they mockingly would prostrate themselves in front of me and say: 'Forgive us, Abba,[83] because we brought trouble on you the entire night.' But I replied to them: 'Depart from me, all of you who work iniquity,[84] and do not put the Lord's servant to the test.'

(25) "As for you, my children, love stillness and silence, cultivate knowledge, and train yourselves in order that during frequent conversation with God you may present your mind to him as pure, so that your prayers are not hindered in his presence.[85] Ascetics who live among the people of the world have a wholesome occupation and their conscience is praiseworthy. They train themselves in good works and occupy themselves with upright and holy deeds by practicing hospitality, devoting themselves to the duties of charity, giving alms, visiting the sick,[86] and performing other works of this kind; in doing these, they always bestow some blessing on others yet keep themselves chaste.[87] Praiseworthy indeed, very praiseworthy, are the men who please God through their good deeds and are "unabashed doers" of God's commandments.[88] But nevertheless, all these things concern earthly deeds and are carried out with respect to corruptible matters.

---

83. *Abba* (= "father") was a title of respect that monastic disciples used for revered spiritual elders; see L. Regnault, *Abba, dis-moi une parole* (Solesmes: Abbaye St-Pierre, 1984), 7–8. For the use of this form of address in later eastern monasticism, see T. Derda and E. Wipszycka, "L'emploi des titres *abba, apa* et *papas* dans l'Église byzantine," *JJP* 24 (1994): 23–56.

84. Ps 6.9.

85. Cf. 1 Pt 3.7.

86. In the early Christian centuries the visitation, caring for, and praying over the sick, which is mandated by the NT (Mt 25.36; Jas 5.14), was a pastoral ministry over which specially appointed Christian widows had charge; see G. Dunn, "Widows and other Women in the Pastoral Ministry of Cyprian of Carthage," *Augustinianum* 45 (2005): 295–307. By the same token, visitation of the sick was regarded as a responsibility also of bishops and priests (e.g., Polycarp, *epist. ad Php.* 6.1; John Chrysostom, *sacerd.* 3.16) and of lay ascetics (e.g., Basil, *reg. fus. tract.* 7 [PG 31:928–29]; Jerome, *epist.* 54.12).

87. Cf 1 Tm 5.22.

88. 2 Tm 2.15.

"But he who labors in the training of his mind and hones the spiritual faculties within himself is to be deemed far superior to these men. He prepares a place within himself for the Holy Spirit to dwell. He acquires a sort of obliviousness to earthly things and is concerned about heavenly and eternal things. For he always makes himself stand firmly in God's sight. Casting all cares for present reality behind his back, he is bound only by the passion of divine longing and, because he is occupied with hymns, psalms, and praising God, he is unable to be sated both day and night."

(26) Narrating these and many similar things to us for three straight days, the blessed John restored and renewed our souls. As we were about to depart, he blessed us: "Go in peace, my children. By the way, I want you to be aware that today word of the pious emperor Theodosius's victory over the tyrant Eugenius was announced at Alexandria.[89] Moreover, Theodosius himself must die not long afterward." After we had left him, we discovered that these events actually did transpire as he had predicted.

A few days later some brothers caught up with us and related to us that the holy John died in peace and that his death occurred as follows. For three days he allowed nobody to see him and then, bowing on his knees in prayer,[90] he gave up his spirit and went to the Lord, to whom be glory forever and ever. Amen.

---

89. Theodosius's army defeated the battalions of Eugenius and his co-conspirator Arbogast in a stunning and improbable victory on the banks of the Frigidus River in northern Italy on 6 September 394. Eugenius was executed, and Arbogast, sensing the hopelessness of the situation, took his own life several days later; see S. Williams and G. Friell, *Theodosius: The Empire at Bay* (New Haven: Yale University Press, 1998), 134–35. Palladius (*hist. Laus.* 35.2) alludes to this same instance of long-distance clairvoyance by John.

90. The Greek text specifies that John's corpse subsequently was discovered in a kneeling position, the obvious implication being that he had died while praying. Similarly, according to Jerome (*v. Paul.* 15.1–2), Paul of Thebes's corpse remained in a kneeling position, with head upright and hands raised toward heaven, and Antony, upon discovering it, mistook Paul for being deep in prayer. These two descriptions are typical of idealized corpse-discovery (and death) scenes in late antique hagiography, in which the bodies of departed saints conventionally are portrayed as manifesting signs of their serene departures into eternal life. For further examples, see Athanasius, *v. Ant.* 92.1; Gregory of Nyssa, *v. Macr.* 25; Jerome, *epist.* 108.29; Uranius, *obit. Paul. Nol.* 10; Gerontios, *v. Mel.* 68; Ennodius, *v. Epiph.* p. 382 Hartel; Hilary of Arles, *v. Hon.* 34.

CHAPTER 2
OR

E ALSO VISITED another amazing man in the Thebaid[1] named Or. He was the father of many monasteries,[2] and his monastic habit had an angelic splendor to it. He was ninety years old at the time, his beard was long and resplendently white, and he was so joyous in his face and mien that from the looks of him he possessed something greater than is in human nature.

Earlier, while living in the remotest part of the desert, he had become well-practiced in a good many ascetic exercises, but later he established monasteries near the city. In the region surrounding his dwelling he planted groves of trees of various species by sowing the seedlings all by himself. As was affirmed to us by many of the holy fathers, there was no shrubbery at all in this region prior to his arrival. He planted this woodland so that the brothers whom he hoped to gather there would not need to venture farther out to find wood, for he made provisions also for what is necessary for the welfare of their bodies but especially of their salvation and faith.

(2) When he was in the desert, he would eat herbs and some roots, and these tasted delectable to him. He would drink water whenever he had found it,[3] and he would spend all day and

1. Palladius includes a brief entry on a certain Or in his *Lausiac History* (9), but he places him in Nitria instead of in the Thebaid, where Rufinus and Sozomen (*hist. eccl.* 6.28) situate him. In an attempt to identify both monks as one and the same and to resolve this discrepancy, R. T. Meyer, *Palladius: The Lausiac History* (New York: Paulist Press, 1965), 176n98, suggests that Or "lived on the border and ruled monasteries in both areas."

2. Rufinus omits the anonymous Greek author's specification that Or supervised "a thousand brothers" within this monastic setting.

3. As a general rule, desert anchorites gravitated towards, and settled in,

night in prayer and hymnody. When he reached an advanced age, an angel appeared to him in a vision in the desert and said: "You will be a great nation, and a populous multitude will be entrusted to you. There will be many myriads of people who will be saved through you.[4] Indeed, however many you will have brought to salvation while you are in this life, that is how many over whom you will receive authority in the age to come. Have no fear, for you will never lack any of the things needed for the body's sustenance as often as you ask God for them." After hearing this, he went to the region closer to the city and initially began living by himself in a small hut he had built for himself, occasionally eating only vegetables he had gathered, though only after prolonged fasts.

At first he was illiterate, but after he had gone from the desert to the region closer to dwelling-places, which I just mentioned, a grace was divinely bestowed upon him: when the brothers handed him a book, he began reading it as if he had always been able to read. Power over demons also was conferred on him, such that many of those whom the demons were

---

areas based upon the availability of water, in whatever form it could be procured (Paphnutius, *narr. On.* 7; Theodoret, *hist. rel.* 2.2; John of Ephesus, *Lives* p. 106). Some were able to retrieve water from pre-existing, manmade conduits such as cisterns. Antony, for instance, lived in an abandoned Roman fort for twenty years and during that time enjoyed a continuous water supply from its cistern (Athanasius, *v. Ant.* 12.4). Euthymius, after settling on a mountaintop in the Judean desert, furnished himself with potable water by repairing a cistern that had collapsed (Cyril of Scythopolis, *v. Euth.* p. 22), while his fellow Palestinian monk Sabas, when he lived in a cave near Siloam, obtained his water from a nearby cistern called Heptastomus (Cyril of Scythopolis, *v. Sab.* p. 98). Anchorites such as Abba Or who lived in the wild and did not have ready access to working cisterns had to be more resourceful than their better equipped counterparts, whether by digging their own wells in the desert (Palladius, *hist. Laus.* 39.3; Cyril of Scythopolis, *v. Sab.* p. 198) or by collecting dew from his cave's rocks with a sponge (Palladius, *hist. Laus.* 27.1) and rainwater from the grooves in rocks (Cyril of Scythopolis, *v. Cyr.* p. 232).

4. The prophetic commissioning of Or is intended to be reminiscent of the call of Abraham ("Go from your country and your kindred and your father's house to the land that I will show you. And I will make of you a great nation" [Gn 12.1–2]) as well as of the Lord's subsequent promises to him that his spiritual offspring would be as limitless as the stars in the sky and the grains of sand on the seashore (Gn 15.5; 22.17).

tormenting were brought to him, even against their will,[5] and with ear-splitting shouts proclaimed his excellence. He also performed many other types of healings.

(3) In the meantime, great throngs of monks were gathering around him. When we had arrived in their midst, he was most delighted at seeing us. After greeting us and saying a prayer (as was his custom), he washed the feet of his visitors with his own hands and began teaching us things from the Scriptures that pertain to the betterment of our lives and faith. For the grace of teaching also was conferred on him by God. He accordingly explained to us scores of passages from the Scriptures in expert fashion, and then he returned to his prayers.

It was his custom not to consume food for the body before partaking of the Communion of Christ for the spirit. After receiving it and giving thanks, he urged us to have a meal, but he nevertheless sat with us and never stopped inculcating something about spiritual pursuits. He told us the following story: "I know a certain man in the desert who for three straight years consumed no earthly food. For every third day an angel of God would bring him heavenly sustenance, and this was both his food and drink. Again, I know with regard to such a man that demons came to him under the guise of a heavenly army and in angels' dress, driving fiery chariots arrayed in dense formation as if they were escorting some king.[6] The one who evidently was regarded by the rest as the king said to him: 'You have accomplished everything, my good man. All that remains is for you to worship me and for me to take you up like Elijah.'[7]

5. Cf. Athanasius, *v. Ant.* 64.2.

6. Or, of course, is speaking about himself in the third person, and he frames his experience in formulaic language allusively evoking Paul's account of his own ecstatic rapture to the third heaven: "I know a man in Christ who fourteen years ago was caught up to the third heaven.... And I know with regard to such a man that he was caught up into paradise" (2 Cor 12.2–4). For one commentary on this Pauline passage, see R. Spittler, "The Limits of Ecstasy: An Exegesis of 2 Corinthians 12:1–10," in G. Hawthorne, ed., *Current Issues in Biblical and Patristic Interpretation* (Grand Rapids: Eerdmans, 1975), 259–66; cf. also J.D. Tabor, *Things Unutterable: Paul's Ascent to Paradise in its Greco-Roman, Judaic, and Early Christian Contexts* (New York: University Press of America, 1986).

7. Cf. 2 Kgs 2.11.

"The monk, upon hearing this, said in his heart: 'What is this? Every day I worship the Savior, who is my king. If this person were he, how could he demand from me what he knows I do all the time?' Then he replied to him: 'I have my king whom I worship every day without ceasing; you, however, are not my king.' At these words the enemy immediately was nowhere in sight." Relating this to us as if he were referring to another man, he recounted his own deeds under another's identity. Nevertheless, the fathers who were with him affirmed to us that *he* was the one who had seen and heard these things.

(4) He was an eminent father, and among the rest of his good deeds he also would do the following for brothers who came and wanted to live with him. He summoned together the brothers who lived with him, and in one day he had them build a cell for the newly arrived brother.[8] There was great enthusiasm for this endeavor on the part of the brothers, as every single one of them hastened to bring bricks or spread mortar or serve water or carry pieces of timber. Once the cell had been completed, Or had it equipped with all the necessary amenities.

One time when a certain deceitful brother showed up and had hidden his clothes so as to appear naked, Or chastised him in front of everyone and produced the clothes the brother had hidden. All were so fearful that nobody from that point on dared to perpetrate a deception in his presence. Very great indeed were the spiritual virtue and the immensity of the divine grace within him, which he had cultivated through strenuous asceticism and purity of faith. Moreover, the throngs of brothers who lived with him had been filled with so much grace that when they convened at church, they looked like choirs of angels[9] radiant in their clothing and inner being and ceaseless in their hymnody and praise of God, as they imitated the virtues of heaven.

8. Cf. the case of the Theban solitary Dorotheus, who spent his days collecting stones in the desert, which he used to build cells for monks who could not build their own (Palladius, *hist. Laus.* 2.2).

9. On desert monks being likened to heavenly choirs, see Palladius, *hist. Laus.* 44.2.

CHAPTER 3
AMMON

E ALSO VISITED another man in the Thebaid named Ammon,[1] the father of around three thousand monks who are called Tabennisiots.[2] They practice an extraordinary asceticism. It is their custom to wear tunics[3] like baggy linen shirts; to be covered by a sheepskin cape which stretches from the nape of the neck down to the flank; to conceal their heads as well with hoods especially when there is a gathering for a meal; and to veil even their faces with these so that nobody catches sight of another eating sparingly.

(2) While eating they observe such absolute silence that you would not think that a single man is in the refectory. In every aspect of their conduct they behave in a group as if they are alone, as each one's asceticism is so inconspicuous that it cannot be noticed by another. As such, when they sit down to

1. Ammon was a common Egyptian name in this period. The Ammon of the *LHM* is not to be confused with the homonymous bishop who authored the famous letter to Bishop Theophilus of Alexandria recounting his experience with Pachomian monasticism. For an analysis of this work, see J.E. Goehring, *The Letter of Ammon and Pachomian Monasticism* (Berlin: De Gruyter, 1986).

2. This was a standard late fourth-century epithet for monks who followed Pachomius's *Rule;* see A. Veilleux, "Monasticism and Gnosis in Egypt," in B.A. Pearson and J.E. Goehring, eds., *The Roots of Egyptian Christianity* (Philadelphia: Augsburg Fortress Publishers, 1986), 271–306 (277). This epithet was applied to Pachomian monks across the board, whether or not they actually lived in the monastery Pachomius had founded at Tabennisi around 320. On his founding of this first of his monastic communities, see M. Jullien, "A la recherche de Tabenne et des autres monastères fondés par saint Pachôme," *Études* 89 (1901): 238–58.

3. Lat. *colobium,* a short-sleeved monastic tunic made of linen.

dine, they seem to pick at their food more than actually eat it, meaning that they are seated at the table but do not satisfy their appetite. Abstaining from what the eyes and hands take in certainly is a superior form of self-control.

CHAPTER 4

BES

E ALSO VISITED another old man named Bes, who surpasses everyone in meekness.[1] The brothers who lived by him affirmed that neither an oath nor a lie ever came out of his mouth and that no man ever saw him angry or speak an unnecessary and idle word.[2] To the contrary, his life was characterized by the utmost stillness, his manner was peaceful, and in every respect he was a man who for all intents and purposes had attained the angelic state. Additionally, his humility was astounding, and he considered himself of no account in all regards. In fact, when we insisted on hearing from him some word of edification, we barely succeeded at getting him to say a few things to us about meekness.

(2) Once, when a certain wild animal called a hippopotamus[3] was ravaging the neighboring territory, he went there at

1. The assertion that a holy person excels all others in some or other virtue is a *topos* of late antique hagiography. See, e.g., Gregory of Nyssa, *v. Macr.* 6; Gregory of Nazianzus, *orat.* 7.6; 8.8; 18.11; 24.6; 43.10, 76; Jerome, *epist.* 108.3; John Cassian, *coll.* 3.1; 19.2; Palladius, *hist. Laus.* 41.2; 48.1; 61.1; Gerontios, *v. Mel.*, prol.; Anon., *v. Olymp.* 13; Cyril of Scythopolis, *v. Euth.* p. 11 Schwartz; *v. Sab.* p. 89 Schwartz.

2. Cf. *AP* Or 2: "They said of Abba Or that he never lied, nor swore, nor hurt anyone, nor spoke without necessity" (Ward, *Sayings,* 246). See also John Moschus, *prat. spir.* 191.

3. Ancient Egyptians regarded the hippopotamus as a terrifying animal on account of its ferocity and destructiveness, and so Bes's routing of one would have earned him the reverence of the local populace. According to Pliny the Elder (*nat. hist.* 8.96), M. Aemilius Scaurus displayed the first hippopotamus ever shown in Rome during his aedilician games in 58 BCE. While Romans in the early centuries CE might see the occasional hippopotamus (along with other exotic African animals) in staged hunts (*venationes*) on the arena floor of the Colosseum, probably very few of Rufinus's contemporary western

the urging of its farmers. After laying eyes on the savage beast, he said to it: "In the name of Jesus Christ, I order you not to ravage this land any more." Thereupon it was put to flight, as if by an angel in hot pursuit, and it completely vanished. They also asserted that on another occasion he drove off a crocodile in a similar way.[4]

---

readers had ever heard of a hippopotamus, much less seen one with their own eyes; hence his use of the phraseology "a certain wild animal called a hippo-potamus," which assumes his readership's ignorance of this species of animal.

4. The same miracle is ascribed to Pachomius by his anonymous biogra-pher (*Life of Pachomius SBo* 20). Cf. Athanasius, *v. Ant.* 52, where Antony wards off a menacing pack of hyenas sent by the devil. On beasts fleeing from desert monks out of fear, cf. *AP* Theodore 23.

CHAPTER 5
OXYRHYNCHUS

WE ALSO CAME to a certain other city in the Thebaid called Oxyrhynchus,[1] where we discovered such outstanding examples of piety that nobody could adequately describe them. For we saw it filled with monks on the inside and completely surrounded by monks on the outside.[2] Whatever public buildings had been in it, along with the temples devoted to ancient pagan religion, now were the dwellings of monks, and throughout the entire city one could see many more monasteries than houses. Moreover, because the city is very large and densely populated, there are twelve churches in which the people gather together as a community, whereas the monasteries have their own oratories.[3]

1. On the history of Roman Oxyrhynchus in its cultural and other aspects, see A. K. Bowman et al., eds., *Oxyrhynchus: A City and its Texts* (London: Egypt Exploration Society, 2007); J. Krüger, *Oxyrhynchus in der Kaiserzeit: Studien zur Topographie und Literaturrezeption* (Frankfurt: Peter Lang, 1990).

2. Prior to the fourth century, Oxyrhynchus had been a stronghold of pagan religious cults; see J. Whitehorne, "The Pagan Cults of Roman Oxyrhynchus," *ANRW* II, 18.5, 3050–91. By the late fourth century, however, there was a sizeable Christian population there, though it was nowhere nearly as large (or rather, all-encompassing) as Rufinus and his Greek model lead us to believe. Their romanticized depiction of Oxyrhynchus is a rhetorical construct that is supposed to give the impression that paganism had been routed from this city by the late fourth century and had been replaced by confessional Christianity and monasticism. Indeed, the extensive papyrological record from this period reveals a starkly different landscape in which pagans and Christians coexisted; see A. Luijendijk, *Greetings in the Lord: Early Christians and the Oxyrhynchus Papyri* (Cambridge, MA: Harvard University Press, 2008), 3–6.

3. I.e., non-monastic Christians assemble for worship and prayer in these twelve churches, but the monks do so in the oratories of their individual monasteries.

(2) Neither the city's gates, nor its watchtowers, nor even a single nook of it, is without monks' habitations. Offering hymns and praise to God day and night in every quarter of the city, they transform the entire municipality into something of a unified church of God. For no heretic or pagan[4] is found there, but all the citizens are Christians, all are catholics, such that it makes absolutely no difference whether the bishop[5] conducts liturgical prayer in the street or in church. What is more, the city's magistrates, leading officials, and the rest of the citizens assiduously station watchmen by each gate so that if a stranger or pauper arrives at any one of them, he may obtain the necessities of life once he is rushed to the watchman who caught sight of him.

(3) How could I fittingly recount how we were treated by the common folk who saw us pass through their city and ran up to us and paid homage to us as if we were angels? Or what about the monks and virgins themselves, numberless crowds of whom are in that city (as I mentioned earlier)? For, upon making an inquiry of the holy bishop of that place, we learned that there are twenty thousand virgins and ten thousand monks there.[6] Words do not suffice, and modesty does not allow me, to express the affection and esteem that each of them showed us,

4. Lat. *paganus,* one of the most common derogatory epithets in patristic Latin for "pagan." See J. Zeiller, *Paganus: Étude de terminologie historique* (Paris: Éditions de Boccard, 1917).

5. This bishop, who remains unnamed in both the *GHM* and *LHM*, is identified as a certain Hierakion by A. Papaconstantinou, "Les évêques byzantins d'Oxyrhynchus," *ZPE* 111 (1996): 171–74 (173); cf. K.A. Worp, "A Checklist of Bishops in Byzantine Egypt (A.D. 325–c.750)," *ZPE* 100 (1994): 283–318 (288–89), who omits Hierakion from his inventory of fourth-century Oxyrhynchan bishops. Hierakion presumably was the founder of the *Ekklēsia abba Hierakiōnos* (Church of Abba Hierakion) in Oxyrhynchus, which is mentioned in several papyri (e.g., *POxy* 7.1053,23; *POxy* 18.2206,4; *POxy* 24.2419,3).

6. In his *Life of Peter the Iberian* (87), John Rufus speaks of Oxyrhynchus in comparable terms as "a great and prosperous city of the Thebaid, throughout which the grace of Christ reigned, such that all of the [inhabitants] were Christians, and the company of monks who were dwelling in the monasteries surrounding it [was] not less than ten thousand"; ed. and trans. C. Horn and R. Phenix, *John Rufus: The Lives of Peter the Iberian, Theodosius of Jerusalem, and the Monk Romanus* (Leiden: Brill, 2008), 129.

how our cloaks were torn as each one of them grabbed us and
hoped to bring us back to their own abodes. We also visited
a great many holy fathers there who possess various divine
charisms: some minister in the Word of God; others, in asceticism; and still others, in signs and miracles.

CHAPTER 6
THEON

NOT FAR FROM the city,[1] in the area that borders on the desert, we also visited another holy man named Theon, an anchorite confined to his cell.[2] He is said to have practiced the discipline of silence for thirty years,[3] and he performed so many miracles that he was deemed a prophet among the locals. Every day a huge crowd of sick people would come to him. He would reach his hand toward them through the window, rest it on everyone's head, give his blessing, and send them away cured of all illness.

(2) In his appearance he was so dignified and had such an awe-inspiring expression on his face that he looked like an angel among men; he was delightful to gaze at and was full of all grace. As we found out, a short time earlier robbers had come at night to attack him, thinking that they would find gold at his residence. Through prayer alone he bound them, such that they were stuck at his doorstep and unable to move at all. In the morning, once the throngs had come to him as usual and had

1. I.e., Oxyrhynchus.
2. Lat. *cellula*. In classical Latin a *cellula* is a small room (e.g., a slave's quarters), but starting in the fourth century this diminutive acquired, in Christian monastic discourse, the specialized meaning of a hermit's cell; and as cenobitic monasticism spread, it could refer also to individual rooms within a monastery.
3. Similarly, Apollonius of Tyana took a vow of silence lasting five years (Philostratus, *Life of Apollonius of Tyana* 1.14). Self-imposed silence was a much praised virtue in early Christian monastic culture; see, e.g., Basil, *epist.* 2.2; Gregory of Nazianzus, *orat.* 32.14; *AP* Arsenius 2; Jerome, *epist.* 24.5; cf. P. Antin, *Recueil sur saint Jérôme* (Brussels: Latomus, 1968), 297–304; P. Burton, *Language in the* Confessions *of Augustine* (Oxford: Oxford University Press, 2007), 6–7; H. G. Ingenkamp, "Geschwätzigkeit," *RLAC* 10 (1978): 829–37.

seen the robbers at his door, they wanted to have them burned alive. Compelled by the necessity of the situation,[4] he made only one brief remark to them: "Let them leave unharmed, otherwise the charism of healing will depart from me." When the people heard this, they did not dare to contradict him and sent the robbers away. Seeing how they were dealt with, the robbers relinquished their criminal inclination, repented of their past misdeeds, and sought refuge at the nearby monasteries, and there they adopted the manner and routine of a more respectable life.[5]

(3) Theon was proficient in not only Coptic and Greek but also Latin,[6] as we learned from him and from those who lived by him. Hoping to give us relief and comfort amidst the arduousness of our travels, he wrote a message for us on a slate and demonstrated the grace and teaching in what he conveyed.

Moreover, his food did not need to be cooked.[7] Finally, they said that at night he would go to the desert and enjoy the bustling company of its wildlife. He would repay them for being submissive by drawing water from his well and offering them bowls of it. Clear proof of this is that scores of footprints of gazelles, wild goats, and wild asses were visible around his cell.

---

4. I.e., he would not have broken his silence if it were not for these extreme circumstances.

5. A similar story with a comparable outcome is told in *APanon* 337 (=*APsys* 16.21): "Brigands once came to the monastery of an elder and said to him: 'We have come to take everything in your cell,' and he said: 'Take whatever you like, my sons,' so they took what they found in the cell and went their way, but they missed one pouch that was hanging there. So the elder took it and ran after them, calling out and saying: 'Take this [pouch] that you overlooked in our cell, my sons.' They wondered at the forbearance of the elder and restored everything in the cell to him; they apologized, saying to each other: 'This truly is a man of God'" (Wortley, *Anonymous Sayings*, 221).

6. Although Theon writes down a short message for the party in his native Coptic as well as in Greek and Latin, this need not imply advanced literacy or a mastery of either Greek or Latin. In any event, the fact that he evidently had at least some literacy in Greek and Latin would have made him unusual among contemporary native Egyptian monks, most of whom were monolingual in Coptic; see S. Torallas-Tovar, "Linguistic Identity in Graeco-Roman Egypt," in A. Papaconstantinou, ed., *The Multilingual Experience in Egypt from the Ptolemies to the Abbasids* (Aldershot, 2010), 17–43 (36).

7. The *GHM* (6.4) specifies that Theon's diet consisted of raw vegetables.

CHAPTER 7
APOLLO

E ALSO VISITED another holy man, named Apollo,[1] in the Thebaid in the region outlying Hermopolis.[2] They say that the Savior came there with Mary and Joseph from the territory of Judea, in accordance with Isaiah's prophecy: "Behold, the Lord is seated on a swift cloud and will come to Egypt, and the manmade idols of the Egyptians will be shaken at his presence and will fall to the ground."[3] We saw there also the very temple in which they say all the idols tumbled over and were shattered after the Savior had entered it.[4]

1. Rufinus gives the Latinized form of his name as Apollonius, which appears in the *GHM* as "Apollo" (*Apollō*). In this translation I have preferred the Greek form to the Latin one so as to distinguish this monk from the deacon-martyr Apollonius, who is featured in Chapter 19 of both the Latin and the Greek *HM*.

2. Hermopolis Magna was situated near the northern border of the Egyptian province of the Thebaid. It was a thriving city that boasted seven-story buildings, according to one Oxyrhynchus papyrus; see K. Lembke, C. Fluck, and G. Vittmann, *Ägyptens späte Blüte: Die Römer am Nil* (Mainz: Philipp von Zabern, 2004), 29. In the late fourth century it was an agricultural center with an estimated population of around 58,000; see R. Alston and R. D. Alston, "Urbanism and the Urban Community in Roman Egypt," *JEA* 83 (1997): 199–216 (202–3). It also was an important Roman military installation, and between 340 and 538 it was garrisoned by the 500-troop unit known in the papyri as *Equites Mauri Scutarii;* see J. G. Keenan, "Soldier and Civilian in Byzantine Hermopolis," in A. Bülow-Jacobsen, ed., *Proceedings of the 20th International Congress of Papyrologists, Copenhagen, 23–29 August 1992* (Njalsgade: Museum Tusculanum Press, 1994), 444–51. Apollo's community actually was located outside Bawit, which was south of Hermopolis, but Rufinus makes Hermopolis the geographical frame of reference because it was far more prominent at the time than its neighbor to the south.

3. Is 19.1.

4. This is the earliest documented reference to an oral tradition that is

As I was saying, we visited Apollo, who oversaw hermitages at the base of a certain mountain in the neighboring desert. For he was the father of around five hundred monks[5] and was extraordinarily renowned in all the regions of the Thebaid. His works were great, and God performed through him many mir-

---

not attested in writing again until the early seventh century in the Latin apocryphal Gospel of Pseudo-Matthew, according to which Mary and the infant Jesus went to the city of Sotinen in the region of Hermopolis and entered a temple dedicated to 365 pagan idols, whereupon every idol fell to the ground and broke into pieces. Pseudo-Matthew, like Rufinus, quotes Is 19.1 and claims that the incident prophetically fulfills this verse. For the Latin text of the Pseudo-Matthew passage, see J. Gijsel and R. Beyers, *Pseudo-Matthaei Textus et Commentarius* (Turnhout: Brepols, 1997), 473–75, and for an English translation, see W. Schneemelcher, ed., *New Testament Apocrypha*, vol. 1 (Cambridge: James Clarke & Co., 1991), 464. The Holy Family's flight to Egypt is discussed in the canonical Gospels only once (Mt 2.13–23), and no mention is made of this incident or of their specific whereabouts while in Egypt. On the extra-canonical development of the tradition about their time in Egypt, see O. Meinardus, "The Itinerary of the Holy Family in Egypt," *SOCC* 7 (1962): 1–45; F. Manns, "La fuite en Égypte dans l'Évangile apocryphe du Pseudo-Matthieu," *Augustinianum* 23 (1983): 227–35.

5. At least three Coptic monks named Apollo are known to have founded monasteries; see M. Krause, *Das Apa-Apollon-Kloster zu Bawit: Untersuchungen unveröffentlicher Urkunden als Beitrag zur Geschichte des ägyptischen Mönchtums* (diss., Karl-Marx-Universität, 1958); M. Krause and K. Wessel, "Bawit," in K. Wessel and M. Restle, eds., *Reallexikon zur byzantinische Kunst*, I (Stuttgart: Hiersemann, 1966), 569–83 (572–73); H. Torp, "La date de la fondation du monastère d'Apa Apollo de Baouit et de son abandon," *MEFRA* 77 (1965): 153–77 (154–56). It has been hypothesized that the Apollo at Bawit may be the same Apollo after whom a monastery at Titkooh was named; see R.G. Coquin, "Apollon de Titkooh ou /et Apollon de Bawît?" *Orientalia* n.s. 46 (1977): 435–46. For a critical edition of Greek and Coptic documents produced at Apollo's monastery at Bawit during the sixth through ninth centuries, see S.J. Clackson, *Coptic and Greek Texts relating to the Hermopolite Monastery of Apa Apollo* (Oxford: Griffith Institute, 2000). No evident traces of Apollo's original monastery survive. The featureless style of the oldest extant buildings indicates a date no earlier than the mid-fifth century; see R. Milburn, *Early Christian Art and Architecture* (Berkeley: University of California Press, 1988), 148. See further H. Torp, "Le monastère copte de Baouit: Quelques notes d'introduction," in H. Torp, ed., *Acta ad archaeologiam et artium historiam pertinentia* (Rome: Institutum Romanum Norvegiae, 1981), 1–8; D.L. Brooks Hedstrom, *The Monastic Landscape of Late Antique Egypt* (Cambridge: Cambridge University Press, 2017), 200–221.

acles and a tremendous number of signs and wonders.[6] From childhood he had been brought up in self-control, and when he reached adulthood, the grace of God continually increased in him.[7] He was around eighty years old when we visited him and witnessed him enjoying pre-eminence among the community of hermitages. Not to mention that those who were recognized as his disciples were excellent and supremely distinguished, such that almost all of them could work miracles.

(2) They relate that when he was fifteen years old he withdrew to the desert. After forty years of devoting himself to spiritual exercises there, they say that the voice of God came to him: "Apollo, through you I will destroy the wisdom of the wise in Egypt and will confute the understanding of the intelligent.[8] You also will destroy for me the wise men of Babylon, and you will overthrow every form of demon-worship. Therefore, go now to the inhabited region, for you will bear me a peculiar and excellent people which is eager to do good works."[9] He replied: "Lord, keep arrogance away from me so that I do not by chance exalt myself over my brothers and fall away from all your blessings." The divine voice answered him back: "Place your hand on your neck and tightly clamp what you grab onto and bury it under the sand." Right away he put his hand on his neck and grasped what looked like an Ethiopian boy. He promptly thrust him under the sand as he cried out: "I am the demon of pride!"[10] After this a voice came to him from God:

6. Cf. Acts 2.22: "Jesus of Nazareth, a man approved of God among you by miracles and wonders and signs, which God did by him ..." Rufinus borrows phraseology from this biblical passage in order to invest Apollo with Christlike thaumaturgical prowess.

7. Cf. Lk 2.40. Athanasius (*v. Ant.* 1.2) applies this same verse to the child Antony.

8. Is 29.14. The author of the *GHM* makes a pun on the etymological derivation of Apollo's name (Ἀπολλῶ, *Apollō*) when he quotes this biblical verse (ἀπολέσω, *apolesō*, "I will destroy," from ἀπόλλυμι, *apollumi*), but this pun is lost in Rufinus's Latin translation.

9. Cf. Ti 2.14.

10. Ethiopians conventionally were objectified as demons in early monastic literature (e.g., Athanasius, *v. Ant.* 6.1; John Cassian, *coll.* 1.21; *AP* Heraclides 1; Gregory of Tours, *glor. mart.* 28; John Moschus, *prat. spir.* 30, 66; Adomnán, *v. Col.* 3.8), and in most cases their gender is understood as being male, but

"Go now, for you will receive everything you ask of God."[11] As a result, he went to the regions that people inhabit. These events occurred during the reign of the tyrant Julian.[12]

In that area near the desert was a cave in which he lived. Occupying himself ceaselessly with prayers day and night,[13] he performed these prayers (so they said) while bending his knees a hundred times throughout the day and just as often at night.[14] He ate food that was more heavenly than human. His clothing was a sleeveless tunic made of tow, which among those monks is called a *lebiton,* as well as a linen cloth with which he covered his neck and head. They related that these garments had remained with him in the desert but never became worn out.[15]

(3) So then, he passed his time in a nearby part of the desert

---

occasionally we hear of demons taking the form of Ethiopian women (Palladius, *hist. Laus.* 23.5; George of Sykeon, *v. Theod. Syk.* 86). Cf. J. M. Courtès, "The Theme of 'Ethiopia' and 'Ethiopians' in Patristic Literature," in D. Bindman and H. L. Gates, eds., *The Image of the Black in Western Art from the Early Christian Era to the "Age of Discovery": From Demonic Threat to the Incarnation of Sainthood,* vol. II/1 (Cambridge, MA: Harvard University Press, 2010), 199–214; P. Frost, "Attitudes towards Blacks in the Early Christian Era," *SecCent* 8 (1991): 1–11; D. Brakke, "Ethiopian Demons: Male Sexuality, the Black-Skinned Other, and the Monastic Self," *JHSex* 10 (2001): 501–35; A. Nugent, "Black Demons in the Desert," *ABR* 49 (1998): 209–21.

11. Cf. Jn 11.22.

12. I.e., between November 361 and June 363, when Julian reigned as sole emperor of both the eastern and the western Roman Empire. Rufinus calls him a "tyrant" (*tyrannus*) on account of his open opposition to Christianity.

13. In desert monasticism unceasing prayer, a concept based on Paul's imperative, "Pray constantly" (1 Thes 5.17), was an essential exercise for not only communing with God but also warding off demonic attacks and unclean thoughts. See, e.g., A. Guillaumont, "Le problème de la prière continuelle dans le monachisme ancien," in Guillaumont, *Études sur la spiritualité de l'Orient chrétien* (Bégrolles-en-Mauges: Abbaye de Bellefontaine, 1996), 131–41; I. Hausherr, "Hésychasme et prière," *OCA* 176 (1966): 255–306; C. Stewart, "John Cassian on Unceasing Prayer," *MonStud* 15 (1984): 159–77.

14. Other desert monks adopted their own peculiar prayer rituals. For instance, according to Palladius (*hist. Laus.* 20.1), Paul of Pherme knew three hundred prayers by heart and would collect that many pebbles, hold them in his lap, and after reciting each prayer would cast off a pebble, and then he would repeat this cycle when his lap was empty of stones.

15. Cf. Dt 8.4.

in the power of the Spirit, performing miracles and astounding cures, which no words will suffice to describe on account of their immeasurable greatness, according to what we learned from the elders who lived with him. Glowing reports about him spread far and wide.[16] After he had begun to be revered by all as something of a prophet or apostle, monks from neighboring regions flocked to him from various locales, and all of them individually offered to him, as if to their father, precious gifts: their own souls. Welcoming each and every one of them with the utmost care, he admonished some to focus on doing good works and others on acquiring spiritual understanding, but he first modeled by his own conduct what he desired to teach them by his words. So as to foster a sense of fraternal love, he encouraged all to dine with him on Sunday, but on the other days he allowed them to exercise discretion about dietary abstinence, each according to his own ability. Nevertheless, he kept to his usual customs of abstinence by consuming only vegetables and did not condone the usage or assistance of fire.[17]

During the reign of Julian (to whom I referred earlier), Apollo heard that a certain brother had been arrested over the issue of military service and was being detained in prison.[18] He and the brothers visited him in order to lift his spirits and to remind him to hold fast in these dire circumstances and also to think nothing of, and laugh at, impending perils.[19] "The

16. Cf. Lk 4.14.

17. I.e., he ate his vegetables uncooked.

18. This monk had been jailed for evading compulsory military service and was being detained in prison until he could be drafted properly. This passage in fact is the sole literary *testimonium* for the emperor Julian's forcible conscription of monks; see D. Woods, "An Unnoticed Official: The *Praepositus Saltus*," *CQ* n.s. 44 (1994): 245–51 (248n23). Julian was not the only fourth-century emperor to adopt this policy. According to the *Lives of Pachomius* (*SBo* 7; *G*[1] 4–5), Pachomius as a young man was, along with many others, detained for a while against his will as a military conscript during the reign of Constantine.

19. What Rufinus leaves unsaid is that these visitors would also have brought food to their fellow monks, for prisons in contemporary Roman Egypt did not provide any food for their detainees; see S. Torallas-Tovar, "Violence in the Process of Arrest and Imprisonment in Late Antique Egypt," in H.A. Drake, ed., *Violence in Late Antiquity: Perceptions and Practices* (Aldershot:

time of trial is at hand," he said, "and during it the hearts of
the faithful are to be tested and exposed through temptations."
As he was firming up the resolve of the young man with these
and other words, the garrison commander showed up and was
irate at how Apollo presumed to come in [without permission].
He had the prison's doors locked from the outside and impris-
oned Apollo and all who had come with him, so that he could
keep them for compulsory military service. He assigned several
guards to them and left.[20] In the middle of the night, an angel appeared before them aglow with a dazzling brightness. As
the guards stood dumbfounded and petrified, the angel threw
open the doors of the prison. At that point they fell at the feet
of the holy men and begged them to leave, saying that they
would rather die on their account than stand in the way of the
divine power that was protecting them.[21] In the morning, the
garrison commander and his chief officers rushed to the prison and urged all the detainees to depart. The reason, he said,
is that his house had been destroyed by a great earthquake and
that every one of his most prized servants had died as a result.
Upon hearing this, the holy men sang a hymn and praised God
and retreated to the desert as one body—"having," like the
apostles, "one heart and soul."[22]

Ashgate, 2006), 103–12 (108). On incarceration in late antique Egypt, see further S. Torallas-Tovar, "Las prisiones en el Egipto Bizantino según los papiros
griegos y coptos," *Erytheia* 19 (1999): 47–55; idem, "Arresto y encarcelamien-
to en el Egipto romano tardío y bizantino," in S. Torallas-Tovar and I. Pérez
Martín, eds., *Castigo y reclusión en el mundo antiguo* (Madrid, 2003), 209–23.

20. On the police force in late antique Egypt, see R.S. Bagnall, "Army and
Police in Roman Upper Egypt," *JARCE* 14 (1977): 67–86; C. Drecoll, *Die Litur-
gien im römischen Kaiserreich des 3 und 4 Jh. n. Chr.* (Stuttgart, 1997); S. Torallas-
Tovar, "The Police in Byzantine Egypt: The Hierarchy in the Papyri from the
Fourth to the Seventh Centuries," in A. MacDonald and C. Riggs, eds., *Current
Research in Egyptology* (Oxford: Oxbow Books, 2001), 115–23.

21. The account of Apollo's escape is a composite of elements drawn freely
from three different apostolic jailbreak narratives in Acts: "all of the apostles" at
Jerusalem (5.17–25), Peter at Jerusalem (12.1–19), and Paul and Silas at Philip-
pi (16.25–40). For a complete intertextual analysis, see Cain, *The Greek Historia monachorum in Aegypto*, 161–65. For another hagiographic story modeled
on Peter's jailbreak, see D.W. Johnson, trans., *A Panegyric on Macarius, Bishop of
Tkôw, Attributed to Dioscorus of Alexandria* (Louvain: Peeters, 1980), 26.

22. Cf. Acts 4.32: "Now the full number of those who believed were of one

(4) The elderly father taught his monks to progress daily in the virtues and to drive away, right from their very first appearance, the traps the devil lays through one's thoughts. This is why he would say: "Let the serpent's head be crushed, and its whole body becomes lifeless.[23] God commands us to be wary of the serpent's head so that we do not at all entertain evil and unclean thoughts, even from their inception, in our hearts. How much less appropriate is it, then, to allow sordid fantasies, which God prohibits from being entertained even at their inception, to permeate our minds?"

Apollo also would admonish that each monk strive to surpass each other in the virtues and that nobody allow himself to be inferior to his neighbor. "You will know that you are progressing in the virtues," he would say, "if you have no strong inclination towards earthly desires. For this is the beginning of the gifts of God. Now, if any of you should reach the point of performing signs and wonders, he should not be prideful about this or be exalted in his own mind as if he were better than everyone else. He must not reveal to everyone the gift of grace he has received, otherwise he leads himself astray and is deceived and will lose the grace."

He had, then, this wonderful capacity to teach with his words, as we ourselves experienced in part, but he had a greater grace with respect to his deeds. For whatever he had asked of God, he received without delay. What is more, he saw scores

---

heart and soul." Rufinus is superimposing on Apollo's monks the same idealized sense of holy solidarity that is said to have pervaded the earliest Christian community at Jerusalem. Early Christian authors typically interpreted this verse as Scriptural support for the ascetic life. Thus, for example, *APanon* 389 (cf. *APsys* 18.44): "The elders used to say that each one ought to assume responsibility for his neighbour's situation: to suffer with him in everything, to rejoice and to weep with him. One should have the same sentiments as though wearing the same body and be afflicted as though one suffered affliction oneself, as it is written: 'We are a single body in Christ' [Rom 12.5] and 'The multitude of the believers had but one heart and a single soul' [Acts 4.32]" (Wortley, *Anonymous Sayings*, 249). See further L. Verheijen, "Spiritualité et vie monastique chez S. Augustin: L'utilisation monastique des Actes des Apôtres 4:32–35," in C. Kannengiesser, ed., *Jean Chrysostome et Augustin: Actes du colloque de Chantilly 22–24 septembre 1974* (Paris: Beauchesne, 1975), 93–123.

23. Cf. Gn 3.15.

of visions. One concerns his older brother, who for a long time had led a perfect life with him and died in the desert. Apollo saw him in a dream-vision seated on a throne of the apostles (his brother had become one of them) and also saw that he had left him an inheritance of virtues and grace. When he pleaded on his own behalf that the Lord swiftly take him up and give him rest with his brother in heaven, the Lord and Savior replied that he had to spend a little more time on earth, until there is a multitude of zealous imitators of his way of life. For, he said, a populous nation of monks, a pious army, would be entrusted to him, and he would earn from God a reward commensurate with such great deserts.

(5) This came to pass according to Apollo's vision, as monks from every quarter flocked to him,[24] attracted by his reputation and teaching and especially his pattern of life, and a huge number renounced the world. They formed a wonderful community around him in the aforementioned part of the mountain and with one mind shared a common way of life and the same table. We beheld them looking truly like a heavenly and angelic army adorned in all the virtues. To be sure, none among them wore dirty clothes. Rather, they were resplendent on account of the brightness of their garments as much as of their souls, such that, in the words of Scripture, "the thirsty desert rejoiced, and its many children were spotted in the wilderness."[25] Although this was said about the church,[26] it nevertheless has been fulfilled historically in the deserts of Egypt.[27] For where in the cit-

24. Apollo's reputation as a holy man and thaumaturge is what made him a magnet for prospective disciples. These recruits likely were almost exclusively Egyptian and not from other parts of the Empire, for Egyptian monasticism, like Syrian monasticism, was primarily a local affair; see D. Chitty, *The Desert a City* (Oxford: Blackwell, 1966), 46; L. Regnault, *La vie quotidienne des Pères du désert en Égypte au IVe siècle* (Paris: Hachette, 1990), 35–36.

25. Cf. Is 35.1; 54.1.

26. For the early Christian interpretation of these two verses from Isaiah as prophecies for the flowering of the church, see R. Wilken, *The Church's Bible* (Grand Rapids: Eerdmans, 2007), 253–55, 436–38, and on the prominence of the book of Isaiah as a messianic text in early Christianity, see J. F. A. Sawyer, *The Fifth Gospel: Isaiah in the History of Christianity* (Cambridge: Cambridge University Press, 1996), 42–64.

27. The Isaiah passages just quoted were interpreted by some ascetic authors

ies do such great multitudes come to salvation that are as vast
as those the deserts of Egypt have produced? The multitudes
of monks in the deserts are almost as vast as the number of
people in the cities. Hence it seems to me that a saying of the
Apostle has been fulfilled in them: "Where sin abounds, grace
abounds that much more."[28]

At one time an obscene idolatry flourished in Egypt as in no
other nation. They worshiped dogs, apes, and other abomina-
tions. They believed that garlic, onions, and other vegetables
are gods, as we learned from Father Apollo himself, who explained to us the reasons for their ancient superstition: "The
Egyptians once believed that the ox is a god because they used
it to cultivate their fields and procure food and the necessities
of life. But they also believed that the Nile's water is a god because it irrigated all the regions of Egypt, and they worshiped
the soil because it was more fertile than soil anywhere else.
They worshiped dogs, apes, and various kinds of plants and
vegetables because they thought that these would save them
during Pharaoh's reign. Their preoccupation with each one
of these seems to have originated when he was drowned while
pursuing our fathers, and everyone reckoned as his god that
which kept him from following Pharaoh, saying: 'This was my
god today so that I would not follow Pharaoh and be drowned
along with him.'" These were the words of holy Apollo. But it
is necessary to focus much more on the substance of his deeds
and virtues.

At one time there were around ten pagan villages situated
near him in which a demonic superstition was practiced with
supreme devotion. There was a huge temple and an idol inside
it, which by custom was carried by priests who, in the manner
of bacchic revelers, made a procession with the rest of the villagers and conducted profane rites in order to secure the favor

---

as foreshadowing the proliferation of desert monasticism. See P.W. van der
Horst, "The Role of Scripture in Cyril of Scythopolis's *Lives of the Monks of Pal-
estine*," in J. Patrich, ed., *The Sabaite Heritage in the Orthodox Church from the Fifth
Century to the Present* (Leuven: Peeters, 2001), 127–45 (129).

28. Rom 5.20. In his *Ecclesiastical History* (11.8), Rufinus quotes the same
verse as being fulfilled by monks' colonization of the desert regions in Egypt.

of the river's waters.[29] It so happened that when religious rituals of this kind were being performed, blessed Apollo was making his way through the area with a group of the brothers, and he saw the hordes of hapless, demonically-controlled people passing through the countryside in a bacchic frenzy, as if controlled by some demon. He had mercy on their folly, bent his knees, called upon our Lord and Savior, and made all who were under the spell of demonic rites stop dead in their tracks along with their idol, and he kept them from being able to make a single step in any direction.[30] They remained there the entire day being roasted by the searing heat and at a loss as to how it had come about that they were stuck motionless in one spot.

(6) At one point their priests said that there was a Christian named Apollo who lived in the territory of the neighboring desert and that this was his doing and that unless he were appeased, their lives would continue to be in danger. But when people from all around who had heard about this converged to marvel at such a great sight and asked what caused such an ominous event, they admitted that they had absolutely no idea. They did nevertheless say that suspicion fell on Apollo,

29. The priests were carrying the local god's bark shrine to the Nile's bank in the hope that this god would ensure the river's inundation that year. In antiquity the Nile usually would flood annually in July, August, and September, depending on the timing of the annual torrential rainfall in the Ethiopian highlands, which was the source of its inundation. This flooding was essential to agriculture because the overflowing waters irrigated the soil and also deposited silt, which acted as a fertilizer. If the flood came too late, sowing and harvest were delayed, and if it came too little, the area of cultivation was reduced and the crop-yield suffered. Throughout Egyptian history, there developed an increasingly institutionalized Nile cult in which priests and villagers would perform rites annually to incur the divine river's favor. On the development and ritualistic aspects of the Nile cult, see D. Bonneau, *La crue du Nil, divinité égyptienne, à travers mille ans d'histoire* (Paris: Klincksieck, 1964), 393–98; Bonneau, "Les fêtes de la crue du Nil: Problèmes de lieux, de dates et d'organisation," *RdE* 23 (1971): 49–65; D. Frankfurter, *Religion in Roman Egypt: Assimilation and Resistance* (Princeton: Princeton University Press, 1998), 42–46.

30. Cf. Sulpicius Severus, *v. Mart.* 12.1–5, where Martin causes a group of pagan mourners carrying a dead body to its tomb to remain motionless but then removes the curse when he realizes that they are practicing funerary rites and not idolatrous sacrifices.

whom they begged to be appeased on their behalf. Then some of them said that their instincts were right, for they confirmed that they had seen him passing by on that road, yet they did not hesitate to resort to alternative measures they figured would do some good. They brought oxen by whose sheer might one would think the idol could be moved. But since they had not made any headway even by doing this and despaired of every source of help, they sent ambassadors to the man of God and promised that if he released them from these bonds, he would loose the bonds of folly that were on them. When this was reported to him, he went down to them without delay and, after only offering a prayer to God, released all of them.

Right away they all rushed toward him as one body, believing in our God who saves and giving thanks. As for the idol, which was made of wood, they threw it into the fire at once. Moreover, after following the man of God and learning from him how to have faith in the Lord, they were put into communion with the church of God. In fact, a good many of them remained with Apollo and even now live in monasteries. In any event, word of this wondrous deed spread everywhere, and consequently many were converted to faith in the Lord. The end result was that scarcely any pagan remained in that district any longer.

(7) A little while later there was a boundary dispute between two villages. After this had been reported to the man of God, he went down to them in a hurry to make peace. But, being enraged over the quarrel, they were not at all amenable to a peaceful solution, especially because the members of one faction put a great deal of confidence in the might of a certain brigand who was seen as the agitator of the dispute. When Apollo saw that he was standing in the way of peace, he said to him: "Friend, if you are willing to submit to me for the sake of peace, I will entreat my God and he will forgive your sins." Upon hearing this, the man immediately fell at Apollo's knees and humbly beseeched him.[31] At that point Apollo turned to-

---

31. Self-prostration before a holy person was a common reverential gesture in Christian antiquity; see, e.g., Acts 10.25; Basil, *epist.* 45.1; Jerome, *epist.* 108.7, 117.8; *v. Hilar.* 23.3, 28.1; Sulpicius Severus, *dial.* 1.1.2, 3.2.7; *v. Mart.* 9.1, 16.7; *epist.* 2.4; Prudentius, *perist.* 9.5–6; Theodoret, *hist. rel.* 2.17.

ward the crowds that had followed the man and sent away all
of them in peace. As they withdrew, he stayed with the man of
God, begging to receive what had been promised by him. Then
Apollo, taking hold of him and escorting him to the monasteries, taught him that he must change his way of life and patiently
seek mercy from God and faithfully await the fulfillment of the
promise, for he said that all things are possible for him who
believes.[32]

When night came, they fell asleep at the same time in the
monastery, and in a dream-vision both saw themselves in heav-
en standing before the judgment seat of Christ, and they also
saw the angels of God and all the saints worshiping the Lord.
After beholding these things and worshiping God themselves,
the voice of the Lord came to them: "Even though there is no
fellowship between light and darkness, and although the believ-
er shares nothing with the unbeliever,[33] the salvation of that
man on whose behalf you have prayed is granted to you, Apollo." After hearing many other things during their heavenly vision—things that speech cannot express nor the ears hear[34]—
they awoke and recounted to the brothers what they had seen.
As each man described one and the same dream, there grew an
extraordinary sense of wonderment. In any event, that brigand,
now a saint, stayed with the brothers from then on and transformed his life and character into a state of total innocence
and piety as if he had been turned from a wolf into a lamb. The
prophecy of Isaiah found complete fulfillment in him: "Wolves
will feed with lambs, and the lion and ox will eat together."[35]
We saw there even some men of Ethiopian extraction who lived
with the monks and excelled many of them in their spiritual
virtue and observance of ascetic discipline, such that in them
this Scripture was fulfilled: "Ethiopia will stretch out her hands
to God."[36]

32. Mk 9.22.
33. 2 Cor 6.14–15.
34. Cf. 1 Cor 2.9.
35. Is 65.25.
36. Ps 67.32 LXX. For the patristic application of this verse to the conversion of Ethiopians, see J. M. Courtès, "The Theme of 'Ethiopia' and 'Ethiopians' in Patristic Literature," in Bindman and Gates, eds., *The Image of the Black*

(8) Among the deeds of holy Apollo this one also was related. Once a quarrel arose between two villages, one Christian and the other pagan. A huge number of armed villagers from both sides came out. It just so happened that holy Apollo arrived on the scene. As he was encouraging them to be at peace, one of them, who stood poised to fight as the leader of the pagans and the reason for that conflict[37]—a savage and ferocious man— spiritedly defied him, asserting that he would not allow there to be peace as long as he lived.[38] At that point Apollo said: "It will be as you choose. For nobody else besides you will perish. Also, when you are dead, your tomb will not be the earth but the bellies of wild beasts and vultures." Straightaway his statement became fact, for nobody else from either side died except him alone. Although they had buried him in the sand, in the morning they returned and found that he had been dug up by wild animals, ripped to shreds, and devoured by vultures.[39] Overtaken by a sense of wonderment that the man of God's statement had been fulfilled, all of them were converted to faith in the Lord Savior and proclaimed Apollo a prophet of God.

We should not forget about a deed we learned had been performed by him still in the early days when he had begun to live with a few brothers in a cave. It was the holy day of Easter. The vigil and Eucharist had been celebrated inside the cave and a meal prepared from items they had at their disposal. They had only a few dry loaves of bread[40] and vegetables from among those that had been soaked in salt and customarily were preserved by these men for later consumption. Apollo addressed

---

in Western Art from the Early Christian Era to the "Age of Discovery," 199–214 (204). For full reference see p. 106n10 above.

37. Cf. Virgil, Aen. 11.361. See Introduction, p. 20.

38. Lit. "until his own death" (usque ad mortem suam).

39. Cf. Athanasius, v. Ant. 86.1–7, where Antony curses the military commander Balacius, who as a result is brutally attacked by a horse and dies three days later.

40. Bread was a staple of the ancient Mediterranean diet; see N. Jasny, "The Daily Bread of the Ancient Greeks and Romans," Osiris 9 (1950): 227–53. When seasoned with salt, it was a popular dish among ascetics; see, e.g., Theodoret, hist. rel. 2.13. Gregory of Nazianzus (orat. 43.61) claims that it was Basil's favorite meal.

the brothers who were with him: "If we have faith and are truly faithful servants of Christ, let each of us ask of God for whatever he desires to eat on the festal day." Considering themselves unworthy of this grace, however, they allowed these requests of God to be made by Apollo since he surpassed them in age and moral excellence. Then he prayed to the Lord very vigorously. When he had finished, they all responded: "Amen." Then all of a sudden they saw some men, complete strangers to them, standing at the cave's door. They brought so many alimentary delights that hardly anyone has ever seen such a variety of things. Included among them were some varieties of fruits that have never been seen at all in the lands of Egypt, and their size was extraordinary: grapes, nuts,[41] figs,[42] pomegranates (all procured out of season), honeycombs and likewise honey,[43] an abundance of milk, and also giant dates[44] and loaves of the whitest bread, which were hot despite seeming to come from a foreign country. As soon as the men who had brought these items handed them over, they left as if in a hurry to return to the one who had sent them. Then the monks thanked the Lord and began to dine on what had been brought to them—there was such an overflow that the daily provisions were enough to last until Pentecost—and they were confident that God sent these items to them for their religious celebration.

41. Nuts were a regular component of the eastern monastic diet, and they also were consumed by all social classes in the late Roman Empire; see M. van der Veen, "Food as Embodied Material Culture: Diversity and Change in Plant Food Consumption in Roman Britain," *JRA* 21 (2008): 83–109.

42. Figs are frequently mentioned in the literary sources as being part of the diet of monks (e.g., Jerome, *v. Hilar.* 3.1, 5; John Cassian, *coll.* 8.1, *inst.* 5.40; Palladius, *hist. Laus.* 36.3), but Jerome regarded them as a delicacy (*adv. Iov.* 2.5).

43. In Roman times honey was used most commonly as a culinary sweetener (D. Brothwell, *Food in Antiquity* [Baltimore: Johns Hopkins University Press, 1998], 73–80), but peasant farmers also enjoyed it raw for dessert or as a snack. Athenaeus (*deipn.* 10.419) says that Pythagoras subsisted almost exclusively on honey.

44. Dates, the fruit of the date palm tree, were a popular delicacy in Roman culture. They often were used as a culinary flavoring, and eastern monks scavenged for them in nature (e.g., John Cassian, *inst.* 10.24; Palladius, *hist. Laus.* 36.2).

We discovered also that one of the brothers, who lacked the grace of humility and gentleness, begged Apollo to ask the Lord that he be granted this spiritual gift. As Apollo prayed, such a profound grace of gentleness and humility came upon him that all the brothers were awestruck by the calmness and meekness of a man in whom they had seen none of these beforehand.

(9) Once there arose a famine in the Thebaid. The inhabitants of that territory, aware that the monks who served the Lord with Apollo often were fed through the grace of the Lord even when they did not have any food, all went together with their wives and children to ask him for food and a blessing. Without hesitating at all, he brought out provisions stored up for the brothers' use and distributed these liberally to each person. In fact, when only three baskets of bread remained, even though the famine was still decimating the populace, he ordered that the only baskets left, which were supposed to provide the monks with food for one day, be brought out. In the hearing of all the people whom the famine had forced to come together, he raised his hands to God and said: "Is the hand of the Lord not strong enough to multiply these? For the Holy Spirit says: 'The bread in these baskets will not run out until all of us are satisfied with new returns.'"[45] As a great many who had been present at that time confirmed, for four straight months bread never once stopped being dished out of the baskets, and there was not at any time the possibility of a shortage.[46] They

45. Cf. 1 Kgs 17.14.

46. This story is modeled primarily on the biblical accounts of Christ's feeding of the 4,000 (Mt 15.32–9; Mk 8.1–9) and 5,000 (Mt 14.15–21; Mk 6.35–44; Lk 9.12–17; Jn 6.5–14), but it draws vital elements also from the account of an increase miracle attributed to Elijah (1 Kgs 17.10–16). It is also worth noting that Apollo's miracle closely resembles one said by Cyril of Scythopolis (v. Euth. pp. 27–28 Schwartz) to have occurred in Euthymius's laura. When 400 hungry Armenians showed up at his doorstep, Euthymius ordered his cellarer, Domitian, to feed them. Domitian said that this would be impossible since there was hardly enough bread to sustain their own modest community of thirteen brothers, but Euthymius told him to proceed as ordered. Domitian then went to the pantry and found it overflowing with bread loaves, wine, and oil. These foodstuffs continued to multiply for the next three months, keeping the monks amply satisfied. Besa (v. Shen. 27–28) similarly tells of how Shenoute made his monastery's bread-store become completely

asserted that on another occasion Apollo had done the same with grain and oil.

It is related that the devil, irritated by these miracles, said to him: "Are you Elijah or one of the other prophets or apostles, that you have presumed to do these things?"[47] He replied: "Why do you say that? Were not the prophets and apostles men who bequeathed to us both their faith and grace? Or was God present then, but now he is absent? God can do anything, and what he can do, he can do at any time.[48] So then, if God is good, why are you evil?" As I said earlier, we learned by faithful testimony from the elder holy monks that these deeds had been performed through Apollo.[49] Although their account ought to be taken as trustworthy, what we ourselves beheld with our own eyes nevertheless has given more credence to matters. For we saw baskets full of bread loaves being carried to empty tables, and when the tables were covered with loaves, which were consumed to the point of complete satiety, the baskets nonetheless were full when they were gathered up again.

(10) I will not be silent about another amazing thing we saw while we were with him. There were three of us brothers when

---

full in an instant in order to feed the hungry crowds begging for food. For comparable stories about saints' miraculous provision of food, see Palladius, *hist. Laus.* 51.1; Callinicus, *v. Hyp.* 20.1–3; Besa, *v. Shen.* 138–43; Gregory of Tours, *glor. mart.* 9; Adomnán, *v. Col.* 2.3; John Moschus, *prat. spir.* 179; John Rufus, *v. Pet. Ib.* 67.

47. This contumelious question echoes the response of Christ's disciples when he asked them who people believed him to be: "And they told him, 'John the Baptist; and others say, Elijah; and others one of the prophets'" (Mk 8.28).

48. Cf. Lk 1.37.

49. By the phrase *per eum gesta* Rufinus implies that God was the one who performed miracles through the human agency of Apollo. The idea that God performs miracles through the agency of his human servants is rooted in the Bible (e.g., 2 Kgs 5.1), and it also is a commonplace of late antique monastic hagiography. See, for instance, Athanasius, *v. Ant.* 38.2, 40.6, 49.1, 54.4, 56.1, 61.3, 70.2, 80.6, 84.1; Sulpicius Severus, *dial.* 1.10; Anon., *v. Pach. SBo* 45; Callinicus, *v. Hyp.* 25.1, 28.50, 36.6, 38.2, 44.30; Theodoret, *hist. rel.* 9.15; Anon., *v. Dan. Styl.* 88; John Moschus, *prat. spir.* 40, 56; Cyril of Scythopolis, *v. Euth.* p. 20 Schwartz; Gregory of Tours, *lib. mir. Mart.* 1.12.4 and *glor. conf.* 23; Adomnán, *v. Col.* 2.43; George of Sykeon, *v. Theod. Syk.* 61, 119, 138.

we were on our way to see him.[50] Lo and behold, we were still some distance from his monastery and brothers who had been informed by him about our arrival three days earlier ran up to us as they were singing psalms. For this is what they ordinarily do when any monks arrive. Falling prostrate with their faces to the ground, they kissed us, and, pointing us out to one another, they said: "These are the brothers whose arrival father Apollo had foretold three days ago,[51] saying that in three days three brothers coming from Jerusalem would be here." Some of the brothers accordingly went in front of us, others followed, but each group was singing psalms.

As we began to draw near, the holy man, having heard the sound of psalmody, came forth to meet us. Upon seeing us, he immediately fell prostrate on the ground and then got up and welcomed us with a kiss. When we entered the monastery, a prayer was said first (as was the custom), and then he washed our feet with his own hands and attended to everything else pertaining to the refreshment of the body.[52] It was his custom to do these things for all who come to visit him, such that the brothers who live with him do not eat before receiving the Eucharist around the ninth hour of the day.[53]

Afterward they would remain there until evening while they heard the word of God and were taught without interruption about fulfilling the Lord's commandments. After this some of them who already had eaten would withdraw to the desert and spend the entire night reflecting on the divine Scriptures. Others would remain in the same place where they had gathered together, and they would stay wide awake until daybreak singing hymns and praising God, just as I myself witnessed

50. The party consisted of seven monks from Jerusalem, but for some unknown reason four of them temporarily split off from the three who went on to visit with Apollo for a week.

51. Antony too is said to have predicted the arrival of his visitors even months beforehand (Athanasius, *v. Ant.* 62.1).

52. Fourth-century Egyptian ascetics were renowned for being hospitable, not only to their own kind but also to pilgrims. See G. Gould, *The Desert Fathers on Monastic Community* (Oxford: Oxford University Press, 1993), 142–50; Regnault, *La vie quotidienne,* 162–63.

53. I.e., three o'clock in the afternoon.

firsthand. Around the ninth hour, a number of them who had come down from the mountain would receive the grace of the Lord[54] and immediately depart, being satisfied with only this spiritual food. They would do this on most days.

(11) They possessed extraordinary joyfulness and gladness and a degree of exultation that cannot be attained on earth by any human being. Not a single sad person at all was found among them, though if someone seemed a little melancholy, Father Apollo immediately would inquire about the reason for his glumness. Even if someone had wanted to conceal the reason, Apollo often divulged what was hidden in his heart in such a way that the one under duress would understand. Furthermore, he would admonish them that those whose salvation is in God and whose hope is in the kingdom of heaven certainly must not have sadness. He said: "Let the pagans be sad, let the Jews wail, let sinners mourn without end, but let the righteous rejoice. For if they who love what is earthly rejoice in perishable and transitory things, why should we, who have the hope of such a great glory and the expectation of eternal life, not rejoice in complete exultation? Or did not the Apostle admonish us: 'Be glad always, pray without ceasing, give thanks in all things'?"[55] In any event, who could adequately describe the excellence of his teaching and words? This is why I think it is better to be silent about them than to speak out in an insufficiently worthy manner.

Apollo conversed with us extensively in private about the practicalities of abstinence and chaste living and also extensively about being dedicated to hospitality.[56] He assiduously taught us that we should welcome visiting brothers as if we were welcoming the Lord's arrival. He said: "Tradition requires that brothers be shown reverence so that their arrival may be regarded unquestionably as the Lord's arrival.[57] For in this

54. I.e., through the Eucharist.

55. 1 Thes 5.16–18.

56. See R. Greer, "Hospitality in the First Five Centuries of the Church," *MonStud* 10 (1974): 29–48; H. Waddell, *The Desert Fathers* (Ann Arbor, 1957), 113–14. On the reception of guests in eastern monastic culture, see, e.g., Athanasius, *v. Ant.* 17.7, 67.1; John Cassian, *coll.* 1.12.

57. Rufinus dilutes the pithy apophthegm found in the *GHM* (8.55): "You

way Abraham welcomed those who indeed looked like men,[58] yet he saw the Lord in them. Meanwhile, the example of holy Lot, who forcefully brought angels to the guest quarters of his home,[59] teaches us to make brothers accept bodily refreshment even against their will."

Apollo also admonished: "If possible, monks should communicate daily in Christ's Mysteries,[60] lest they distance themselves from God by distancing themselves from these. But as for him who frequently receives them, it should be as if he frequently is receiving the Savior, because the Savior himself says: 'He who eats my flesh and drinks my blood will remain in me, and I in him.'[61] The commemoration of the Lord's suffering, when it is constantly observed by monks, confers immense benefit on them as an example of patience.[62] Implicit in this is also the reminder for each and every person to strive always to be found prepared so that he not be deemed unworthy of the Lord's Mys-

---

have seen your brother, you have seen the Lord your God" (εἶδες γάρ, φησί, τὸν ἀδελφόν σου, εἶδες κύριον τὸν θεόν σου). This sententious saying did not originate with Apollo but in fact had been in currency for at least two centuries. It is found elsewhere in Clement of Alexandria (*strom.* 1.19.94.5, 2.15.70.5), and a similar formulation in Latin is attested as early as Tertullian (*orat.* 26). Cf. J.B. Bauer, "*Vidisti fratrem vidisti dominum tuum* (Agraphon 144 Resch und 126 Resch)," *ZKG* 100 (1989): 71–76, who hypothesizes that this saying originated with Melito of Sardis.

58. Cf. Gn 18.2. In early monastic literature Abraham frequently is held up as a scriptural paradigm for monastic hospitality; see, e.g., *AP* Nisterus 2; Theodoret, *hist. rel.* 17.7.

59. Cf. Gn 19.1–3. Evagrius of Pontus also cites Lot as the archetypal host; see R. Sinkewicz, *Evagrius of Pontus: The Greek Ascetic Corpus* (Oxford: Oxford University Press, 2003), 20, 51, 241.

60. Some Egyptian monks partook of the Eucharist on a daily basis, but others did so less frequently; see H. Ashley Hall, "The Role of the Eucharist in the Lives of the Desert Fathers," *StudPatr* 39 (2006): 367–72. Cf. E. Dekkers, "Les anciens moines cultivaient-ils la liturgie?" *La Maison-Dieu* 51 (1957): 31–54 (41), who asserts that monks generally communed less frequently than "ordinary" Christians.

61. Jn 6.57.

62. Rufinus's phrase *ad exemplum patientiae* ("as an example of patience") has a twofold sense: monks learn patience not only by contemplation of the Lord's patience through suffering but also by the disciplined practice of daily Communion.

teries."[63] He added that the forgiveness of sins also is bestowed on believers through the Mysteries.

(12) Apollo advised that the canonical fasts—the ones on Wednesdays and Fridays—not be broken except for some significant and unavoidable reason, because on a Wednesday Judas conceived the idea to betray the Lord and on a Friday the Savior was crucified.[64] So then, he who breaks the established fasts on these days without an avoidable reason will seem as if he either is joining the betrayer in betraying the Savior or is joining the crucifiers in crucifying him. Apollo said that if on the aforementioned days any of the brothers happens to come and wants to eat before the ninth hour because he is exhausted from manual labor, a table should be set only for him, but if he does not wish to eat, then he should not be forced. For this is the widely observed tradition surrounding this practice.[65]

He severely censured those who grow their hair long, wear iron around their neck, or perform any gesture which is done ostentatiously to attract attention.[66] He said: "There is no doubt

63. Cf. 2 Cor 9.3–4.

64. From perhaps as early as the late first century and down through the fourth century, Wednesday and Friday were normal fasting days for Christians, though a few sources indicate that during the fourth century fasting was observed also on Saturday by some churches. See F.J.E. Boddens Hosang, *Establishing Boundaries: Christian-Jewish Relations in Early Council Texts and the Writings of Church Fathers* (Leiden: Brill, 2010), 61–66.

65. Cf. John Cassian, *coll.* 2.25–26.

66. This allusive criticism, which is echoed by Jerome (*epist.* 22.28), is leveled at contemporary Syrian ascetics, some of whom were notorious for wearing heavy iron chains (as a self-mortifying exercise) and for letting their hair grow long and become disheveled. As Chitty, *The Desert a City*, 17n36, points out, chain-wearing among ascetics was a predominately Syrian phenomenon. For some examples, see Palladius, *hist. Laus.* 44.2; Theodoret, *hist. rel.* 3.19; 4.6, 12; 11.1, 3; 21.8; 23.1; 24.6, 10; 29.4–5. On the ascetic impulse in general in early Syrian Christianity, see S. Ashbrook Harvey, *Asceticism and Society in Crisis: John of Ephesus and the 'Lives of the Eastern Saints'* (Berkeley: University of California Press, 1990), 1–21; S. Griffith, "Asceticism in the Church of Syria: The Hermeneutics of Early Syrian Asceticism," in V. Wimbush and R. Valantasis, eds., *Asceticism* (New York: Oxford University Press, 1995), 220–45. In other ancient literary sources, especially ones biased in favor of Egyptian monasticism, it is specifically Syrian ascetics who often are accused of practicing the kind of insincere ascetic piety ascribed to them by Apollo. For Cassian's

that they seek praise from men[67] and act like this to show off, even though it is commanded that fasts be done in secret[68] so that they may be known only to God, who sees what is done in secret and repays in plain view.[69] It seems instead that they are not content to be monitored and rewarded by him who sees what is secret, but rather they crave popular acclaim. Every expression of asceticism should be made in secret so that the body may be fatigued from fasts, yet in such a way that praise not be sought from men but that recompense be sought from God."

Throughout the entire week Apollo spoke to us about these and many other things pertaining to the monastic lifestyle, and he showed how trustworthy his teaching was by the authoritative example of his deeds. When we got ready to leave, he escorted us a little way and exhorted us: "Before all else, be at peace among yourselves, and do not be separated from one another." Then he turned to the brothers who together with him were escorting us and said: "Which of you is ready to take

---

generally negative appraisal of Syrian asceticism vis-à-vis its Egyptian counterpart, see C. Gaspar, "Cassian's Syrian Monastic Contemporaries," in C. Badilita and A. Jakab, eds., *Jean Cassien entre l'Orient et l'Occident* (Paris: Beauchesne, 2003), 15–32.

67. Cf. 1 Thes 2.6.

68. Cf. Mt 6.16–18.

69. Cf. Mt 6.6. Apollo is evoking Christ's condemnation of Pharisaical prayer and his exhortation to his disciples to pray "in secret" (Mt 6.5–6). The typological casting of hypocritical ascetics (and clergymen) as haughty, morally depraved Pharisees was a polemical tactic adopted by many patristic authors. For instance, Jerome incorporated two verbal allusions to Christ's denunciations of the Pharisees when admonishing the young priest Nepotian: "I do not want you to pray on street corners [cf. Mt 6.5], lest the wind of popular approval interrupt the straight course of your prayers. I do not want you to lengthen your tassels or show off your phylacteries and wrap yourself in pharisaical self-seeking [cf. Mt 23.5b], against the better judgment of your conscience. It is better to carry these things in your heart than on your body, and better to be looked at with favor by God than by men" (*epist.* 52.13); for analysis of this passage, see Cain, *Jerome and the Monastic Clergy*, 243–44. For other examples, see Gregory of Nazianzus, *orat.* 2.70; Augustine, *op. mon.* 28.36; Jerome, *comm. in Zach.* 14.10–11, ll. 415–17; Gregory the Great, *reg. past.* 1.1; cf. A. Cain, "Origen, Jerome, and the *senatus Pharisaeorum*," *Latomus* 65 (2006): 727–34.

them to the neighboring hermitages of the fathers?" Almost all of them most readily volunteered and expressed their willingness to accompany us, and then the holy father selected three because they were fluent in Greek and Coptic[70] (so that they could interpret for us if the need ever arose) and because they would be able to edify us with their words of encouragement. As he sent them off with us, he instructed them not to leave our side before we saw all the fathers and monasteries we wanted to see, even though nobody is capable of going around to them all. He accordingly sent us off by blessing us and worded the blessing as follows: "May the Lord bless you from Zion, and may you see the prosperity of Jerusalem all the days of your life."[71]

70. The anonymous Greek author puts Latin on this list, but Rufinus omits it.

71. Ps 127.5. Apollo's choice of scriptural benediction is apt, of course, because the monastic pilgrims came from Jerusalem.

CHAPTER 8
AMOUN

HAT WE HEARD about Amoun, a certain holy man whose dwelling-place we saw in the desert, I did not think should be passed over in silence. After we had made it to where he was and were heading towards the southern part of the desert, we spotted in the sand the tracks of a giant serpent whose massive size made it seem like a wood-beam had been dragged through the sand. When we saw this, we were stricken with overwhelming fear. The brothers who were escorting us, however, encouraged us not to be afraid at all but rather to muster courage and to follow the serpent by its tracks. They said: "You assuredly will see how strong our faith is when you watch us put the serpent to death. We have killed many serpents, snakes, and horned vipers with our own hands. For we find in Scripture how the Savior grants to those who believe in him the ability to trample underfoot serpents and scorpions and every power of the Enemy."[1]

---

1. Cf. Lk 10.19: "Behold, I have given you authority to tread upon serpents and scorpions, and over all the power of the enemy; and nothing shall hurt you" (RSV). This Lucan verse, which is conceptually reminiscent of Ps 90.13 LXX ("On the asp and cobra you will tread, and you will trample underfoot the lion and serpent"), is part of Jesus's reply to his seventy-two disciples who had returned from their missionary travels and ecstatically reported that even demons had submitted to them. He affirmed their newfound power over the demonic realm and Satan himself (the "enemy" in this passage; see I.H. Marshall, *The Gospel of Luke* [Grand Rapids: Eerdmans, 1978], 429) but immediately exhorted them to rejoice not that spirits submit to them but that their names are written in heaven. On Christians' immunity from lethal snakebites, see Mk 16.18; Acts 28.3–6; *Life of Pachomius* (*SBo* 98–99; *G*[1] 21); Theodoret, *hist. rel.* 2.6; 22.5–6; cf. Athanasius, *v. Ant.* 24.5. On snake-handling by both pagans and Christians, see J.A. Kelhoffer, *Miracle and Mission: The Authentication*

As they were saying this, we were becoming more and more terrified on account, I believe, of weakness caused by lack of faith. We begged them not to want to follow the serpent's tracks but instead that we continue on the planned route. Nevertheless, one of them, impatient because of his impetuosity, pressed on after the serpent. After he had located its cave not far away, he called out to us to go and see what was going to happen. One of the brothers, however, who had a hermitage nearby ran up to us and forbade us to go, saying that the beast was of enormous size and that we were unable to handle even the sight and spectacle of it, primarily because we had beheld nothing like it. He acknowledged that he often had seen the beast, whose immensity was indeed unparalleled and whose length stretched out to fifteen cubits.[2] After he had dissuaded us from going to the place, he hastened over to the brother who was waiting for us there and stood ready to destroy the beast, and he pulled him away. Although he did not want to leave unless he killed the beast, the other brother brought him back with him and with much pleading changed his mind. After he had returned to us, he chastised our cowardice and lack of faith.

(2) Then we traveled to the cell of the brother who had approached us. After being welcomed by him with the utmost kindness, we rested. He told us that in the area where he was living there was a holy man whose disciple he himself was. The man's name was Amoun, and the Lord performed a great many miracles through him. Among other stories the brother told us the following one about Amoun.

"Robbers frequently would come to him and steal his bread, the only thing he ate, as well as any other provisions for his extremely temperate way of life. He often was harassed by them, and so one day he went out to the desert, and on his way back he commanded two giant serpents to accompany him. He ordered them to stand guard at the door of the hermitage. The robbers came as usual. They beheld the guards on the door-

---

of Missionaries and their Message in the Longer Ending of Mark (Tübingen: Mohr Siebeck, 2000), 407–16.

2. I.e., about twenty-two feet long.

step, and as they looked on, they were scared to death and
frantic. Becoming suddenly stupefied, they fell to the ground.
When the old man realized what had happened, he went out
and found them half-dead. As he approached them and helped
them up, he chided them: 'You see how much more savage
you are than wild animals, for they obey us on God's account,
whereas you neither fear God nor respect the life of God's servants.' Nevertheless, he took them into the hermitage and sat
them at the table and instructed them to eat. Struck inwardly by compunction and abandoning every vestige of cruelty in
their intentions, they instantly became superior to many who
had begun to serve the Lord before them. Indeed, through
their repentance they progressed so far that not long afterward
they even were performing the same signs and miracles.

(3) "On another occasion, when an enormous serpent was
laying waste to the surrounding territory and killing a lot of
people, the locals came to Amoun and begged him to rid their
territory of the beast. In the hope of arousing the old man's
sense of compassion, they brought with them the son of a shep-
herd, a boy who had become terrified merely at the sight of the
serpent and had fainted. He was carried in, swollen and tee-
tering on death after having come into contact with only the
beast's noxious breath. Then Amoun anointed the boy with oil
and made him whole again. He set his mind on killing the serpent, but in the meantime he did not want to promise them
anything but gave them the impression that he was unable to
help. Early in the morning he awoke and went to the beast's
haunt. He bent his knees on the ground and called upon the
Lord in prayer. At that point the beast let out foul-smelling
snorts and shrill hissing and started to lunge at him with tremendous force. But fearing none of this, he turned to the serpent and said: 'May Christ the Son of God, who will slay the
great sea-monster,[3] slay you.' As soon as the old man said this,

3. Amoun is alluding to Is 27.1: "On that day the Lord with his cruel and
great and strong sword will punish Leviathan the fleeing serpent, Leviathan
the twisting serpent, and he will kill the dragon that is in the sea." On this
verse in its original context, see B.W. Anderson, "The Slaying of the Flee-

the fiercely menacing serpent vomited up all of its venom together with its breath and made a loud noise as it burst in half.[4]
The people who lived nearby came together and were dumbfounded by the astounding occurrence. They could not stand
the pungency of the foul smell and heaped large mounds of
sand on top of it. Father Amoun stood there, because they did
not dare to approach the beast without him there, even though
it was dead."

---

ing, Twisting Serpent: Isaiah 27:1 in Context," in L.M. Hopfe, ed., *Uncovering Ancient Stones: Essays in Memory of H. Neil Richardson* (Winona Lake, IN:
Eisenbraums, 1994), 3–15; J. Day, "God and Leviathan in Isaiah 27:1," *BSac*
155 (1998): 423–36; E.M. McGuire, "Yahweh and the Leviathan: An Exegesis
of Isaiah 27:1," *RQ* 13 (1970): 165–79.

4. Similarly, Abba Ammonas "by the power of God" made a basilisk burst
asunder at his command (*AP* Ammonas 2; Ward, *Sayings*, 26).

CHAPTER 9
COPRES

HERE WAS a certain priest named Copres,[1] a holy man around eighty years old, who had a hermitage in that desert. He performed many miracles, healing illnesses and effecting cures but also exorcising demons and performing many wondrous feats, some of which he did because we were there. After laying eyes on us, greeting us with a kiss, and washing our feet after prayer (as was customary), he asked us about what was happening in the world.[2] But we urged him to tell us instead about some of his exploits and to explain on the grounds of what deeds or merits the Lord had conferred such a great grace on him. He readily obliged and described for us his own way of life and that of his predecessors. He asserted that

1. There are at least two other fourth-century Egyptian monks by this name who are attested in the literary sources; see *AP* Copres 1–3; *Letter of Ammon* 29. Many more people by this name are known from the papyri; see, e.g., R. J. S. Barrett-Lennard, *Christian Healing after the New Testament: Some Approaches to Illness in the Second, Third and Fourth Centuries* (Lanham, MD: University Press of America, 1994), 12–14, 16, 65; M. Malouta, "The Terminology of Fatherlessness in Roman Egypt: ἀπάτωρ and χρηματίζων μητρός," in J. Frösén, T. Purola, and E. Salmenkivi, eds., *Proceedings of the 24th International Congress of Papyrology, Helsinki, 1–7 August, 2004* (Helsinki, 2007), 615–24 (620–24).

2. Once when Macarius the Great was traversing the desert, he met two monks who had lived in complete isolation for four decades, and they were inquisitive in the same way as Copres, asking Macarius: "How is the world? Is the water [of the Nile] rising in due time? Is the world enjoying prosperity?" (*AP* Macarius the Great 2; Ward, *Sayings*, 126). Similarly, Paul of Thebes, when Antony had traversed the desert to meet him, asked his visitor: "Tell me, how is the human race faring? Are there new roofs rising in the ancient cities?" (Jerome, *v. Paul.* 10.1).

they had been far more eminent than he and that he followed their examples,[3] which were by no means insignificant.

"What you see in us, my children, is nothing special in comparison to the holy fathers. For instance, there was a certain very noble man[4] named Patermuthius, who preceded us. He was the first monk in this area, and he was the first in this whole desert to show the way of salvation to us all. He initially was a pagan,[5] a brigand-chief and tomb-robber[6] notorious for crimes of all sorts. The opportunity for salvation came to him in the following way. One night he ventured to the residence of a certain virgin consecrated to God, intending to burglarize it. After he had climbed onto the roof using tricks familiar to schemers of

---

3. Another example of cross-generational comparison among Egyptian monks is provided by the following anecdote about the ascetic Elias: "The old men said of Abba Agathon to Abba Elias, in Egypt, 'He is a good abba.' The old man answered them, 'In comparison with his own generation, he is good.' They said to him, 'And what is he in comparison with the ancients?' He gave them this answer, 'I have said to you that in comparison with his generation he is good but as to that of the ancients, in Scetis I have seen a man who, like Joshua the son of Nun, could make the sun stand still in the heavens.' At these words they were astounded and gave glory to God" (Ward, *Sayings*, 71).

4. Rufinus's characterization of Patermuthius as a "very noble man" (*vir nobilissimus*) and thus belonging to the upper classes of late Roman society—a designation not found in the *GHM*—is somewhat puzzling inasmuch as almost in the same breath he identifies Patermuthius as a one-time career criminal, and a robber in particular. Generally speaking, thieves in the Roman world tended to arise from the lower classes, for they resorted to crime because they did not have the financial wherewithal to live a comfortable, law-abiding life; see J. M. Kelly, *Roman Litigation* (Oxford: Oxford University Press, 1966), 162–63. On their marginalized status, see V. Neri, *I Marginali nell' occidente tardoantico* (Bari: Edipuglia, 1998), 289–418.

5. Lat. *gentilis,* one of the many pejorative terms, along with *paganus* and *ethnicus,* that Latin patristic authors applied to pagans. This was the term preferred by Augustine; see C. Mohrmann, *Die altchristliche Sondersprache in den Sermones des hl. Augustinus* (Nijmegen: Latinitas Christianorum primaeva, 1932), 110.

6. See J. Gascou, "La vie de Patermouthios moine et fossoyeur (*Historia Monachorum* X)," in C. Décobert, ed., *Itinéraires d'Égypte. Mélanges M. Martin* (Cairo: IFAO, 1992), 107–14; cf. T. Baumeister, "Ägyptisches Lokalkolorit in der *Historia monachorum in Aegypto*," in U. Zanetti and E. Lucchesi, eds., *Aegyptus Christiana: Mélanges d'hagiographie égyptienne et orientale dédiés à la mémoire du P. Paul Devos bollandiste* (Geneva: Patrick Cramer, 2004), 165–74 (168–71).

his ilk, he wondered by what kind of cunning or through what point of entry he could sneak into the innermost room of the residence. Perplexed by the challenge of carrying out the task, he spent most of the night on the roof without any success.

(2) "After many vain attempts to figure it out, he was worn out and overcome by sleep. In a vision he saw someone dressed in regal garb standing next to him who said: 'Quit these crimes now, and stop spilling human blood. Devote your sleepless nights to pious toil rather than to detestable thefts, become a soldier in the heavenly and angelic military, live according to the spiritual virtues from here on out, and I will make you commander and leader of this military.' After listening joyously to what was being offered to him, he was shown an army of monks and was ordered to assume command over them. Upon waking up, he saw the virgin standing in front of him inquiring about who he was, whence he came, and why he was there. As if dumbstruck, he did not reply except to ask her to point him in the direction of the church. As soon as she had recognized God's work afoot in the matter, she escorted the man to the church and handed him over to the priests. Falling at their feet, he begged to become a Christian and to be given the chance to repent. Because they realized that this man was a perpetrator of every sort of crime, the priests were skeptical about whether he was telling the truth. Once his persistence had given assurance that he was, they admonished him to disavow his crimes completely if wanted to be a Christian.

"From then on, after taking the first steps in his religious devotion, he begged for instructions on how to enter upon the path of salvation.[7] They gave him three verses from the first Psalm. After contemplating them carefully, he said that they were enough to show him the path of salvation and to give him a knowledge of holiness. He stayed with them for three days and then proceeded to the desert. There he lingered for a con-

7. Patermuthius took "the first steps in his religious devotion (*religio*)" by renouncing his life of crime and embracing the ethical norms of Christianity; his zeal, however, was so intense that he was not content to be an ordinary professing Christian but wanted to become a monk, that is, "to enter upon the path of salvation (*viam salutis*)."

siderable amount of time, persevering day and night in tearful prayer; for food he ate the roots of wild plants. After having returned to the church, he manifested, in not only his words but also his actions and deeds, the three verses of the Psalm he had learned from the priests.

"The priests were amazed because the man who had instantaneously been converted at once undertook the harshest possible asceticism. They gave him more fulsome lessons from the divine Scriptures and urged him to live with them. So as not to seem disobedient, he spent a week with them but again ventured out into the desert. He lived there for seven straight years practicing every form of asceticism and attained the fullness of grace from God, to the point that he committed almost all the Scriptures to memory.[8] On Sunday he would eat only bread provided by God. For when he would pray, he would get up from his prayer and find bread placed there, which nobody had brought. Once he had eaten it with thanksgiving, it was enough to fill him until the following Sunday.

(3) "After a long period of time Patermuthius returned from the desert, and through the example of his asceticism he induced as many people as possible to imitate him. Among these was a certain young man who approached him in the hope of being his disciple. Patermuthius clothed him in monks' garb (a sleeveless tunic, hood, and goatskin cloak) and then taught him about the rest of the lifestyle guidelines for monks. Patermuthius dutifully attended to the burial of any Christian who had died. When the young man, that disciple of his, had seen him dressing the dead in burial clothing with the utmost care, he said to him: 'When I am dead, teacher, I want you to dress me like this and bury me.' Patermuthius said: 'I will do so. I will dress you splendidly for burial until you say, "That's enough."'

---

8. Rote memorization of Scripture, and especially of the Psalter (see Gregory of Nyssa, *v. Macr.* 3; Jerome, *epist.* 125.11; George of Sykeon, *v. Theod. Syk.* 13), was a crucial component of Egyptian monastic culture: see, e.g., Palladius, *hist. Laus.* 11.4; 18.25; 32.12; 37.1; Epiphanius, *pan.* 67.1.4; Burton-Christie, *The Word in the Desert*, 107, 117, 161. Jerome praises Origen (*epist.* 84.8), Hilarion (*v. Hilar.* 4.3), and his patron Paula (*epist.* 108.26) for knowing all of Scripture by heart, and he recommends that a virgin commit the entire Bible to memory (*epist.* 107.12; 128.4; cf. *epist.* 22.17).

"Not long afterward the young man died, and the prophetic word came to pass. For after Patermuthius had fitted him with many layers of burial clothes, he addressed him in the presence of everyone: 'Are these enough for your burial, my child, or do you want me to add anything?' Then, as all were listening, the dead man let out a cry, even though his face had already been wrapped and his expression had become stiff.[9] He said: 'That's enough, Father. You've done what you had promised.'[10] Those present were dumbfounded and greatly astonished at so amazing a feat of his. In any event, as soon as the young man had been buried, Patermuthius returned to the desert with the greatest eagerness, shunning ostentation.

(4) "On one occasion he came back from the desert to visit the brothers he had trained. When one of them was on his deathbed, the Lord revealed to Patermuthius that the brother was about to die. It was nearly evening, so he hurried so that he could see him.[11] The town, however, where the ailing man was bedridden was still a long way off. Patermuthius did not want to enter the town at night, and at the same time he reflected on the Savior's sayings, 'Walk while you have the light among you,'[12] and, 'He who walks in the light does not stumble.'[13] When he saw the sun already setting, he said to it: 'In the

9. I.e., from *rigor mortis*.

10. A syncopated version of this story, with Patermuthius's name removed, is found in the *Anonymous Sayings of the Desert Fathers* (Wortley, *Anonymous Sayings,* 13).

11. Patermuthius, with his sense of extreme urgency, may be contrasted with Abba Theodore, whom a gravely ill Abba Joseph summoned to come and see him before he died. Theodore received the summons in the middle of the week and sent a message to Joseph, saying: "If you wait until Saturday, I shall come; but if you depart, we shall see one another in the world to come" (*AP* Theodore of Pherme 19).

12. Jn 12.35. Patermuthius quotes this verse out of context: Jesus is referring to himself figuratively as the "light" of the world, and when he encourages his followers to walk by the light of day, he means that they should try to benefit from his presence for as long as he is with them in body. In Johannine parlance "day" refers to Jesus's ministry on earth, and "night" symbolizes his crucifixion and death (cf. Jn 9.4–5). On the life and light motifs in the canonical Johannine corpus, see A.J. Köstenberger, *A Theology of John's Gospel and Letters* (Grand Rapids: Eerdmans, 2009), 344–49.

13. Jn 11.9. This is an especially apt verse for Patermuthius to quote as he

name of our Lord Jesus Christ, stand still in your course for
a little while and wait until I reach the town.'[14] Although it already had begun to set, it stopped and did not go down before
the man of God reached the town.[15] This was made evident to
all who lived there. For as they stood and gazed at the sun's
halting during its descent, all marveled at why it did not set for
so many hours.[16] When they saw Patermuthius emerging from
the desert, they asked him the meaning of the solar spectacle.
He replied to them: 'Do you not remember the saying of our
Lord and Savior, "If you have faith like a grain of mustard seed,
you will perform greater works than these?"'[17] Once they understood, a great many of them were stricken with tremendous

---

journeys to visit his dying disciple, for Jesus makes the remark on his way to
see his own gravely ill friend and disciple, Lazarus, who had already died from
his illness (much like Patermuthius's disciple) and had been entombed for
four days by the time Jesus arrived in Bethany to see him.

14. Cf. Christ's ability to control the elements (Mk 6.45–52; Lk 8.22–25).
Like Patermuthius, Abba Bessarion, one of the pioneering monks at Scetis, is
said to have made the sun stand still until he could complete a journey to a fellow monk (*AP* Bessarion 3). Abba Elias claims that he once saw a monk from
the first generation of monastic settlers at Scetis (Bessarion?), "a man who,
like Joshua the son of Nun, could make the sun stand still in the heavens" (*AP*
Elias 2). Late antique holy men were not the only Christians to be credited
with making the sun stand still. According to the *Chanson de Roland* (laisses
179–80), Charlemagne prayed to God for the same miracle and was granted
it, so that his troops had enough daylight to chase and overtake the fleeing
Saracen army.

15. Patermuthius's solar miracle is meant typologically to evoke one of
the most famous events in the annals of Old Testament history, when Joshua
called on the Lord at Gibeon and commanded the sun and moon to stand
still for approximately a day so that he could finish decimating the armies of
the Amorite coalition (Jos 10.12–14); for a conspectus of scholarly hypotheses
that have attempted to explain this celestial phenomenon, see R. Nelson, *Joshua: A Commentary* (Louisville: John Knox Press, 1997), 141–45.

16. Rufinus emphasizes their sense of wonderment at the spectacle, for
it was regarded as a scientific "fact" in Greco-Roman antiquity that the sun
cannot be stopped in its course; see R.M. Grant, *Miracle and Natural Law in
Graeco-Roman and Early Christian Thought* (Amsterdam: Wipf and Stock, 1952),
57–58.

17. Mt 17.20. This verse is quoted elsewhere in late antique monastic hagiography to explain the divine origin of monks' wonder-working powers; see
Athanasius, *v. Ant.* 83.2; Jerome, *v. Hilar.* 29.5.

fear and joined themselves to him as disciples and began following him.

"After he had entered the home of the brother for whose
sake he had been in a hurry and found that he had already
died, he said a prayer, approached the bed, kissed him, and
said: 'Which do you prefer, to depart and be with Christ or
to remain in the flesh?' At that point he regained his breath
of life, sat up slightly, and said: 'Why are you summoning me
back, Father? It is better for me to leave and be with Christ; I do
not need to remain in the flesh.'[18] Patermuthius replied: 'Very
well then, my son, sleep in peace, and pray for me.' At once he
lay back on the bed and went to sleep.[19] Those who were present were dumbfounded and said: 'Truly he is a man of God.'
Then he dressed the young man for burial in a fitting way (as
was his custom), and after spending a whole sleepless night in
psalmody and hymnody, he buried the youth with dignity.

(5) "He visited another bedridden brother. When Patermuthius saw that he was having difficulty accepting the repose
of death and was being severely reproached by the anxiety of
his conscience, he said to him: 'Why are you ill prepared for
the journey? The way I see it, your conscience sticks by you as
the accuser of your negligence.' Then he begged him: 'I im-

---

18. Cf. Phil 1.23–24.

19. The metaphorical identification of sleep with death was a convention
of classical Greek and Latin literature; see, e.g., Hesiod, *theog.* 756; Homer,
Il. 11.241; Aeschylus, *Choeph.* 906; Plato, *apol.* 40C–D; Xenophon, *Cyr.* 8.7.21;
Lucretius, *rer. nat.* 3.909–10; Cicero, *Tusc. disp.* 1.97; Horace, *carm.* 1.24.5–6;
Virgil, *Aen.* 6.278. This identification had wide currency among the Hebrews
from at least as early as the sixth century BCE (e.g., 1 Kgs 1.21; 2 Kgs 4.32;
1 Chr 16.13–14; Jb 3.11–14; Is 14.8). The NT writers employ it as well, especially in connection with the doctrine of the resurrection (e.g., Mt 9.24; Jn
11.11–13; 1 Cor 7.39; Eph 5.14; 1 Thes 4.13–15; 2 Pt 3.4). For some patristic
expressions of the metaphor of death as sleep, see Irenaeus, *adv. haer.* 4.48.2;
Clement of Alexandria, *protr.* 9.84.2; Origen, *c. Cels.* 2.73; Methodius, *resurr.*
1.51; Tertullian, *resurr. carn.* 24; Cyprian, *epist.* 1.2; Ambrose, *bon. mort.* 8.34;
Prudentius, *cath.* 10.53–56; Augustine, *nat. orig. an.* 4.28; Paulinus of Nola,
epist. 13.9; cf. A.C. Rush, *Death and Burial in Christian Antiquity* (Washington,
DC: The Catholic University of America Press, 1941), 1–22; C.L. Thompson,
"Taedium vitae" in Roman Sepulchral Inscriptions (Lancaster: Kessinger Publish-
ing, 1912), 19–31.

plore you, intercede with God for me to give me a short period of time in which I may change my life.' Patermuthius said: 'Now that you have finished the time allotted for life, you ask for a period of repentance. What were you doing during this whole time of your life? Were you not able to heal your wounds but instead were always adding newer ones?' As he continued to beseech him, the old man said: 'If you do not keep adding evils to your evils, we will pray to God for you. For he is good and patient and concedes to you a little more time in life so that you may settle all your debts.'

"After this Patermuthius prayed to God, and when he arose from prayer he said to him: 'Behold, the Lord has given you three years in this life for the sole purpose of your becoming sincerely repentant.' Taking his hand, he lifted him from the bed.[20] He got up and without any delay followed Patermuthius to the desert. When the three years were up, Patermuthius summoned him back to the place whence he had taken him, presenting him to God no longer as a man but as a man-turned-angel, such that all were astonished at his conversion. After a great many brothers had gathered around him, Patermuthius put him front-and-center, and the entire night he introduced teaching to the brothers about the salutary effects of repentance and conversion, drawing his subject matter from this man's example. But as he was speaking, that brother became drowsy and promptly fell asleep permanently. Then a prayer was said over him, all the customary rites of burial were completed, and Patermuthius hastily made off for the desert.

"Patermuthius often crossed the raging Nile River on foot with the water up to his knees.[21] Another time, when the doors were closed and the brothers were sitting on a roof-terrace, he came to them[22] and was whisked away, in the twinkling of an eye, to whatever place he wanted, no matter how far away it was.

20. Acts 3.7.

21. Cf. Abba Bessarion, who crossed a river with the water coming up only to his ankles (*AP* Bessarion 2). The implication is that both Patermuthius and Bessarion only imperfectly imitated Christ's ability to walk on water (cf. Mt 14.22–33; Mk 6.45–52; Jn 6.16–21).

22. Cf. Jn 20.26.

During the first stage of his conversion,[23] when he was in the desert and had been fasting for a week, they say that a man came to him in his solitude carrying bread and water and exhorted him to consume the food. Another time a demon stood next to him and showed him many hoards of gold buried underground, which he claimed had belonged to Pharaoh.[24] Patermuthius is said to have replied to him: 'May your money perish with you!'[25] God did these and many similar things through him.[26] But nevertheless there were many fathers before us, of whom the world was not worthy,[27] who performed heavenly signs and wonders. Why, then, are you astonished if we insignificant men do insignificant things by healing the lame and blind, which doctors also are able to do through their skill?"

(6) As the old man Copres was telling us these things, one of our brothers, as if out of disbelief at what was being said, began to lose interest and to doze off from boredom. After he had fallen asleep, in a vision he saw the old man Copres holding a book, inscribed with golden letters,[28] from which his stories appeared to be taken. He also saw a venerable man with white hair and a resplendent countenance[29] standing beside Copres

23. In ancient monastic terms, conversion (*conversio*) was viewed as a gradual process of achieving spiritual perfection.

24. Cf. Dt 33.19.

25. Acts 8.20 (Peter's rebuke of Simon Magus for attempting to buy the Holy Spirit's miracle-working power). Antony quoted this same verse to the devil upon finding an expensive silver dish on a road and suspecting that the devil had put it there to tempt him (Athanasius, *v. Ant.* 11.4).

26. Rufinus omits the account in the *GHM* (10.21–22) about how Patermuthius once was physically translocated to Paradise and ate some of its fruit and even brought back to his fellow monks a huge succulent fig. So potent was this fruit that if a sick man caught even just a whiff of it, he would instantly be cured of his ailment.

27. Heb 11.38.

28. The decorative golden lettering presumably symbolizes the precious value of the stories Copres told.

29. This white-haired figure represents God and is a possible allusion to the Ancient of Days of Dn 7.9, the only time in the OT that God is portrayed as an old man with white hair. Many scholars have argued that this OT depiction evokes El, the supreme god of the Ugaritic pantheon, who also is portrayed in anthropomorphic terms as an old man. For a conspectus of scholarly

who said to him in a very threatening manner: "Why are you not listening attentively to what is being read aloud but instead doze off in your disbelief?" He awoke in a state of consternation and right away related to us, discreetly in Latin, what he had seen.

While this was going on, we saw a peasant coming to the old man's door with a container full of sand and waiting until Copres finished his story-telling. When we saw him, we asked the priest what this peasant with the sand wanted. The old man replied to us: "My children, it certainly is not appropriate for me to publicize this to you, lest we look as if we are boasting and lest the reward for our hard work vanish. Nevertheless, for your edification and benefit, and because you have come on such a long journey to visit us, I will not allow even this to be concealed from you, but 'I declare the works of the Lord'[30] which he has seen fit to bring to pass through us.

"The neighboring land of this region, which is now farmed, used to be very barren and infertile, to the point that if it ever took seed by forcible planting, it scarcely gave a double return. For certain worms infiltrated the very stalks of shoots and chewed off the nascent crop.[31] Now, the farmers in that area used to be pagans. After we had taught them to believe in the Lord and to have faith in Christ, they came to us, having already become Christians, and begged us to pray to the Lord for their crops. We told them that we certainly would pray but that they needed faith in God's eyes to entitle them to receive this. They filled the folds of their tunics with sand that had been trodden by us, brought it to us, and begged us to bless it in the Lord's name. I said to them, 'According to your faith, let it be done for you.'[32] Then they took the sand with them, mixed it

---

opinion, see J. Eggler, *Influences and Traditions Underlying the Vision of Daniel 7:2–14* (Göttingen: Vandenhoeck & Ruprecht, 2000), 58–70.

30. Ps 117.17.

31. On the perennial threat that worms and other pests posed to rural farmers during this period, see D. Stathakopoulos, *Famine and Pestilence in the Late Roman and Early Byzantine Empire: A Systematic Survey of Subsistence Crises and Epidemics* (Aldershot: Ashgate, 2004), 41–46.

32. Cf. Mt 9.29.

with seeds they were about to sow, spread it throughout their fields, and reaped more produce than any stretch of land anywhere in Egypt was able to reap. From that point on it has been their custom to come to us each year and make the same request of us.

(7) "I also will not conceal from you what the Lord provided to me as a means for glorifying his name.[33] Once I had gone down to the city and encountered there a certain man, a teacher among the Manichaeans,[34] who was deceiving the people. I debated with him, but he was very crafty and I could not defeat him with words. I feared that the onlookers would be endangered if he left the scene appearing to be superior to me in speaking, so I said to the crowds who were listening: 'Light a huge fire in the middle of the street, and let us both walk into the flames. Whichever of us is not burned by it, rest assured that his is the true faith.'[35] Once I had said this, the common

33. That it is God who performs healings and other miracles *through* his saints is a notion rooted in the Bible (see, e.g., 2 Kgs 5.1) and duly emphasized in hagiographic literature; cf. Athanasius, *v. Ant.* 49.1, 56.1; Anon., *v. Pach. SBo* 45; *G*¹ 45; Theodoret, *hist. rel.*, prol. 10, 9.15; Anon., *v. Dan. Styl.* 88; John Moschus, *prat. spir.* 40, 56; Cyril of Scythopolis, *v. Euth.* p. 20; John of Ephesus, *Lives* pp. 7, 26, 71, 82–83, 422; Gregory of Tours, *lib. mir. Mart.* 1.12.4; Adomnán, *v. Col.* 2.43; Gregory of Tours, *glor. conf.* 23; George of Sykeon, *v. Theod. Syk.* 119, 138.

34. This Manichaean's urban proselytizing is by no means surprising, for by the late fourth century Manichaeism (and Manichaean monasticism) had a well-established presence in Egypt. See, e.g., D.W. Johnson, "Coptic Reactions to Gnosticism and Manichaeism," *Le Muséon* 100 (1987): 199–209; L. Koenen, "Manichäischer Mission und Klöster in Ägypten," in G. Grimm, ed., *Das römisch-byzantinische Ägypten*, 2 (Mainz: Philipp von Zabern, 1983), 93–108; W. Seston, "L'Égypte manichéenne," *Chronique d'Égypte* 14 (1939): 362–72; G. Stroumsa, "The Manichaean Challenge to Egyptian Christianity," in B. Pearson and J. Goehring, eds., *The Roots of Egyptian Christianity* (Philadelphia: Augsburg Fortress Publishers, 1986), 307–19; M. Tardieu, "Les manichéens en Égypte," *BSFE* 94 (1982): 5–19; J. Vergote, "L'expansion du manichéisme en Égypte," in C. Laga and J. Munitiz, eds., *After Chalcedon: Studies in Theology and Church History* (Leuven: Katholieke Universiteit, 1985), 471–78. See more generally P. Brown, "The Diffusion of Manichaeism in the Roman Empire," *JRS* 59 (1969): 92–103.

35. By his very act of initiating a public confrontation with the Manichaean, in the form first of debates and then (more dramatically) of an ordeal by

folk were satisfied, and a huge fire was lit. Then I grabbed him
and started dragging him with me toward the fire. He said:
'Not this way! Each of us should enter the fire individually. But
you must go first because you are the one who proposed this.'
Signing myself with the Cross in Christ's name,[36] I walked in.
The flames actually began to part and disperse this way and
that and to go out of their way to avoid contact with me. I stood
in the midst of the fire for almost half an hour, and, by the
Lord's name, I was not harmed in any respect whatsoever.

"The people looking on cheered in great amazement and
praised God. They started to pressure the Manichaean to enter the fire, but he resisted and backed away. Then the crowds

---

fire, Copres, of course, was trying to incite the mob against his theological opponent—if not directly to provoke violence against him, then at least to secure
the local majority's condemnation of him. S.N.C. Lieu, *Manichaeism in the
Later Roman Empire and Medieval China* (Tübingen: Mohr Siebeck, 1985), 195,
suggests that Copres was emboldened by an imperial edict of 383 that granted
the "faculty to bring charges against the Manichaeans by common consent to
those who observed the right religion." This is a tantalizing possibility; however, we have no way of knowing whether Copres's confrontation occurred
before or after 383. At any rate, Copres is not the only late antique holy man
on record to have adverted to fire-miracles to exact divine justice against his
opponents; see M. Gaddis, *There is No Crime for Those Who Have Christ: Religious
Violence in the Christian Roman Empire* (Berkeley: University of California Press,
2005), 185–86.

36. Self-signing with the Cross is a devotional practice whose origins are
shrouded in mystery. It is first attested in the literary sources in the third century. According to Origen (*sel. in Hiez.* [PG 13:800–801]), all believers make
this symbol on their forehead prior to beginning any task and especially at
the beginning of prayer or Scriptural reading. Tertullian (*cor.* 3) states that
true Christians sign themselves on the forehead every time they step out of
the house and engage in every possible mundane activity from putting on
their clothes to reclining on couches by lamplight. In the post-Constantinian
period, when the Cross became, more so than ever before, a universally recognized symbol of Christianity (P. Stockmeier, *Theologie und Kult des Kreuzes
bei Johannes Chrysostomos* [Trier: Paulinus-Verlag, 1966], 212–17), the gesture
naturally continued to be an important expression of popular piety. Cyril of
Jerusalem (*cat.* 4.14, 13.36), for instance, notes that believers sign themselves
at every possible moment, from the moment of waking until bedtime. In Copres's case, self-signing was a way of entrusting his personal safety to God as
he prepared to enter the flames.

seized him and hurled him into the midst of the fire, and the flames, immediately engulfing and searing him, left him burned on half of his body.[37] The people drove him out of the city in shame, crying out and saying: 'Let the deceiver be burned alive!' But as for me, they took me with them and escorted me to the church as they praised the Lord.

"Another time, while I was passing by a certain temple, I saw pagans sacrificing there and said to them: 'Why are you offering sacrifices to idols, which cannot speak and have no sensation, although you are rational beings? Do you really have less sensation than the things to which you are offering sacrifice?' With this statement the Lord imparted understanding to them; they abandoned their error, followed me, and believed in our God the Savior.

(8) "I once had a small garden next to the hermitage, in which we grew vegetables for the brothers who visited. A certain pagan sneaked in during the night and stole the vegetables. After he had taken them to his house, he put them over fire to cook them. A blazing fire had been under them for three straight hours, yet they could not become hot or tender or even warm up a little but maintained the same greenness they had when they were stolen. Not even the water itself could reach a moderately warm temperature. Returning to his senses,[38] the thief grabbed the vegetables from the oven and brought them back to us. Kneeling at our feet, he begged for his sin to be forgiven and to become a Christian, and he got what he wanted.[39] Furthermore, it happened that on the same day a great

37. Rufinus has the Manichaean half-burned (*semiustum*), but a later Syriac version of this story told by Anan-Isho has him entirely consumed by fire; see E. A. Budge, ed., *Paradisus patrum*, vol. 2 (Oxford: Clarendon Press, 1904), 416.

38. Cf. Lk 15.17.

39. Another example of a foiled theft from a monk, which (like this one) ends formulaically with the conversion of the thief, is found in an anecdote about Abba Gelasius (*AP* Gelasius 1). Gelasius owned a costly edition of the Bible but left it in the church so that it could be used by all the brothers. One of them stole it and went into the city to sell it. The prospective purchaser took the Bible to Gelasius and asked him to estimate its value. Gelasius told the man that it was not worth the thief's asking price. When the thief found out

many brothers visited us as guests, and those very vegetables provided them with just the right amount to eat. So, thanking the Lord for his miracles, we expressed a twofold joy—for the man's salvation and for God's kindness."

that the book had been shown to Gelasius, he was moved by compunction over his crime and returned the Bible to him, begging for forgiveness and asking to become Gelasius's disciple.

CHAPTER 10
SOUROUS

O THE foregoing story Copres added this one:

"Once Abba Sourous, Isaiah, and Paul met one another on a riverbank. They were righteous men who practiced the purest asceticism and were completely devoted to the monastic life. They were on their way to visit a certain holy man named Anouph. The hermitage to which they were heading was three days' worth of travel away. Since they wanted to cross the river but had no means of going across, they said to one another: 'Let us ask as a gift from the Lord that we not be barred from a journey for a noble end.' They turned to Abba Sourous and said: 'You ask the Lord, for we know that he will grant what you request.'

"He enjoined them to kneel in prayer along with him, and then he prostrated himself before the Lord. Once the prayer was finished and they had gotten up, behold, they saw a boat pulling up to the riverbank, ready and outfitted for the journey they were about to take. They climbed into it and were ferried so quickly upstream that they completed within one hour the entire journey they were going to make in three days. When they had touched down on land, Isaiah said: 'The Lord has shown me the man whom we are hastening to see, running up to us and exposing the secrets of each one of our hearts.' Paul said: 'The Lord has revealed to me that in three days he will take him from this world.'

(2) "After they had started on the road leading from the river to the monastery and had made it a little way, the aforementioned man whom they were coming to visit ran up to them, greeted them, and said: 'Blessed be the Lord, who shows you to me now in the flesh and showed you to me beforehand in

spirit.' Then he began to recount the merits that each man had in God's eyes as well as the deeds of each. Paul said: 'Since the Lord has shown us that he will take you from this world in three days, we ask that you tell us about your virtues and deeds whereby you have pleased the Lord and that you not be afraid of seeming boastful. For as you are about to depart the world, leave to your successors the memory of your feats so that they may imitate them.'

"Then Anouph said: 'I recall having done nothing great, but nonetheless, from the time I confessed our Savior's name during persecution,[1] I have made sure that no lie came out of my mouth after confessing the truth[2] and that I have loved nothing earthly after I had fallen in love with heavenly things. The Lord's grace has not failed me in these respects. He has never made me go without earthly food but through the agency of angels has provided me with all the food I have desired. The Lord has concealed from me nothing about what transpires in the earthly realm. His light has never been absent from my heart; I would be awakened by it and not seek bodily sleep because I always have had the longing to see him. He also always stationed his angel by my side, who taught me about all the individual powers in the world. The light in my mind has never gone out. No matter what I have sought from the Lord, I have attained it immediately all at once.[3] He often has shown

1. Rufinus does not elaborate on this "persecution" but instead allows Anouph to remain something of a timeless hero of Egyptian monastic lore precisely because no references in the text tie him down to a specific set of historical circumstances.

2. *AP* Anoub 2: "Abba Anoub said, 'Since the day when the name of Christ was invoked upon me, no lie has come out of my mouth'" (Ward, *Sayings*, 33). Similarly, the Syrian monk Malkha claimed: "No lie has come out of my lips; I have not spoken evil words to men or reviled any man" (Brooks, *John of Ephesus*, 371).

3. *Sine more consecutus sum.* The prepositional phrase *sine more* ("in an unusual way," "unprecedentedly," etc.) is attested in Latin literature (e.g., Virgil, *Aen.* 5.693; 7.371; 8.635; Statius, *Theb.* 11.524), and this theoretically could be what Rufinus had written, in which case it would reinforce Anouph's exceptionalism in receiving things from God in privileged ways. Nevertheless, *sine mora* ("immediately") makes more sense, not only because it accords with one of the running themes of the *LHM,* namely that the Egyptian monks are

me multitudes of angels standing beside him. I also have seen throngs of the righteous, companies of martyrs, and assemblies of monks and of all the saints—at any rate those whose sole occupation is perpetually to praise and bless the Lord in sincerity of heart and faith. On the one hand, I have seen Satan and his angels handed over to everlasting fires, and on the other hand, I have seen the righteous reveling in everlasting joy.'

"After Anouph had related to them these and many other similar things over the course of three days, he died. Right away they saw his soul intercepted by angels and carried aloft to the heavens with such fanfare that even they heard the sound of hymnody. His soul was praising the Lord as it departed with the angels."

---

granted their prayer requests without delay, but also because the Greek original has the adverb εὐθύς here. I therefore have assumed *sine mora* to be Rufinus's intended phraseology, and *sine more* to be a scribal error.

CHAPTER 11
HELLE

[Copres continues his storytelling.]

" HERE ALSO WAS another holy man named Helle. From the time he was a boy,[1] he had been brought up in the

---

1. Rufinus is invoking the hagiographic literary *topos* of the "elderly child" (*puer senex*, παιδαριογέρων) who from a very early age displays the wisdom, self-discipline, and all-around virtuousness that otherwise are found only in lifelong veterans of the ascetic life. This *topos*—in its Christian incarnation, that is—has its roots in the Bible: cf. Christ at the age of twelve holding intelligent discussions with rabbis about Scripture and Jewish law (Lk 2.39–52). In the Greek hagiographic tradition the prototype of ascetic precocity in childhood is none other than Antony. Athanasius opens the *Life of Antony* by painting an idyllic picture of his upbringing. As a boy he had no desire to associate with his rowdy peers, but rather he preferred, like Jacob, to lead a quiet and abstemious lifestyle at home under the watchful supervision of his pious parents whom he routinely accompanied to church (*v. Ant.* 1.2–3). There are numerous other examples of this *topos* in Greek and Latin hagiographic literature: see, e.g., Eusebius, *hist. eccl.* 6.2; Pontius, *v. Cyp.* 5.1; Gregory of Nyssa, *v. Greg. Thaum.* p. 8 Heil; Gregory of Nazianzus, *orat.* 43.23; Jerome, *epist.* 24.3; *v. Hilar.* 2.2; Sulpicius Severus, *v. Mart.* 2.2; Palladius, *hist. Laus.* 17.2; Cyril of Scythopolis, *v. Euth.* p. 13 Schwartz. It is written of the Lyonnese martyr Vettius Epagathus that, "young though he was, his life had reached such a peak of perfection that the same could be said of him as was said of the old man Zachary: that he had indeed walked blamelessly in all the commandments and precepts of the Lord ..." (H. Musurillo, ed. and trans., *The Acts of the Christian Martyrs* [Oxford: Oxford University Press, 1972], 69). The literary convention of the *puer senex* was not confined to males, nor even to Christians. Young girls could be portrayed as being precocious far beyond their years; a case in point is the Neoplatonist mystic Sosipatra, who "while she was still a small child seemed to bring a blessing on everything, such beauty and decorum illumined her infant years" (Eunapius, *Lives of the Philosophers* 467). On the *topos*, see further M. Amerise, *Girolamo e la senectus: Età della vita*

146

Lord's service, in complete chastity and under the auspices of the purest precepts, and he deserved the highest reward. As a result, when he was still a boy in the monastery, if there was a demand for fire from a nearby area, he would carry red-hot coals without his tunic being singed.[2] All the brothers who witnessed this were in awe and aspired to imitate the zeal he displayed in his lifestyle and virtuousness.

"Once when he was alone in the desert, there arose in him the longing to eat honey. He fixated his gaze on a honeycomb stuck to a rock.[3] But, realizing that this was a trick of the Enemy, he immediately rebuked himself and said: 'Depart from me, deceptive and seductive desire! For it is written: "Walk by the Spirit, and you will not gratify the desire of the flesh."'[4] Abandoning this place at once, he departed and ventured into the desert and there began to mortify himself with fasts in order to punish the flesh's desire. During the third week of his fasting, he saw var-

---

e morte nell'epistolario (Rome, 2008), 122–28; M. Bambeck, *"Puer et puella senes bei Ambrosius von Mailand: Zur altchristlichen Vorgeschichte eines literarischen Topos,"* *RomForsch* 84 (1972): 257–313; T. Carp, *"Puer senex* in Roman and Medieval Thought,"* *Latomus* 39 (1980): 736–39. On infant prodigies in the Greco-Roman world, see M. Kleijwegt, *Ancient Youth: The Ambiguity of Youth and the Absence of Adolescence in Greco-Roman Society* (Amsterdam: J.C. Gieben, 1991), 123–31.

2. The description of Helle's pyrokinetic ability is somewhat different in the *GHM* (10.1): "He would often carry fire in his bosom to his neighboring brothers" (τοῖς πλησίον ἀδελφοῖς αὐτοῦ πολλάκις πῦρ ἐν κόλπῳ ἐβάσταζεν). There is a phraseological echo here of Prv 6.27: "Shall anyone carry fire in his bosom and not burn his clothes?" (ἀποδήσει τις πῦρ ἐν κόλπῳ, τὰ δὲ ἱμάτια οὐ κατακαύσει;). The anonymous author of the *GHM* cleverly uses this intertext to make the point that Helle could do what the biblical writer pronounced to be impossible. Rufinus, however, dispenses with this biblical allusion altogether. For other examples of saintly monks handling and transporting hot coals without being burned, see Anon., *v. Pach. SBo* 14; John Moschus, *prat. spir.* 27.

3. Although honey seems in general not to have been on the menu of cloistered monks in late antiquity (see B. Layton, "Social Structure and Food Consumption in an Early Christian Monastery: The Evidence of Shenoute's *Canons* and the White Monastery Federation A.D. 385–465," *Mus* 115 [2002]: 25–55 [45]), monks living in the desert as solitaries partook of wild honey in the absence of more substantive food. Helle craves the honey (stored inside the honeycomb) for its natural sweetness, but it is a delicacy that his conscience forbids him from enjoying.

4. Gal 5.16; cf. 2 Cor 12.18.

ious kinds of fruit scattered about in the desert. Recognizing the Enemy's deceits, he said: 'I will neither eat nor touch them, lest I cause my brother—that is, my soul—to stumble.'[5] For it is written: "Man does not subsist on food alone."'[6]

"When he was fasting the following week, he gradually fell asleep, and an angel appeared before him in a vision and said: 'Get up now and do not hesitate to eat what you find placed next to you.' He got up and saw a spring full of gently flowing water, and its edges were surrounded all around by delicate and sweet-smelling plants. He walked up to it and started picking and eating them and drawing a cupful of water from the spring. He swore that he had never in all his life drunk anything so sweet and delectable.[7] In that very place he also found a cave, into which he retreated to rest for a while. When the time and need arrived for taking care of his broken-down body,[8] he lacked nothing at all of what he asked for from the Lord, thanks to the grace of God.

---

5. 1 Cor 8.13.

6. Mt 4.4. In many vital respects this story closely mirrors the one given by Matthew and Luke of the Temptation of Christ (Mt 4.1–11; Lk 4.1–13). Both stories share the same dramatic setting, the "desert," and both protagonists, waging spiritual warfare all alone, are tempted by hostile forces—Jesus by Satan, and Helle by a personified sinful impulse ("deceptive and seductive desire"). Like Christ, Helle rebukes his tempter with Scriptural texts introduced by the standard formula "it is written." The second verse, "Man does not subsist on food alone," establishes a firm and indeed explicit intertextual link to the Matthean and Lucan accounts of the Temptation, for Christ uttered these same words when he was rebuffing Satan for challenging him to transform a nearby stone into bread with which he could sate his esurient stomach. Not coincidentally, a stone is an inanimate accomplice in Helle's temptation as well: a honeycomb stuck to it is what catches the eye of the starving monk.

7. Not all anchorites were so fortunate. The Egyptian monk Pior, for instance, lived in an inhospitable part of the desert and had no choice but to survive for a long time on extremely bitter-tasting water (ὕδωρ πικρότατον) produced by a well he had dug—a feat of endurance that made him the stuff of local urban legend (Palladius, *hist. Laus.* 39.3).

8. Lat. *corpusculum*. Among ascetic authors, this diminutive often assumed a pejorative denotation and signified disdain for the material part of man. Here it has this shade of meaning, but it also has the complementary pathetic sense of "poor body" that has been enervated by prolonged fasting. See Cain, *Jerome's Epitaph on Paula,* 120.

(2) "One time he was on his way to visit brothers who were in need and was bringing them provisions necessary for the body's welfare. During the journey he became overwhelmed by the weight of what he was carrying. He saw in the distance wild asses traversing the desert and exclaimed: 'In the name of our Lord Jesus Christ, one of you should come and relieve my burden.' Behold, one in the herd approached him in complete submission. Then Helle put the load onto it and mounted it, as it offered its services willingly, and he was carried with maximum swiftness by the wild ass to his destination, the brothers' cells.[9]

"Another time, on a Sunday, he came to a certain monastery of brothers. He saw that they were not observing the solemnity of the day[10] and then asked why they were not doing so. They replied that a priest was not present because he was stranded on the other side of the river, for nobody dared to cross it for fear of a crocodile. He said: 'If you wish, I will go and escort him back to you.' Right away he went to the riverbank, where he called upon the Lord's name. The monstrous animal showed up. Although it used to be in the habit of appearing in order to threaten people, now it appeared in order to transport the righteous man.[11] It submitted to him in great fear and then it took him on its back and ferried him to the opposite bank.[12] He promptly went to the priest and exhorted him to come to the brothers.

"Helle was dressed in very tattered and squalid clothes. The priest was caught off guard and asked who he was, where he was from, and what he wanted. When he realized that he was a man of God, he began following him to the river. When he objected that a boat for transport was nowhere in sight, Abba Helle said: 'Have no fear, Father. At this very moment I will get

9. Cf. *AP* Antony 14, for an anecdote about a young monk who, seeing some old crippled men having difficulty walking on a country road, ordered wild asses to come and carry them until they could be taken to see Antony.

10. I.e., they were not celebrating the Eucharist.

11. Cf. Athanasius, *v. Ant.* 15.1, where Antony crosses a canal amidst crocodiles that neither lunge at him nor show any aggression whatsoever.

12. Cf. Theodoret, *hist. rel.* 6.2, 10–11: Symeon the Elder had the charism of taming lions and making them do his bidding.

a boat ready.' He cried out in a loud voice and commanded the beast to appear. As soon as it heard his voice, it appeared and gently adjusted its back for transporting. Helle was the first to get on. He then invited the priest: 'Climb on and don't be at all afraid.' After laying eyes on the monstrous animal, however, he was terrified and started pulling back and retreating. Immense astonishment and fear overtook all who were there[13] as they watched Helle cross the river channel, ferried by a crocodile. When he dismounted, he took the beast with him onto dry land and said to it: 'For you, death is preferable to being implicated in the guilt of so many heinous acts and murders.' It immediately rolled over and died.

(3) "For the next three days Helle stayed in the monastery and imparted spiritual teaching to the brothers, even divulging the inmost thoughts and secret intentions of some and exposing one as being driven by the spirit of fornication, another by the spirit of anger, still another by lust for money, and some also as being led astray by the spirit of arrogance and pride. He confirmed the meekness of one, the righteousness of another, and the patience of yet another. By indiscriminately adducing the vices of some and the virtues of others, he facilitated growth for them all in an amazingly effective way. Each person individually recognized that his inner disposition was as Helle had declared, and they were struck by compunction and were changed for the better.

"Moreover, as he was about to set out, he said to them: 'Get vegetables ready for the brothers' arrival.' Just as they were preparing them, the brothers showed up. As soon as they had been greeted as honored guests, Helle made off for the desert.' A certain one of the brothers actually begged Helle for permission to live with him in the desert. Helle replied that it is an onerous undertaking and that resisting the demons' temptations requires significant effort. The young man was even more obstinately insistent, promising that he would endure all things patiently for the privilege of Helle granting him the richness of his companionship. Once he had given his permission, the

___
13. I.e., the terrified priest and the monks on the other shore, to which Helle is now returning.

young man followed him to the desert, and Helle ordered him to dwell in the cave right beside him.

"Around that time demons swooped in at night and first tormented the young man with foul and unclean thoughts; then they assaulted him violently and attempted to kill him. He darted to the cell of holy Helle and explained the nature of the evil forces by which he was being assailed. Then the old man comforted him with a few words, admonished him about the virtues of faith and perseverance, and at once sent him back to the cave from which he had fled. With his finger Helle drew a furrow in the sand around the exterior of the young man's cell, and in the Lord's name he ordered that the demons not dare to transgress the established line. Owing to the power of Helle's declaration, the youth remained there with a feeling of security from there on out.

(4) "This was related about his time in the desert. Helle often would partake of heavenly food. The brothers visited him, and since he had nothing to offer them, there appeared a youth who brought him bread and necessary provisions and placed these in front of his cave but then vanished. Helle said to the brothers: 'Let us bless the Lord, who has provided us with a table of food in the desert.'"[14]

Father Copres told us these and a great many other stories about the holy fathers' way of life and exploits. With the utmost affection he instructed us, and, after edifying us with his words, he led us into the garden and pointed out palm trees growing dates and other fruit trees that he had planted. He said: "The faith of the peasant farmers motivated me to plant these in the desert. For when I saw that they had such great faith as to gather sand trodden by us and spread it throughout their fields and transform sterile land into lush land positively teeming in fruitfulness, I said: 'It would be shameful if we were found inferior in faith to those whose faith in God has been affirmed through us.'"

14. Cf. Ps 77.19.

CHAPTER 12
ELIAS

E ALSO VISITED another venerable old man, named Elias,[1] in the territory outlying the city of Antinoë, the capital city of the Thebaid.[2] Word had it that he was nearly one hundred and ten years old, and they said that the spirit of Elijah truly had rested on him.[3] Many amazing

1. Palladius (*hist. Laus.* 51.1), who met this same Elias, recounts the following anecdote about him: "There was Elias, too, who lived as a solitary in a cave in this vicinity. He led a most holy life of self-control. One day a good many brethren visited him, for the place was along the road, and he ran out of bread. And he assured us: 'At my wits' end I entered the cell and found three loaves. There were twenty of them. When they had eaten enough, one loaf remained. This furnished me food for twenty-five days'" (ACW 34:133). Like Palladius, Rufinus and the anonymous author of the *GHM* report on Elias's meager diet of bread. Palladius implies that Elias's mountain cave was readily accessible to passersby, but these other two give quite a different impression, emphasizing how difficult the route to his cave was to navigate.

2. Antinoë (Antinoöpolis), situated on the east bank of the Nile, was the administrative center of the Thebaid, founded by the emperor Hadrian over two and a half centuries earlier. Hadrian built up this colony as part of his ambitious plan to Romanize this portion of Egypt; see, e.g., Calandra, "La città e il nome: Progetto politico e utopia nella fondazione di Antinoe," in C. Carsana and M. Schettino, eds., *Utopia e utopie nel pensiero storico antico* (Rome: Bretschneider, 2008), 133–59. In *hist. Laus.* 58, Palladius profiles several ascetics who lived in the vicinity of Antinoë.

3. To reinforce the typological connection forged here between the biblical prophet Elijah and the Egyptian monk Elias, which already is facilitated by homonymity, Rufinus captures the collective judgment of the monastic locals using phraseology that intentionally recalls what the "sons of the prophets" in Israel are quoted as saying: "The spirit of Elijah has rested upon Elisha" (2 Kgs 2.15). The implication is that, just as Elisha had been the prophetic heir to Elijah, so also was Elias believed to be the successor to his biblical namesake. In imitation of Elijah, to whom many desert monks looked as the Old Testament prototype of their lifestyle, Elias consummately embodied the ideal of

stories are told about him. For instance, they assert that he had spent seventy years in an exceedingly desolate and lonely place: no words will accurately capture how frightening and foreboding this desert is. During this entire period of his life the old man remained there, ignorant of the places humans normally inhabit.

(2) The foot-path leading to him was narrow and steep and could barely be spotted by travelers. The place in which he lived was a formidable cave that struck onlookers with much dread. His limbs quivered, and he had tremors caused by his advanced age. Even still, every day he would work miracles ceaselessly and completely heal those coming to him who were afflicted with every kind of ailment. All the fathers, to a one, affirmed that nobody at all recalled when he had withdrawn to the desert. His food into his extreme old age was a tiny bit of bread and a tiny bit of olives, and they asserted that during his youth he often fasted a whole week at a time.

---

monastic solitude in the wilderness, and, as Rufinus goes on to relate, he also resembled the Tishbite in his prolific thaumaturgy.

CHAPTER 13
PITYRION

N THE meantime, as we were leaving the Thebaid, we saw overhanging the river[1] a certain rugged mountain[2] that was foreboding to behold on account of its steep layering of jutting rocks, and throughout its craggy precipices were caves that were difficult to access. In these a great many monks dwelled, and their father was named Pityrion.

He was one of the disciples of blessed Antony, and after Antony's death he lived with holy Ammonas.[3] After Ammonas's death he established himself on this mountain. So great was the abundance of virtues in him, so great his gift of healing and his power over demons, that he alone deservedly obtained a twofold inheritance from the two eminent men.[4] He edified

---

1. I.e., the Nile.

2. The party of seven monks is now at Pispir, Antony's "outer mountain" (cf. Palladius, *hist. Laus.* 21.1), where Antony's disciple Pityrion oversaw a community of cave-dwelling monks. The location of this community may be the recently excavated monastic site of Gebel Naqlun in the area of Medinet-el-Fayyum. See D. Moschos, "Kontinuität und Umbruch in mittelägyptischen Mönchsgruppen nach der *Historia monachorum in Aegypto*," *JbAC* 12 (2008): 267–85 (274–76).

3. Ammonas was Antony's successor at Mount Pispir. There survive fourteen letters of spiritual direction he wrote to his disciples (all fourteen are extant in Syriac translations, and eight survive in their original Greek). For a translation of these letters, see D. Chitty, trans., *The Letters of Ammonas, Successor of Saint Antony* (Oxford: SLG Press, 1979), and for studies of them, see D. Brakke, "The Making of Monastic Demonology: Three Ascetic Teachers on Withdrawal and Resistance," *ChH* 70 (2001): 32–41; B. McNary-Zak, *Useful Servanthood: A Study of Spiritual Formation in the Writings of Abba Ammonas* (Kalamazoo: Cistercian Publications, 2010).

4. It is a *topos* of early monastic hagiography that charisms can be passed

us with many exhortations and strengthened us with substantial teaching, especially about the discernment of spirits.[5] He said that there are certain demons who attend each and every specific vice and who bend the soul's impulses toward every evil deed when they see these impulses being swayed by passions and vices. So, if anyone wants to master the demons, he must first master his own vices and passions. For whatever vice (arising from an individual passion) you cast off, you will be able also to banish from your besieged bodies the demon assigned to this vice. We must strive to overcome individual vices one step at a time so that we may be able to overcome also the demons who attend such vices.

(2) He was in the habit of eating, on the second day of the week, a little gruel made with spelt and was unable to eat any other food because neither his age nor his personal custom allowed it.

---

down from masters to worthy disciples; see B. Flusin, *Miracle et histoire dans l'œuvre de Cyrille de Scythopolis* (Paris: Études Augustiniennes, 1983), 187–91.

5. Athanasius highlights the ability to discern spirits as one of Antony's chief gifts (*v. Ant.* 88.1).

CHAPTER 14
EULOGIUS

E ALSO VISITED another holy father, named Eulogius,[1] who would receive so much grace from the Lord when he celebrated the Eucharist that he would discern the merits and faults of each person who approached the altar. In a word, he held back some of the monks wishing to approach for Communion, saying: "How have you dared to approach the Mysteries, seeing that your mind and intentions are set on evil?" He then would say: "Tonight you entertained thoughts about fornicating. You said in your heart: 'It does not matter whether a righteous man or a sinner approaches the Mysteries.' Another person has doubt in his heart, saying: 'How can Communion sanctify me?'" He therefore would bar individual people from partaking in the Mysteries and say to them: "Stay back a while and do penance so that you may be purified through atonement and tears and then be deemed worthy of Christ's Communion."

1. The name Eulogius (Εὐλόγιος) is rarely attested in the papyri before the fourth century but then became quite popular; see R.S. Bagnall, "Conversion and Onomastics: A Reply," *ZPE* 69 (1987): 243–50 (244).

CHAPTER 15
APELLES AND JOHN

N THE neighboring region[1] we also visited another priest, named Apelles, a righteous man. He used to be a blacksmith and made necessary utensils for the brothers. One time, when he was up late for metal-working in the still of the night, the devil, having assumed the appearance of a beautiful woman, came to him as if he were bringing something for his work. At that point Apelles grabbed a piece of red-hot iron from the furnace with his bare hand and pushed it into her face. She fled, crying out and wailing so loudly that all the brothers who lived around him heard her wailing as she ran away. From then on that man could handle red-hot iron with his bare hand without being injured.[2]

When we visited him, he welcomed us most warmly, and we asked him to tell us about his virtues and the virtues of those he knew of who are exceptional for their holy way of life. He said: "In the neighboring desert there is a certain brother named John who is advanced in age and excels everyone else in his way of life, character, and asceticism. Upon first withdrawing to the desert, he stood underneath the crag of a large rock and prayed for three straight years,[3] without interruption. He

---

1. The *GHM* (13.1) specifies that Apelles lived "in the district of Achoris," but Rufinus curiously omits this detail, saying only that he lived "in the neighboring region" (*in vicina regione*).

2. Cf. the hermit Ammonius, who disciplined his body by applying a hot iron to his limbs until they became ulcerated all over (Palladius, *hist. Laus.* 11.4).

3. Standing was a common posture for prayer in early Christianity (see Mk. 11.25); see G. Bunge, *Earthen Vessels* (San Francisco: Ignatius Press, 2002), 141–43. Standing for prolonged periods while praying was a widely attested

never sat down nor lay down at all, but got only as much sleep as he could catch while standing,[4] and he never ate except on Sunday.

(2) "During that period a priest would come to him and celebrate the Eucharist for him; this was his only Communion and food.[5] One day Satan, wishing to deceive him, made himself look like the priest who customarily would visit him. Arriving before the usual time, he pretended that he had come to partake of the Mysteries. John, however, astutely caught onto the deceit and indignantly said to him: 'O father of every ruse and every deceit, enemy of all righteousness,[6] you do not stop leading astray Christian souls, but you have had the gall to insinuate yourself even into the hallowed and sacrosanct Mysteries themselves.' But Satan replied to him: 'I thought that I could win you over, for this is how I deceived a certain other monk from your cohort, and it resulted in him going mad and losing his mind. He trusted me and I drove him insane, but then so many righteous men prayed for him and barely were able to make him sane again.' The demon said this, and then he ran away from John.

"Moreover, John was persistent in the work he had begun and in persevering in prayer. Because his feet had been immobile for a long time, they split open to the point that bloody pus

---

practice in early monastic culture (see, e.g., *AP* Bessarion 4, Zeno 7), but, as the sources readily admit, this discipline becomes more onerous for monks as their joints weaken with age (see, e.g., Jerome, *epist.* 52.3; Theodoret, *hist. rel.* 4.12, 17.2, 24.1).

4. Abba Bessarion claimed never to have lain down for a period of fourteen years but to have slept either sitting or standing (*AP* Bessarion 8). Bessarion also is credited with complete sleep deprivation for two weeks while standing in a thornbush patch (*AP* Bessarion 6). Palladius (*hist. Laus.* 49.1) claims that the hermit Sisinnius spent three years inside a tomb praying and never once sat or lay down during either the day or the night. Palladius (*hist. Laus.* 19.8) also alleges that Moses the Ethiopian spent six full years' worth of sleepless nights in prayer. According to Abba Arsenius, one hour of sleep per night is sufficient for a monk if he is spiritually stout (*AP* Arsenius 15).

5. One is reminded of the monk Heron, who allegedly ate only once every three months (usually a little wild lettuce) and otherwise was nourished only by the Eucharist (Palladius, *hist. Laus.* 26.2).

6. Cf. Acts 13.10.

oozed out of them.[7] When the three years were up, an angel of the Lord appeared and said to him: 'The Lord Jesus Christ and the Holy Spirit have heard your prayers and heal the wounds of your body and give you an abundance of heavenly food—that is, their word and knowledge.' Touching his mouth and feet, the angel cured him of his sores and did not allow him to feel hunger for food now that he was filled with the gift of knowledge and insight. Moreover, the angel ordered him to pass on to other places and the surrounding desert to visit other brothers as well and to edify them in the word and teaching of the Lord.

(3) "Nevertheless, on Sundays he always would return to the same place for the same reason, to receive the Mysteries, but on the other days he would perform manual labor[8] and make saddles for asses which he wove out of palm leaves,[9] as was

7. Symeon the Stylite likewise developed on his left foot a malignant ulcer from which pus oozed (Theodoret, *hist. rel.* 26.23), and Daniel the Stylite's feet were badly swollen and eaten by worms (Anon., *v. Dan. Styl.* 98). According to the *Life of Pachomius* (*SBo* 19), Pachomius and his brother John would stand all night while they prayed, and this caused their feet to become painfully swollen. Both Rufinus and the anonymous author of the *GHM* report the lurid details about John's pus-filled feet in order ultimately to inspire admiration for his superhuman endurance in prayer. On hagiographers' use of repugnant sensory imagery to dramatize saints' afflictions and thereby to inspire awe in readers for their endurance, see S. Ashbrook Harvey, "On Holy Stench: When the Odor of Sanctity Sickens," *StudPatr* 35 (2001): 90–101.

8. The performance of manual labor, as a means both to keep idle hands busy and to generate income with which to purchase food and other necessities of life, was regarded as a core duty of the anchorite and cenobite alike, and it is promoted as an ideal in late antique monastic literature. On the work ethic of self-sufficiency in desert monasticism in particular, see A. Cain, *The Letters of Jerome: Asceticism, Biblical Exegesis, and the Construction of Christian Authority in Late Antiquity* (Oxford: Oxford University Press, 2009), 24–25; D. Caner, *Wandering, Begging Monks: Spiritual Authority and the Promotion of Monasticism in Late Antiquity* (Berkeley: University of California Press, 2002), 200–203; see also P. Bonnerue, "*Opus* et *labor* dans les règles monastiques anciennes," *StudMon* 35 (1993): 265–91. The ideal of eremitical self-sufficiency is succinctly captured in a saying about Abba Agathon: "He was wise in spirit and active in body. He provided everything he needed for himself, in manual work, food, and clothing" (*AP* Agathon 10).

9. On the use of palm leaves as manufacturing materials in desert Christianity, see Regnault, *La vie quotidienne*, 112–15.

the custom in those parts. One time a crippled man wanted to visit him to be cured. It just so happened that the animal he was about to ride came with a saddle handmade by the man of God. It was fitted on the ass, and as soon as his feet made contact with this saddle, he was healed. John also sent bread that had been blessed to whoever was sick, and as soon as they tasted it, they were healed. The Lord wrought many other miracles and cures through him.

"He possessed the following gift to a greater degree than almost all other men. The conduct of each one of the brothers from the neighboring monasteries would be revealed to him, and as a result he would write to their abbots and advise that this monk and that were being remiss in their duties, that they were not upholding their monastic vow made in the fear of God, or that this monk and that were advancing in faith and spiritual virtue. But he also wrote to the abbots themselves—to one, because he was excessively overbearing toward the brothers and hesitated to show patience, and to another, because he was acting firmly and conscientiously and encouraging the brothers in an appropriate fashion. He also would announce what reward was coming from the Lord to one man for his virtues and what chastisement was coming to another for his laxity. He would describe the deeds, motives, and diligence or carelessness of those who were not there[10] so that when they heard what was said about them, they would be convicted by their conscience and not be able to make any denials.

(4) "All the same, he would teach all to turn their attention from the visible and corporeal to the invisible and incorporeal. He said: 'It is time for us to pass on to these kinds of pursuits, for we must not always remain children and infants,[11] but at some point we must ascend to loftier spiritual things, adopt mature ways of thinking, and advance to a more complete understanding, so that we can shine forth with spiritual virtues.'"

The holy man of God[12] confided to us many other things

10. By "those who were not there" Rufinus means monks who were not present when John's letters were read to the rest of the monastery.

11. Cf. Col 3.1; 1 Cor 14.20.

12. I.e., Apelles.

about John during the course of his most trustworthy account. Recording all of these would take too long, and to some readers they perhaps would seem hardly believable on account of their greatness.[13]

13. Cf. a similar sentiment expressed by Palladius: "I am reluctant to speak or to write of the many great and almost unbelievable events involving the Macarii, those famous men, lest I be accounted a liar" (*hist. Laus.* 17.1).

CHAPTER 16
PAPHNUTIUS

E ALSO VISITED the monastery of holy Paphnutius,[1] a man of God, who had been the most famous anchorite in that region and a resident of the remotest desert in the vicinity of Heracleopolis, a magnificent city in the Thebaid.

From the fathers' most trustworthy account about him we learned that after he had begun living the angelic life,[2] he begged God on one occasion to show him which of the saints he resembled.[3] An angel appeared and answered that he resembled a certain musician who made a living in that town from his talent at making music.[4] Dumbfounded by the unexpected reply, he made a mad dash for the town and eagerly asked around about the man. After finding him, Paphnutius interrogated him about what holy and pious work he had performed, and he painstakingly scrutinized all his deeds. The

---

1. On this common fourth-century Egyptian name, see L. Blumell, *Christian Oxyrhynchus: Texts, Documents, and Sources* (Waco: Baylor University Press, 2015), 581.

2. The ascetic life as the life of angels is a conventional metaphor in late antique monastic literature. See E. Muehlberger, *Angels in Late Ancient Christianity* (Oxford: Oxford University Press, 2013), 148–75.

3. For a similar story, which involves an anonymous desert hermit being told by an angel about a greengrocer whose piety surpasses his, see *APanon* 67 (=*APsys* 20.22).

4. We discover further down, when this musician becomes a monk, that he is a flute-player. The living he made likely would not have been a lucrative one, as professional flute-players occupied one of the lower rungs on the late Roman socio-economic ladder. See C.G. Starr, "An Evening with the Flute-girls," *PP* 33 (1978): 401–10; F. Tambroni, "La vita economica della Roma degli ultimi re," *Athenaeum* 8 (1930): 299–328, 452–87.

musician told the truth: he was a sinner and a man who lived
a very shameful life, and not long before he had been a robber
before falling into the disgraceful profession he now was practicing.[5]

(2) Paphnutius pressed him further, inquiring if by chance
he had done any pious deed even during his robberies. He
said: "I'm aware of nothing good. But I do know that when I
was keeping company with robbers, a virgin consecrated to
God once was kidnapped by us. While the rest of my accomplic-
es were bent on taking away her chastity,[6] I threw myself into
their midst and saved her from being defiled by the robbers. At
night I escorted her back to town and restored her, unviolated,
to her home. Another time I found a respectable-looking woman wandering in the desert. When I asked her where she came
from and under what circumstances she had ended up in this
region, she replied: 'Don't question me, a hopelessly wretched
woman, and don't pry into the reasons, but if it pleases you to
have a slave, take me wherever you wish. I'm miserable! My husband has often been strung up, flogged, and tormented with
every punishment on account of his tax debt. He is incarcerated and only brought out of his cell to be tortured. We had
three sons who had to be sold into slavery on account of the
same debt. I am bitterly unhappy because I am being searched
for, to undergo similar punishments, and I roam from place
to place racked by hunger and misery. Now, for the past three
days, I have been in hiding, wandering through this region
without food.' When I heard this, I felt sorry for her, took her to
a cave, and refreshed her soul, which had become forlorn due
to hunger. I even gave her three hundred gold coins, which she
declared would release her husband, sons, and herself not only
from slavery but also from their penalties. Once I had taken
her back to the city, I handed over the money and freed them
all."

5. In Roman antiquity flute-players proverbially were associated with loose
living, and Rufinus plays on this stereotype when he characterizes this musician as a former robber and an all-around sinner.
6. Lat. *cuperent eripere pudorem*, Rufinus's euphemistic way of expressing that
the robbers were planning to rape the virgin.

Then Father Paphnutius said: "I've done nothing of the sort. Yet, I trust, word has reached even you that the name 'Paphnutius' is famous among monks. For I have had a not insignificant zeal in refining my life with exercises of this kind. Now, God has revealed to me that you enjoy no less esteem in his eyes than I do. So, brother, since you see that in God's eyes you are not held in the lowest regard, do not neglect your soul." Right away he threw away the flutes[7] he was holding and followed Paphnutius to the desert, transforming his musical talent into a spiritual harmony of life and mind. For a full three years he devoted himself to the strictest asceticism and kept himself occupied day and night with psalmody and prayer, and, journeying towards heaven in the spiritual virtues, he died a member of the angelic choirs of saints.

(3) After Paphnutius sent to the Lord, ahead of himself, this man who had been perfected by every exercise in the virtues, he applied himself to more austere discipline than he had exercised before and again beseeched the Lord to show him who resembled him on earth. The voice of the Lord came to him a second time: "Know that you resemble the leading citizen of the nearby town." As soon as he heard this, Paphnutius rushed to him without delay and knocked on the door of his home. The man, who was accustomed to being hospitable to guests, greeted him and led him inside. He also washed his feet and prepared a table for him and provided a meal. As he was dining, Paphnutius began to interrogate his host about what impulse of his, what underlying motivation, guided the performance of each and every thing he did. When he replied with a humble assessment of himself and said he preferred to keep a low profile in the good he did than become well known for it, Paphnutius pressed him, saying that it had been revealed to him by the Lord that he was worthy of being numbered among monks.

But the man, voicing even more humble sentiments about himself, said: "Make no mistake, I am not aware of any good whatsoever in myself, but because the word of God came to you, I am unable to conceal anything from him, from whom

7. *Fistulae,* lit. "reed-pipes," the instruments used by flute-players.

nothing escapes notice.[8] So, I will speak about how I conduct myself in the presence of many people. For the past thirty years nobody has known that I have had an agreement with my wife not to have sexual relations. I did have three sons by her, for it was solely on account of them that I have known my wife; I have not known her besides or beyond this.[9] I have never stopped showing hospitality to guests, even to the extent that I do not allow anyone to greet a visiting out-of-towner before I do. I have never sent a guest away from my home without giving him provisions for travel. I have never disregarded a poor man but instead provided him with what he needed. If I have judged a case, I have not flouted justice by showing favoritism to my son. The fruits of another person's labor[10] have never entered my house. If I have witnessed a dispute, I have not gone on my way until I make peace between the quarreling parties. Nobody has ever caught my servants doing anything blameworthy. My flocks have never harmed others' crops. If someone has wanted to plant seed in my field, I have never forbade him from doing so, nor have I claimed the more fertile and fallow land for myself and left him the more barren land. To the best of my ability, I have never allowed a rich man to oppress a poor man. Throughout my life I have always made it my goal to afflict no one with sorrow. If I have had the authority to judge, I have condemned nobody, but rather I have strived to restore peace between the quarreling parties. In any event, up to now this is how I have led my life, thanks to God's generosity."

(4) When blessed Paphnutius heard this, he kissed his head and blessed him, saying: "'May the Lord bless you from Zion, and may you see the prosperity of Jerusalem.'[11] You have done these things in a fine and fitting manner, but you lack the greatest good of them all: to forsake everything, pursue the wisdom of God, and seek after the treasures of hidden knowl-

8. Cf. Acts 26.26.

9. Rufinus uses the verb *cognoscere* ("to know") in its euphemistic sense to refer to the sexual act. On this usage, see J. N. Adams, *The Latin Sexual Vocabulary* (Baltimore: Johns Hopkins University Press, 1982), 190.

10. I.e., the crops or produce farmed by a fellow citizen.

11. Ps 127.5.

edge—treasures you will not otherwise be able to attain unless you deny yourself, take up your cross, and follow Christ."[12] Upon hearing this, he did not tarry one bit, nor did he put any of his domestic affairs in order, but he became Paphnutius's disciple and accompanied him to the desert. After they had come to the river and did not find a boat anywhere for crossing it, Paphnutius ordered him to go with him on foot into the river, whose depth in those parts was known for being vast. So they crossed the river together with the water barely coming up to their waists. When they reached the desert, Paphnutius situated the man in a cell close to his own hermitage and prescribed a regimen for a spiritual way of life, taught him the practices of advanced monastic devotion, and also entrusted him with the more arcane elements of knowledge. After he had trained him in every respect, Paphnutius devoted himself with renewed vigor to more intense practices, reckoning as paltry his previous efforts, whereby the man who ostensibly had been caught up in the world's affairs was able to be considered comparable to him.

Moreover, Paphnutius passed a fair amount of time in these pursuits and guided to the summit of knowledge the man whom he had taken on as a disciple when he was already perfect in his deeds. One day Paphnutius was sitting in his cell and saw his soul borne up amidst choirs of angels who were singing: "Blessed is the man whom you have chosen and adopted; he will dwell in your tabernacles."[13] Once he heard this, he recognized that the man had been taken from this world. Then Paphnutius steadfastly continued with his fasts and prayers, pushing himself on to greater and more perfect things.

(5) Once again he begged the Lord to show him what mortal he resembled. Again the divine voice responded to him: "You are like the merchant you see approaching you. Get up quickly and meet him. For the man whom I deem you to be like is here." Without delay Paphnutius went down and met a certain Alexandrian merchant sailing down from the Upper Thebaid on three ships carrying merchandise worth twenty thousand gold coins. Since he was pious and zealous about doing good

12. Cf. Mt 19.21; Lk 5.11, 28.
13. Ps 64.5.

works, he had ten sacks of beans hoisted onto his slave boys and took them to the hermitage of the man of God. This was the reason he visited Paphnutius. As soon as Paphnutius saw him, he said: "What are you doing, O soul most precious and worthy of God? Why do you bother yourself with earthly things, seeing that a stake and share in heavenly things have been bestowed on you? Leave these things to those who belong to the earth and think in earthly ways.[14] As for you, become a merchant of God's kingdom, to which you have been summoned, and follow the Savior, to whom you are going to be joined a little later."

The merchant, without hesitating at all, ordered his slave boys to distribute to the poor all that remained (he already had given away a lot on his own). He followed holy Paphnutius to the desert, and Paphnutius situated him in the same spot from which his previous two disciples had been taken to the Lord. He likewise was trained comprehensively by Paphnutius and persevered in spiritual practices and the cultivation of divine wisdom. But after a short time had elapsed, he too was taken up to the assemblies of the righteous.

(6) Not long afterward Paphnutius lost stamina for his arduous ascetic practices and labors. An angel of the Lord stood before him and said: "Come now, blessed one, and enter into the eternal tabernacles which are your due.[15] Behold, with me here are the prophets, who welcome you into their choir. I did not reveal this to you earlier so that you would not become proud and lose any of the fruits of your hard work." He was still in the body for one day longer when some priests came to visit him. He made known to them everything the Lord had revealed to him, telling them that nobody in this world ought to be looked down upon. Even if someone is a robber or involved in the theater,[16] even if he farms the land and appears as if he is bound by marriage, even if he is called a merchant and makes a career

14. Cf. Jn 3.31.
15. Cf. Mt 25.34.
16. I.e., as an actor. Rufinus is alluding to the stigma of *infamia* that the profession of acting carried in the late Roman world. See the essays collected in P. Easterling and E. Hall, eds., *Greek and Roman Actors: Aspects of an Ancient Profession* (Cambridge: Cambridge University Press, 2002).

out of buying and selling—in every sector of human life there nonetheless are souls who please God and act in unseen ways in which God delights. It therefore is an unchanging fact that what meets with God's approval is not so much one's career or how one appears outwardly, but rather his integrity and attitude and the honesty of his deeds.

After Paphnutius had related similar insights about any number of topics, he gave up his spirit. The priests and all the brothers who were with him plainly saw him as he was welcomed by the angels, who were singing a hymn and praising God together.

CHAPTER 17
ISIDORE'S MONASTERY

N THE THEBAID we also visited the very renowned monastery of Isidore which was surrounded by a vast expanse of land and fortified by a wall, and in which spacious accommodations were provided for the one thousand men living there. Inside was a large number of wells, irrigated gardens, and orchards filled with every kind of fruit tree. All necessary provisions were made available to an adequate, or rather an abundant, degree so that none of the monks living inside would have any need to venture outside to find something.

(2) An austere elderly man chosen from among the monastery's leadership sat by the gate. He was responsible for welcoming visitors with the stipulation that they not leave after entering. If it suits them to enter initially, the stipulation cannot be overturned. Even still, what is more striking is that what keeps them there once they have entered is not the rigid stipulation *per se* but rather the contentment and sublimity of their lifestyle. In any event, this old man had a guest-house, near the gate where he was stationed, for putting up visitors and entertaining them with every gesture of kindness.[1] We were ushered

---

1. The *GHM* (17.2) contains the detail, omitted by Rufinus, that overnight visitors were given gifts in the morning as they were sent on their way. On such gifts, which were routinely given by monastic hosts to their guests, see D. Gorce, *Les voyages, l'hospitalité et le port des lettres dans le monde chrétien des IVe et Ve siècles* (Paris: Monastère du Mont-Vierge, 1925), 184–89. Affluent travelers, though, often refused gifts and left monetary donations to express appreciation to their hosts. Such donations were in fact a principal source of revenue for the Christian monasteries of late antique Palestine; see J. Binns, *Ascetics and Ambassadors of Christ: The Monasteries of Palestine 314–631* (Oxford:

in by him and were not allowed to enter the monastery, but nevertheless we learned from him what contentment there was in the monastic regulations therein.

(3) He said that there are only two elderly men who have the freedom to enter and leave because they are in charge of supervising the monks' tasks and fetching needed supplies, but that the rest live in silence and quietude devoting themselves to prayer[2] and pious pursuits and excelling in spiritual virtues to the degree that they all perform miracles. This truly is the greatest miracle of them all: none of them feels discomfort from any illness, but each one confidently foreknows when the end of his life is near.[3] Indicating as much to the rest of his brothers and bidding farewell to everyone, each lies down and dies in a state of happiness.

Oxford University Press, 1994), 85–87; Y. Hirschfeld, *The Judean Desert Monasteries in the Byzantine Period* (New Haven: Yale University Press, 1992), 102–11; D. Savramis, *Zur Soziologie des byzantinischen Mönchtums* (Leiden: Brill, 1962), 46–49.

2. On silence as a component of monastic prayer, see M. Schürer, "Das Reden und Schweigen der Mönche: Zur Wertigkeit des *silentium* im mittelalterlichen Religiosentum," in W. Röcke and J. Weitbrecht, eds., *Askese und Identität in Spätantike, Mittelalter und Früher Neuzeit* (Berlin: De Gruyter, 2010), 107–29; R. Teja, "*Fuge, tace, quiesce:* El silencio de los Padres del desierto," in S. Montero and M. Cruz Cardete, eds., *Religión y silencio: El silencio en las religiones antiguas* (Madrid: Publicaciones UCM, 2007), 201–7; K.T. Ware, "Silence in Prayer: The Meaning of Hesychia," in B. Pennington, ed., *One Yet Two Monastic Traditions East and West* (Kalamazoo: Cistercian Publications, 1976), 22–47.

3. An ascetic's premonition of his own or another's death is a *topos* of late antique hagiographic literature; for primary-source references and discussion, see Cain, *Jerome's Epitaph on Paula,* 439.

CHAPTER 18
SARAPION

N THE district of Arsinoë[1] we also visited the priest Sarapion, the father of many monasteries. Under his supervision were a great many monasteries scattered about, which housed around ten thousand monks. All of them would give to the aforementioned father the vast majority of the proceeds from their own manual labor, which they would collect especially at harvest time as their wage, and, pooling these resources, they would designate them for the relief of the poor.[2] It was the custom not only among them but also among almost all the monks of Egypt to dedicate their labors to gathering produce at harvest time. Everyone sets aside more or less eighty *modii* worth of grain from this haul and they earmark the vast majority of it for the relief of the poor,[3] meaning that

1. Arsinoë (modern-day Medinet el-Fayûm) was the metropolis of the Fayum district in Roman times. It was founded around 2900 BCE as the "City of Crocodiles" (cf. Herodotus, *hist.* 2.148), on account, Strabo (*geogr.* 17.1.38) tells us, of the great honor in which the locals held the crocodiles that infested the waters of its nearby canals, and indeed this city became an important cultic center for the crocodile-headed god Sobek. It officially was renamed Arsinoë during the Ptolemaic period (304–30 BCE).

2. In fourth-century Egyptian monastic culture, manual labor and almsgiving were linked conceptually because monks would use revenue from their work to fund their charitable giving. See, e.g., *Life of Pachomius* (*SBo* 19); *AP* Agathon 27; Jerome, *epist.* 52.3; John Chrysostom, *hom. in Mt.* 68.3 (PG 58:644); John Cassian, *inst.* 5.38; Cyril of Scythopolis, *v. Euth.* p. 14 Schwartz; cf. R. Finn, *Almsgiving in the Later Roman Empire: Christian Promotion and Practice, 313–450* (Oxford: Oxford University Press, 2006), 90–96.

3. For the sake of his readers in the Latin West, Rufinus quantifies the amount of grain using a standard Roman unit of measurement, the *modius*. See P. Mayerson, "The *modius* as a Grain Measure in Papyri from Egypt," *BASP* 43 (2006): 101–6.

not only are the indigent of that region fed, but also ships loaded with grain are dispatched to Alexandria for the purpose of helping the incarcerated or the remaining population of foreigners and the underprivileged. For there are not enough poor people in Egypt to be able to exhaust the resources of the monks' kindness and largesse.

(2) In the regions of Memphis[4] and Babylon[5] we saw countless multitudes of monks,[6] among whom we witnessed various gifts in virtue and endowments in holy character. Furthermore, they say that in that vicinity are the places where Joseph is said to have stockpiled grain,[7] which they also call "Joseph's storehouses." Some indeed think they are the pyramids, in which they say grain was gathered back then.[8]

4. For the history of this city during an earlier period, see D.J. Thompson, *Memphis under the Ptolemies* (Princeton: Princeton University Press, 1988); cf. E. Amélineau, *De Historia Lausiaca quaenam sit huius ad monachorum Aegyptiorum historiam scribendam utilitas* (Paris: Leroux, 1887), 247–50.

5. Memphis and Babylon were located more than sixty kilometers to the northeast of Arsinoë.

6. For the presence of monks in late fourth-century Memphis, see Sulpicius Severus, *dial.* 1.15.

7. See Gn 41.47–49, where Joseph stores grain in preparation for seven years of famine.

8. This identification of the pyramids of Giza with Joseph's grain storehouses is not found in the *GHM*. Rufinus appears to be the earliest literary witness to this Christian tradition, which would last throughout the Middle Ages. On the representation of the pyramids in ancient travel writing, see J. Elsner, "From the Pyramids to Pausanias and Piglet: Monuments, Travel and Writing," in S. Goldhill and R. Osborne, eds., *Art and Text in Ancient Greek Culture* (Cambridge: Cambridge University Press, 1994), 224–54.

CHAPTER 19
APOLLONIUS

HEIR ELDERS[1] related that during the time of the persecution[2] there had lived a monk named Apollonius[3] who led a pristine life among the brothers and
also was ordained a deacon. Consequently, during the time of
persecution he zealously visited all the brothers individually
[in jail] and exhorted them to become martyrs. After he himself had been arrested and thrown into jail,[4] scores of pagans

1. Presumably the senior monks whom the party of seven met during their
travels around Babylon and Memphis (cf. Chapter 18 on Sarapion).

2. This persecution occurred during the reign of the emperor Maximian,
who ruled from 286 to 305. Since the dramatic setting of the account is a period in which Christians were being persecuted, Rufinus frames his account
as something resembling the typical early Christian martyr act. References to
many of these martyr acts in the notes to follow are keyed to Herbert Musurillo's *The Acts of the Christian Martyrs* (Oxford: Oxford University Press, 1972).
For an inventory of the literary *topoi* of early Christian martyr acts, see M.L.
Ricci, "Topica pagana e topica cristiana negli *Acta martyrum*," *AATC* n.s. 28
(1963–64): 37–122.

3. Apollonius (Ἀπολλώνιος), a theonymic name derived from Apollo
(Ἀπόλλων), is one of the most widely attested personal names in the Egyptian
papyri of the Ptolemaic, Roman, and Byzantine periods; see L. Blumell, *Christian Oxyrhynchus: Texts, Documents, and Sources* (Waco: Baylor University Press,
2015), 508.

4. For an overview of arrest procedures, see S. Torallas Tovar, "Violence
in the Process of Arrest and Imprisonment in Late Antique Egypt," in H.A.
Drake, ed., *Violence in Late Antiquity: Perceptions and Practices* (Aldershot: Ashgate, 2006), 103–12. For more specialized studies, see U. Hagedorn, "Das For-
mular der Überstellungsbefehlen aus dem römischen Ägypten (I–III Jh. n.
Ch.)," in H.J. Drexhage and J. Sünskes, eds., *Migratio et Commutatio: Studien
zur alten Geschichte und deren Nachleben* (St Katharinon: Winkel Stiftung, 1989),
102–18; T. Gagos and P.J. Sijpesteijn, "Towards an Explanation of the Typology of the So-called Orders to Arrest," *BASP* 33 (1996): 77–97.

would come to taunt him and lambast him with insulting and vile words. Among them was a flute-player named Philemon who was very well known and beloved by the entire populace. He wore down Apollonius with insults, calling him impious, villainous, a charlatan, a deceiver of many men, and said that he deserved to be hated by all.[5] As he made these and many other worse accusations against him, Apollonius replied: "May God have pity on you, my child, and not hold against you as sin any of these things that you have said." When Philemon had heard this, he was cut to the heart[6] and inwardly he felt the forcefulness of his words beyond human measure and so deeply that he straightway professed himself a Christian.

(2) At once he scrambled from there to the judge's tribunal. In the sight of the entire body of people, he proclaimed: "Judge, you are acting unjustly by punishing pious men who are loved by God, for Christians neither do nor teach anything evil." Upon hearing this, the judge initially thought—a natural assumption, given the venue—that the man was joking. But after he had watched him persist and plead his cause with dogged insistence, he said: "Philemon, you are crazy. You have lost your mind all of a sudden." "I am not crazy! You are a supremely unjust and mad judge for unjustly condemning so many just men! As for myself, I am a Christian[7]—the noblest race of peo-

---

5. On martyrs being visited in prison by pagans who ridicule them, see *Martyrdom of Marian and James* 8 (Musurillo, pp. 204–6); cf. *Martyrdom of Perpetua and Felicity* 5 (Musurillo, p. 112); *Martyrdom of Pionius* 12 (Musurillo, p. 150).

6. Cf. Acts 2.37.

7. *Ego Christianus sum.* Martyrs conventionally affirmed their faith through simple formulaic expressions such as "I am a Christian" (Χριστιανός εἰμι; *Christianus sum*), as Philemon does here. For numerous examples of this refrain in martyrological literature, see, e.g., *Martyrdom of Carpus, Papylus, and Agathonice* (Musurillo, pp. 22, 24, 26); *Martyrdom of Justin, Chariton, Charito, Euelpistus, Hierax, Paeon, and Liberian* 2.5 (Musurillo, p. 44); *Acts of the Scillitan Martyrs* (Musurillo, p. 88); *Martyrdom of Apollonius, also called Sakkeas* (Musurillo, p. 90); *Martyrdom of Pionius* 8 (Musurillo, p. 146); *Acts of St. Cyprian* 1 (Musurillo, p. 168); *Martyrdom of Bishop Fructuosus, Augurius, and Eulogius* 2.3 (Musurillo, p. 176); *Acts of Maximilian* 1.3 (Musurillo, p. 244); *Martyrdom of Julius the Veteran* 1.4 (Musurillo, p. 260); *Martyrdom of Dasius* 7.2 (Musurillo, p. 276); *Martyrdom of Agape, Irene, and Chione* 3 (Musurillo, p. 284). Cf. J.N. Bremmer, "*Christianus sum:* The Early Christian Martyrs and Christ," in G.J.M. Bartelink,

ple." At that point the judge, in the hearing of the people, first
tried to persuade him with a great deal of flattery to turn back
willingly into the person he knew him to be. But when he saw
that Philemon was not budging, he brought all kinds of torture
against him.[8]

(3) Because he was aware that this change of heart had been
brought about by Apollonius's words, the judge had Apollonius
seized, and he subjected him to harsher torture and charged
him with the crime of being a deceiver. But Apollonius said:
"Judge and all who are present and hear me, become followers
of what you call this error and deception of mine."[9] When the
judge heard this, he ordered that Apollonius and Philemon be
burned alive in the sight of the people. But after they entered
the flames, blessed Apollonius cried out to God, as everyone
listened, and said: "Do not deliver to the wild beasts, Lord, the
souls that give praise to you, but show us clearly your salvation,
Lord."[10] Now, as soon as Apollonius said this to God in the

---

A. Hilhorst, and C.H. Kneepkens, eds., *Eulogia: Mélanges offerts à A.A.R. Bastiaensen à l'occasion de son soixante-cinquième anniversaire* (Steenbrugge: Abbatia
S. Petri, 1991), 11–20; A. Ferrua, "*Christianus sum*," *Civiltà Cattolica* 84 (1933):
13–26; J.M. Lieu, "The Audience of Apologetics: The Problem of the Martyr
Acts," in J. Engberg, V.H. Eriksen, and A.K. Petersen, eds., *Contextualising Early Christian Martyrdom* (Frankfurt am Main: Peter Lang, 2011), 205–23; F. Vittinghoff, "*Christianus sum:* Das 'Verbrechen' von Aussenseitern der römischen
Gesellschaft," *Historia* 33 (1984): 331–57.

8. On martyrs being threatened with torture and being accused of insanity
for preferring to die rather than to offer sacrifice to the gods, see *Acts of the
Scillitan Martyrs* 8 (Musurillo, p. 88); *Martyrdom of Pionius* 20.2 (Musurillo, p.
162); *Martyrdom of Conon* 4 (Musurillo, p. 190); *Martyrdom of Agape, Irene, and
Chione* 3 (Musurillo, p. 282); *Martyrdom of Irenaeus Bishop of Sirmium* 3.4 (Musurillo, p. 296); *Martyrdom of Crispina* 6 (Musurillo, p. 302).

9. Martyrs often are portrayed as making bold, even witty, rejoinders to
their inquisitors; see *Martyrdom of Polycarp* 10–11 (Musurillo, p. 11); *Martyrdom
of Carpus, Papylus, and Agathonice* (Musurillo, pp. 22–24); *Martyrs of Lyons* (Musurillo, p. 71); *Martyrdom of Pionius* 7 (Musurillo, p. 145); *Martyrdom of Julius
the Veteran* 3 (Musurillo, p. 262); Prudentius, *perist.* 2 (esp. vv. 113–32, 169–76,
185–312, 397–409).

10. Ps 73.19 LXX; 84.8 LXX. Like other martyrs before him (see, e.g., *Martyrdom of Conon* 6 [Musurillo, p. 190]), Apollonius quotes Scripture as he is
about to be tortured. On the prevalence of Scriptural citations in martyr acts,
see V. Saxer, *Bible et hagiographie: Textes et thèmes bibliques dans les actes des martyrs
authentiques des premiers siècles* (Berne: Peter Lang, 1986).

hearing of the people and the judge, a cloud soaked with dew[11] enveloped the men and extinguished the flames of the fire.[12] The judge and the people, dumbfounded by this,[13] all began to shout in unison: "Only the God of the Christians is great and one!"[14]

(4) The prefect of Alexandria became more savage than his usual self when this had been reported to him. He picked some of the cruelest and most ferocious men from his regiment (they were more beasts than men),[15] and he dispatched them to bring back to Alexandria in chains both the judge who had put his trust in the divine miracles and the ones through whom the power of God had been made manifest. As it would happen, as they all were being escorted back in shackles, the grace of God was present through the faculty of speech, and Apollonius began teaching the arresting officers to have faith in God. They became believers through the Lord's mercy and embraced faith in God with absolute steadfastness of heart. Then they offered themselves in shackles, along with the ones they had come to deliver up, to the judge[16] and likewise pro-

11. The *GHM* (19.8) describes it as "a cloud like a luminous dewy mist" (νεφέλη δροσοειδὴς καὶ φωτεινή). Cf. *Passio sanctorum Montani et Lucii* 3.3: "Earnestly devoting ourselves to constant prayer with all our faith, we obtained directly what we had asked for. No sooner had the flame been lit to devour our bodies when it went out again; the fire of the overheated ovens was lulled by the Lord's dew (*dominico rore*)." This same metaphor recurs in a story told in *APsys* 14.28, where a father-turned-monk, to test his monastic commitment and renunciation of family, casts his young child into a blazing furnace, and the flames immediately become like the morning dew (ἐγένετο παραχρῆμα ὡς δρόσος ἡ φλόξ) (Wortley, *Anonymous Sayings*, 201).

12. On martyrs' miraculous preservation from fiery torture, see, e.g., *Martyrdom of Polycarp* 15 (Musurillo, p. 15); *Martyrs of Lyons* (Musurillo, p. 74).

13. On inquisitors and onlookers expressing stupefaction at the defiance of martyrs, see *Martyrdom of Polycarp* 12 (Musurillo, p. 11); *Martyrdom of Carpus, Papylus, and Agathonice* (Musurillo, p. 26); *Martyrs of Lyons* (Musurillo, p. 66).

14. Cf. Prudentius, *perist.* 2.489–500, where St. Lawrence's heroic martyrdom inspires many pagan senators to convert to Christianity.

15. Arresting officers often are portrayed in martyr acts as being vicious and cruel; see, e.g., *Martyrdom of Marian and James* 5 (Musurillo, p. 198).

16. This is not the same judge before whom Apollonius originally had appeared, for earlier in the narrative Rufinus implies that the first judge became a Christian after witnessing the courtroom miracle.

fessed themselves to be Christians. After noticing them being obstinate and immovable in their faith in God, the prefect ordered all of them alike to be drowned in the sea,[17] though the impious man did not realize what he was doing, for this was not a death but a baptism for the saints.[18] Yet, undoubtedly by the providence of God, the sea's wave pushed back to the shore their bodies whole and uninjured, and they were retrieved and brought back and buried in one grave by people who had arrived at that very moment to pay homage to them. To this day they work many miracles and wonders which astound everyone. The petitions and prayers of every person are received by them and successfully fulfilled, and the Lord honored us too by bringing us there and answering our petitions and prayers.

17. This was an unusual form of capital punishment in the Roman world; see J.P. Callu, "Le jardin des supplices au bas-empire," in *Du châtiment dans la cité: Supplices corporels et peine de mort dans le monde antique* (Rome: École Française, 1984), 313–59 (333); H. Leclercq, "Martyr," *DACL* 10 (1931): 2425–40 (2429). On the theme of casting unchaste women into the sea as a punishment in Greek myth and literature, see F. McHardy, "The 'Trial by Water' in Greek Myth and Literature," *LICS* 7 (2008): 1–20.

18. On the early Christian conceptualization of martyrdom as a form of baptism, see Tertullian, *bapt.* 16.1; *apol.* 50; Origen, *mart.* 30; Cyprian, *epist.* 73.22.2; *orat.* 24; *rebapt.* 14; Gregory of Nazianzus, *orat.* 39.15, 17; Cyril of Jerusalem, *cat.* 3.10. See further E. Ferguson, *Baptism in the Early Church: History, Theology, and Liturgy in the First Five Centuries* (Grand Rapids: Eerdmans, 2009), 417–19; G. Jeanes, "Baptism Portrayed as Martyrdom in the Early Church," *StLit* 23 (1993): 158–76; E.E. Malone, "Martyrdom and Monastic Profession as a Second Baptism," in A. Mayer, J. Quasten, and B. Neunheuser, eds., *Vom christlichen Mysterium* (Düsseldorf: Patmos Verlag, 1951), 115–34.

CHAPTER 20
DIOSCORUS

E ALSO VISITED another venerable father in the Thebaid, a priest named Dioscorus,[1] who had around a hundred monks in his monastery. When it came time for approaching the Mysteries,[2] we observed him apply the greatest care and the greatest diligence in making sure that none of those who approached had a defiled conscience in any respect,[3] meaning that he warned them even about what is wont to befall men during their dreams,[4] either with women appearing to them as imagined forms or through an excess of natural fluid. He said that if such a thing happens without the aid of an imagined form of women, then it is not a sin, for when the naturally occurring fluid in the body exceeds its proper bounds, it must be discharged through its own channels, and for this reason it does not result in sin.

(2) But in cases where visions of women and carnal stimulations occur, he affirmed that there are signs of an already idle soul in the grip of thoughts and allurements of this kind. He said: "Monks must in every regard expel from their thoughts images like these and not in any way allow their senses to suc-

1. The name Dioscorus (Διόσκορος) was very popular in late antique Egypt, with over two thousand attestations in papyri alone.

2. Lat. *sacramenta*.

3. On the necessity of purifying the mind in preparation for Communion, see further John Cassian, *coll.* 23.21.

4. Rufinus is referring elliptically to nocturnal emissions. On the problem posed by nocturnal emissions, see D. Brakke, "The Problematization of Nocturnal Emissions in Early Christian Syria, Egypt, and Gaul," *JECS* 3 (1995): 419–60 (441). See further T. Vivian, "'Everything Made by God is Good': A Letter concerning Sexuality from Saint Athanasius to the Monk Amoun," *ET* 24 (1993): 75–108.

cumb to them; otherwise, they are no different from those who live according to the flesh.[5] To the contrary, if possible they must regulate themselves so that through strenuous asceticism they may control the natural excess and hold in check its emission through the prolongation of prayer and fasting." Finally, he said: "Those who live in pleasure[6] will abstain from everything a doctor deems harmful if bodily sickness requires it; so why should the monk, of whom health of the soul and spirit is demanded, not do this all the more intensively?"

5. Cf. Rom 8.12.
6. Cf. 1 Tm 5.6.

CHAPTER 21
NITRIA

E CAME ALSO to Nitria, the most renowned place in all the monastic regions of Egypt.[1] It is about forty miles from Alexandria and takes the name "Nitria" from a nearby town where natron is collected.[2] This, I surmise, is because divine providence foresaw that in these parts the sins of men would be washed away and erased just as stains are by natron.[3] In any event, in this place one can see around fifty (or not many fewer) monasteries that are near one another and under the supervision of one man. Within these some live together in large groups, some live in small groups, and others

1. Nitria was located on a flat desert promontory overlooking the southwestern streams of the Nile delta. Amoun, who built two cells for himself there between c.315 and c.330, is believed to have been the first monk to settle at Nitria. Over the next several decades monks from all over Egypt flocked there to live; see H. G. Evelyn-White, *The Monasteries of the Wadi'n Natrun, 2: The History of the Monasteries of Nitria and Scetis* (New York: Metropolitan Museum of Art, 1932), 45–59. Already by the middle of the fourth century it had become one of the most celebrated monastic centers in all of Egypt, and so it is not surprising that Rufinus designates it as such.

2. Rufinus's claim that Nitria received its name from the natron extracted from nearby lakebeds is accepted by modern scholars; see, e.g., R. Bagnall and D. Rathbone, *Egypt from Alexander to the Early Christians* (Los Angeles: Getty Publications, 2004), 110.

3. The ancient Egyptians used this naturally occurring mineral as (among many other things) a desiccant to help preserve mummies and food and as a cleaning agent to purify linen, and it also was used in glass production. See S. Aufrère, *L'univers minéral dans la pensée égyptienne*, 2 vols. (Cairo: Institut français d'archéologie orientale), 2.606–36; A. Shortland, "Natron as a Flux in the Early Vitreous Materials Industry: Sources, Beginnings, and Reasons for Decline," *JAS* 33 (2006): 521–30.

live as solitaries.[4] Although they are divided by their dwellings, they are closely connected in spirit, faith, and love, and they remain inseparable.

(2) As we approached this place, and when the brothers realized that foreign travelers were arriving, they all immediately poured out of their cells like a swarm of bees[5] and ran up to meet us with joy and eagerness, most carrying jugs of water and loaves of bread, according to the prophet's rebuke of some when he said: "You did not come out to meet the sons of Israel with bread and water."[6] After welcoming us, they escorted us to the church amidst psalmody, washed our feet, and one by one dried them with the linen cloths they wore, as if to soothe the stress of the journey though in fact to wash away the hardships of human life through mystical traditions.

(3) What can I say now that does justice to their kindness, their courtesy, their love? Each one was determined to bring us to his own monastery and not just to fulfill the duties of hospitality but even more to teach us either about humility, in which they are rich, or about gentleness and other like virtues, which they learn according to different graces but one and the same teaching, as if they had been separated from the world for this very reason. Nowhere would you see love flourishing like this; nowhere would you see kindness put into action as vibrantly as here and hospitality provided as zealously as it is here. Nowhere

---

4. According to Palladius, one of these monasteries housed 210 monks, and another, 150 (*dial.* 17; cf. Sozomen, *hist. eccl.* 6.31).

5. In making this apian analogy, which is his own addition to the *GHM*, Rufinus is subverting the classical Roman historiographic *topos* of bee swarms, representing opposing armies, as a familiar prodigy portending Roman defeat; cf. V. Rosenberger, *Gezähmte Götter. Das Prodigienwesen der römischen Republik* (Stuttgart: Franz Steiner Verlag, 1998), 98–99, 114–15, 135. For the conventional comparison of monks to bees (and their proverbial industriousness), see G. Penco, "Il simbolismo animalesco nella letteratura monastica," *StudMon* 6 (1964): 7–38 (32–34); C. Gindele, "Bienen-, Waben- und Honigvergleiche in der frühen monastischen Literatur," *RBS* 6/7 (1981): 1–26; A. Casiday, "St Aldhelm's Bees (*De virginitate prosa* cc. IV–VI): Some Observations on a Literary Tradition," *ASE* 33 (2004): 1–22; A. Taylor, "Just Like a Mother Bee: Reading and Writing *Vitae metricae* around the Year 1000," *Viator* 36 (2005): 119–48.

6. Neh 13.2.

have I seen meditation on the divine Scriptures and such intense cultivation of divine understanding and knowledge that you would suppose that almost each and every one of them was a trained expert in divine wisdom.

CHAPTER 22
KELLIA

EYOND Nitria, in the inner desert, is another place about ten miles away, which they named "Kellia" on account of the high number of monastic cells scattered throughout the desert.[1] Those who first are trained at Nitria, and who wish to live a more secluded life after passing out of their novitiate, withdraw to this place. For the desert is wide open, and the cells are separated by so much distance that they are neither visible nor audible to one another.

(2) Monks live alone in their cells, and there is remarkable silence and profound quiet there. Only on Saturday and Sunday do they come together at church,[2] and they behold one another as men restored to heaven. If anyone happens to be absent from that gathering, they understand right away that he has been kept away by some bodily ailment, and they all go to visit him, not all at once but at different times, each taking with him whatever he has that could benefit the sick brother.

(3) For no other reason does anybody dare to interrupt the

1. Nitria's original founder, Amoun, established a smaller monastic settlement in 338 so that he and other monks could enjoy more peaceful solitude after Nitria had become overcrowded. For a history of the site and its monastic inhabitants, see A. Guillaumont, "Histoire des moines aux Kellia," *OLP* 8 (1977): 187–203. Kellia was an active monastic settlement for centuries after its founding. In the second half of the twentieth century it was extensively excavated by French and Swiss archeologists. See, e.g., A. Guillaumont, "Les fouilles françaises des Kellia, 1964–1969," and R. Kasser, "Fouilles suisses aux Kellia: Passé, présent, et futur," in R. M. Wilson, ed., *The Future of Coptic Studies* (Leiden: Brill, 1978), 203–8 and 209–19, respectively.

2. Many Egyptian monks appear to have attended mass on both weekend days; see Regnault, *La vie quotidienne,* 179–81; cf. Palladius, *hist. Laus.* 32.3; John Cassian, *coll.* 3.1.

silence of his neighbor unless it is to edify him with a word and
to anoint him with the comfort of advice as one anoints athletes for a contest.[3] Many of them travel three or four miles
to church. Their cells are separated from one another by a significant distance, yet their love is so great, and they are inter-
connected by such great affection towards all the brothers, that
they are a wonder and an example to all. This is why, when they
become aware of anyone wishing to live among them, each one
offers him his own cell.

3. Rufinus is alluding to the widespread Greco-Roman practice of athletes,
and especially pankratiasts and wrestlers, copiously rubbing their bodies with
oil before training exercises and contests.

CHAPTER 23
AMMONIUS

E VISITED a certain venerable father among them named Ammonius,[1] a man on whom the Lord had bestowed the entire fullness of spiritual graces. When you saw the grace he had for love, you would think that you had never seen anything like it. If you considered his humility, you would admit that he far surpasses the rest of the brothers in this gift. Likewise, if you considered his patience, his meekness, his kindness, you would reckon that he excels in each of these to the extent that you would not know which one takes precedence. The Lord had bestowed on him such a great gift of wisdom and knowledge that you would suppose that virtually none of the fathers had penetrated the inner sanctum of universal knowledge to the degree he had. All who laid eyes on him admitted that nobody had been welcomed into the private chamber of God's wisdom as he had been.

(2) He had two brothers [with him at Nitria], Eusebius and Euthymius, for Dioscorus, the oldest among them, was snatched away to the episcopate.[2] They not only were his broth-

---

1. Ammonius (Ἀμμώνιος), a Hellenized form of the Egyptian name Ammon (Ἄμμων), was an extremely popular name in the Roman and early Byzantine period, with over 2,000 attestations in the literature and papyri; cf. W. Clarysse, D.J. Thompson, and U. Luft, *Counting the People in Hellenistic Egypt*, 2 vols. (Cambridge: Cambridge University Press, 2006), 2.320–21.

2. These four collectively were dubbed the "Tall Brothers" on account of their height (Socrates, *hist. eccl.* 6.7; Sozomen, *hist. eccl.* 6.30). Dioscorus the Tall Brother, who is to be distinguished from the Dioscorus featured in chapter 20 of the *LHM,* was installed by Bishop Theophilus of Alexandria as bishop of Hermopolis Parva in 399 (Sozomen, *hist. eccl.* 8.12.2). Socrates (*hist. eccl.* 6.7) adds that Theophilus recruited Dioscorus against his will.

ers[3] by physical relation but they also were his kin in their way of life, monastic training, and the plenitude of their spiritual virtue. Through their mentoring, encouragement, and teaching, they, like a nurse taking care of her young,[4] endeavored to guide to the summit of perfection all the brothers who lived in Nitria.[5] So then, we visited the aforementioned man of God, Ammonius, who had a hermitage surrounded by the kind of wall that in those parts tends to be constructed easily out of unbaked bricks. The hermitage is well-equipped and stocked with all the necessary provisions, and he himself also had dug a well by it.

(3) A certain brother came desiring to find salvation in their midst. He approached the same Ammonius and asked him if there was an empty cell in which he could live. Ammonius said: "I will look around, but until I find one, let him stay in this hermitage. For I am leaving at this very moment to look around." Leaving the man all he had, along with the hermitage itself, Ammonius found a tiny cell some distance away and settled himself into it. He handed over the hermitage and everything in it to the unsuspecting brother who recently had arrived on the scene.[6]

(4) If there were many who happened to come to them and desired to be saved, Ammonius would assemble all the brothers to provide speedy help and would have a hermitage built within a day. After he had completed the requisite number of hermitages for each and every one, those who intended to stay permanently were invited to the church under the pretense of having a meal. While they were detained at the church, all of the brothers would bring provisions from their own cells and

3. According to Palladius (*hist. Laus.* 11.1), the four Tall Brothers also had two sisters.

4. Cf. 1 Thes 2.7.

5. On the Tall Brothers' activities at Nitria, see J. F. Dechow, *Dogma and Mysticism in Early Christianity: Epiphanius of Cyprus and the Legacy of Origen* (Macon, GA: Mercer University Press, 1988), 164–69.

6. John Cassian (*inst.* 5.37) recounts a similar experience he had while visiting Abba Archebius in the desert of Diolcos. Noting his visitor's enthusiasm for the eremitical life, Archebius charitably gave to John his cell together with all of its contents, and then he built himself a new cell.

stock the new cells of the individual newcomers. The charitable giving would be carried out in such a way that the newcomers lacked absolutely no utensils or supplies needed for everyday living, yet what each brother contributed remained a mystery. After returning in the evening, the brothers for whom cells had been built would find all their necessary provisions organized and their residences so well stocked that they noticed nothing at all to be lacking.

CHAPTER 24
DIDYMUS

E VISITED another upright man among the elders, named Didymus.[1] The Lord's grace abounded in him, and even his very countenance reflected this. Scorpions, vipers[2] (beasts they call "horned"), and serpents that in those parts are considered very aggressive due to the sun's heat,[3] he would crush with his bare feet as if they were earthworms, and he would destroy them without suffering any harm whatsoever from them.[4]

1. This otherwise unattested monk is not to be confused with his famous namesake, Didymus the Blind.

2. Lat. *cerastes*, the technical name for the horned viper. Rufinus, evidently anticipating that some of his readers may not recognize this species, parenthetically glosses the word as "beasts they call 'horned'" (*bestias quas cornutas vocant*).

3. Cf. Jerome, *v. Mal.* 9.2, for the observation that desert serpents seek shade in order to avoid the heat of the sun.

4. Similarly, Palladius recounts how one night, while chanting the Psalms, the ascetic Elpidius nonchalantly stomped on a scorpion but showed no reaction when the scorpion stung him (*hist. Laus.* 48.2), while Macarius of Alexandria ripped a poisonous asp in half (*hist. Laus.* 18.10).

CHAPTER 25
CRONIUS (CRONIDES)

E VISITED among them another father named Cronius.[1] He was tremendously old—in fact, he was one hundred ten years old—and was thriving in his virtuous old age and perfect life. He was one of the surviving disciples of blessed Antony. We observed, among the rest of his spiritual virtues, an outstanding grace of humility.

1. Palladius (*hist. Laus.* 21.1) mentions a Cronius as being a "priest of Nitria" in the late fourth century, and this presumably is the same one described here.

CHAPTER 26
ORIGEN

HERE ALSO was another of Antony's disciples, named Origen,)[1] an amazing man in every way who possessed impeccable wisdom. His discourses and the stories he told about the virtues of the supreme teacher, the man of God, edified and greatly invigorated all those who heard them, so much so that you would think that the stories he told were being seen with the eyes.

1. Palladius designates this Origen as a priest and also as a "famous man" (*hist. Laus.* 10.1, 6–7). This Origen is not mentioned in the *GHM*.

CHAPTER 27
EVAGRIUS

E ALSO VISITED there a man named Evagrius, who was extremely wise and wonderful in every way. Among other spiritual virtues, he was bestowed with such a great gift of discerning spirits and of "purifying thoughts" (as the Apostle says)[1] that none other of the fathers is believed to have attained such profound knowledge of lofty spiritual matters. Although he was granted great understanding through personal trials involving the matters themselves[2] and most of all through the grace of God, nevertheless this also happened to him: he was instructed for a long period of time by the blessed Macarius, who, as all are aware, was extremely famous for having God's grace and working miracles and for being distinguished in virtuousness. This Evagrius practiced unbelievable abstinence, yet above all he would admonish any brothers who happened to be engaged in an exercise to subdue the body or to repel from the body the imagined forms brought on by demons, not to drink a large amount when consuming water. For he would say that if the body is inundated with water, it gives rise to more powerful imagined forms and provides more

1. Cf. 2 Cor 10.4.
2. I read *rebus ipsis et experimentis* not literally as "through the matters themselves and through personal trials" but rather as a case of hendiadys, hence "through personal trials involving the matters themselves," these "matters" being a reference to the "lofty spiritual matters" mentioned in the previous sentence. Thus Rufinus is saying that Evagrius achieved his hard-earned enlightenment in divine matters in the crucible of human experience (as well as through the grace of God). Rufinus employs the same hendiadic collocation (*rebus ipsis et experimentis*) in Book 2 of his translation of Origen's commentary on the Song of Songs; see W.A. Baehrens, ed., *Origenes Werke,* vol. 8 (Leipzig: Teubner, 1925), 142.

robust dwelling-places for demons. With the utmost judiciousness he taught many other things about abstinence. Moreover, he himself not only drank water very sparingly, but he also abstained entirely from bread.

(2) The other brothers who lived in those parts contented themselves with only bread and salt, and you would scarcely find anyone in that whole population who used even the least bit of oil.[3] What is more, many among them slept not lying down but in a seated position and, I should say, situated themselves in this way so that they could meditate on the divine sayings.

3. I.e., oil either as a condiment or for cooking.

CHAPTER 28
MACARIUS OF EGYPT

OME OF THE fathers there related to us that two Macarii—one an Egyptian and disciple of the blessed Antony, and the other from Alexandria[1]—shone in those parts like two stars in the sky.[2] They had in common not only their name but also their spiritual virtues and the magnificence of their heavenly graces.[3] Both Macarii were equally mighty in their ascetic practices and spiritual virtues. One excelled the other only because he inherited graces and virtues from the blessed Antony.

(2) They said that one time, when a murder had been committed in a nearby area and a certain innocent man was

---

1. It sometimes is difficult to distinguish between these two Macarii (Macarius the Great and Macarius of Alexandria) in the primary sources; see A. Guillaumont, "Le problème des deux Macaires dans les *Apophthegmata patrum*," *Irénikon* 48 (1975): 41–59.

2. Cf. Phil 2.15. In classical literature solar and astral imagery is used to describe individuals or groups of people who distinguish themselves from everyone else. Thus Apollonius of Rhodes (*Arg.* 1.239–40) says that the Argonauts stand out like bright stars among clouds (οἱ δὲ φαεινοί / ἀστέρες ὣς νεφέεσσι μετέπρεπον). Such imagery was extremely popular with Christian writers. Theophilus of Alexandria, quoted in a letter by Jerome (*epist.* 113.1.2), calls Epiphanius of Salamis a bright star among bishops who has shined throughout the world (*inter episcopos clarum in orbe sidus effulsit*). Theodoret of Cyrrhus likewise compares several Syrian desert monks to the sun (*hist. rel.* 9.16) and stars (*hist. rel.*, prol. 9, 2.20, 4.13). Cyril of Scythopolis likens monks to radiant stars (*v. Euth.* p. 8 Schwartz; *v. Sab.* pp. 90–91 Schwartz; *v. Theog.* p. 241 Schwartz), as does John Cassian in the case of the monks of Scetis (*coll.* 3.1). Numerous hagiographic authors compare their holy subjects to resplendent stars; see, e.g., Jerome, *epist.* 108.3; Paulinus of Nola, *carm.* 19.219–20, 27.15–24; Hilary of Arles, *v. Hon.* 1.

3. Cf. John Cassian, *coll.* 19.9.

charged with the crime, the falsely accused man fled to Macarius's cell. His accusers also came and alleged that they would be in serious trouble if they did not act according to law by detaining and handing over a murderer. The man charged with the crime swore under oath that he was not guilty of murder, and arguments back and forth ensued for a long while. Holy Macarius then asked where the murdered man had been buried. After they had indicated the location, he went to the tomb together with all the accusers. There he bent his knees, invoked Christ's name, and said to the people standing there: "The Lord will now reveal whether the man accused by you is guilty." He raised his voice and called out to the dead man by name. When the man summoned from the grave answered back, Macarius said to him: "By my faith in Christ I call you as a witness to say whether you were murdered by this man who is accused of harming you." At that point he answered from the grave in a clear voice and said he had not been killed by that man. Stupefied, all fell to the ground, threw themselves at Macarius's feet, and begged him to ask him by whom he had been murdered. Then Macarius said: "I will not ask him because I am satisfied that an innocent man is exonerated. It is not my responsibility to expose a guilty man."

(3) A story was told also about another kind of miracle of his. The virgin daughter of a certain father from a nearby town looked to people as if she had been turned into a horse through the illusions of magic,[4] such that she was thought to be a mare and not a girl.[5] They brought her to Macarius. After he had inquired of her parents about what they wanted, they said: "This mare that your eyes see was a virgin girl and our daughter, but wicked men used evil arts to turn her into the animal you see. We therefore ask you to pray to the Lord and change her into what she was." But he said: "This one you point out—I see her as a girl who has nothing animal-like about her. Rather,

4. On the practice of magic during this period, see J. Gager, ed., *Curse Tablets and Binding Spells from the Ancient World* (Oxford: Oxford University Press, 1992).

5. Palladius (*hist. Laus.* 17.6–9) tells a different version of this story, according to which a wife, not a virgin, is changed into a mare.

what you are referring to is not in her body but in the eyes of onlookers, for these are demons' illusions, not how things truly are." After bringing her into his cell along with her parents, he bent his knees and began to pray to the Lord, and at the same time he encouraged the parents to join him in entreating the Lord. Afterward he anointed her with oil in the Lord's name, removed all the visual deceptiveness, and made her appear as a virgin to all, as indeed she used to appear to herself.

(4) Another girl also was brought to him. Her genitals had become so completely putrefied that her skin was rotted out and the inner secrets of nature were exposed.[6] Such a vast number of worms was breeding inside her that nobody came near her out of disgust at the stench. Her parents brought her and laid her down at his doorstep. Macarius had pity on the virgin's suffering and said: "Be calm, my daughter. The Lord has given this to you to be saved, not to die. Therefore, more care must be taken to ensure that your healing does not cause you any danger." After he had persevered in prayer for seven straight days, he blessed oil and anointed her limbs in the Lord's name. He restored her to health in such a way that no womanly shape or beauty appeared in her and that she would interact with men without the hindrance of feminine deceit.

(5) They said further that one time there came to him a certain heretic of the Hieracite sect, which is a brand of heresy found in Egypt.[7] After using his significant talent at speaking to

6. John of Ephesus tells the story of an Armenian-born priest named Aaron who was stricken with "gangrene," which consumed the flesh in his upper thighs and genital region almost down to the bone, causing such extensive damage that for the last eighteen years of his life he had to use a catheter made of lead in order to urinate. See Brooks, *John of Ephesus*, 643–44.

7. The sect of the Hieracites was founded by Hieracas of Leontopolis, an Egyptian ascetic teacher who authored biblical commentaries and hymns (none of which survive) and taught that only sexually abstinent Christians will enter the kingdom of heaven. According to Epiphanius (*pan.* 67.1.5), Hieracas upheld the spiritual nature of the resurrection body, and this tenet of the Hieracites likely inspired the story recorded above about Macarius's resuscitation of a corpse. Palladius (*hist. Laus.* 17.11), later followed by Sozomen (*hist. eccl.* 3.14), mentions this miracle in passing and says that Macarius worked it so that he could confute a "heretic" who denied the bodily resurrection, but he does not specify that this "heretic" was a Hieracite. On Hieracas's teachings

confound the brothers who lived in the desert, this man had the audacity to set forth the depravity of his faith even in Macarius's presence. When the old man stood his ground and refuted him, the heretic eluded his simple words with clever arguments. But when the saint saw that the brothers' faith was in danger, he said: "Why should we wrangle over words to the detriment of those who are listening?[8] Let us go to the graves of the brothers who have gone before us in the Lord, and let all know that to whichever of us the Lord has given the power to raise a dead man from his grave, that man's faith is approved by God." This pronouncement gratified all the brothers who were present. They made their way to the graves, and Macarius urged the Hieracite to call forth a dead man in the Lord's name. But he said: "You are the one who proposed this, so you go first."

(6) Macarius prostrated himself before the Lord in prayer, and when he had finished praying, he lifted his eyes heavenward and said to the Lord: "Lord, show by the raising of this dead man which of us two has the true faith." After saying this, he called out the name of a certain brother who recently had been buried. The dead man answered from the tomb, and then the brothers approached at once and removed the lid. They pulled him out of the grave and presented him alive; the burial bandages in which he had been wrapped had come unfastened. When the Hieracite saw this, he was dumbfounded and turned to run away. All the brothers chased after him and drove him beyond the borders of that territory.[9]

Many other stories also are related about him.[10] They are too numerous to be written down, yet from these few stories the rest of his deeds can be known.

---

and place within the early Egyptian monastic movement, see J.E. Goehring, "Hieracas of Leontopolis: The Making of a Desert Ascetic," in J.E. Goehring, *Ascetics, Society, and the Desert: Studies in Early Egyptian Monasticism* (Harrisburg, PA: Trinity Press International, 1999), 110–36.

8. Cf. 2 Tm 2.14.

9. This story about Macarius resurrecting a dead man is not found in the *GHM*.

10. Cf. Palladius, *hist. Laus.* 17.1–13; John Cassian, *coll.* 15.3.

CHAPTER 29
MACARIUS OF ALEXANDRIA

HE OTHER saintly Macarius also excelled in magnificent virtues, about which others too have written some things[1] that can suffice to capture the greatness of his virtue, and so we omit them for the sake of brevity. In any event, they related that he had been a greater lover of the desert than anyone else, to such a degree that he explored even the remotest, inaccessible parts of the wilderness terrain until he found (so it was said) a place situated in the furthest reaches of the desert, teeming with a variety of fruit-bearing trees and filled with every delectable treat.[2] It was here that he also is said to have chanced upon two brothers. He asked them to let monks be brought there to live since the place was delightful and abundant in everything one possibly could need. They replied that no more people could be brought there, for fear that while on their way through the desert they happen to be led astray by demons. For they avowed that there are many demons in the desert whose torments and deceits the inexperienced masses could not endure. Even still, when he returned to the brothers and told them about the place's amenities, many were incited to go there with him.[3] But when the rest of the el-

---

1. Cf. Rufinus, *hist. eccl.* 2.4; Sozomen, *hist. eccl.* 3.14.

2. Pachomius and other late antique holy men are also said to have visited Paradise and enjoyed its intoxicating scents; see S. Ashbrook Harvey, *Scenting Salvation: Ancient Christianity and the Olfactory Imagination* (Berkeley: University of California Press, 2006), 226.

3. The *GHM* (21.12) adds that when Macarius returned home to his fellow monks, he took with him some fruit as proof of the garden's existence. A much different story about Macarius's visit to the garden is told by Palladius (*hist. Laus.* 18.5–8), who adds that Jannes and Jambres first had built a monument for storing gold and later planted trees there and also dug a well. Macarius

ders found out about the younger brothers' dogged determination, they restrained them with salutary advice: "If it really was planted by Jannes and Jambres,[4] as is alleged, it ought to be regarded as nothing more than a place prepared by the devil to deceive us. For if it really is pleasurable and abundant, as they claim, what will we have to hope for in the world to come if we relish pleasures here?" Expressing these and other sentiments of this kind, they held in check the younger brothers' enthusiasm.

(2) The place where holy Macarius lived is called Scetis.[5] It is in an expansive desert wasteland, a day's and a night's journey from the monasteries of Nitria.[6] The way there is not marked or shown by any footpath or landmarks, but is guided by the appearances and movements of the stars. Water is hard to find, and wherever it is, it has a horrible, bituminous smell and an awful taste. The men there are spiritually perfect, for such a foreboding place does not tolerate any but the dweller who has perfect resolve and supreme endurance. They cultivate the utmost zeal for love among themselves and towards all who have happened to reach them.

The following story is told. Once when someone had brought

---

stumbled upon the monument and garden by accident after traveling for nine straight days through the desert. The demons who lived there forbade him from entering, but they relented and allowed him to come in and look around briefly. Inside the monument he found a hanging brass jar and an iron chain near the well that had become corroded with time. The only fruit he found in the garden was some hollowed-out pomegranates that had been dried out by the sun.

4. Jannes and Jambres were magicians at Pharaoh's court who contended with Moses and Aaron (cf. Ex 7.10–12; they are mentioned by name in 2 Tm 3.8). According to one legend, they planted a garden in the Egyptian desert in their attempt to make a copy of Eden. On this and other legends surrounding these two figures, see A. Pietersma, *The Apocryphon of Jannes and Jambres the Magicians, edited with Introduction, Translation, and Commentary* (Leiden: Brill, 1994), 1–43.

5. Along with Nitria and Kellia, Scetis was one of the three great monastic centers in fourth-century Lower Egypt. Around 330 Macarius the Egyptian settled there, and by the late fourth century it had become a prominent colony of monastic hermits consisting of a constellation of individual cells scattered throughout the desert plain. John Cassian lived there from c.380 until 399.

6. Scetis was located forty miles south of Nitria.

a bunch of grapes to holy Macarius, he sent it to another brother who was of weaker constitution because, in accordance with the principle of love, he thought not of his own good but that of another.[7] That man then gave thanks to God for the brother's gift, but nevertheless he, thinking about his neighbor more than about himself, handed it off to another, and this other man did likewise. As a result, after the bunch of grapes had made the rounds in all the individual cells scattered throughout the desert, with nobody knowing who had been the first to send it, it finally was given to the one who had sent it. Holy Macarius, thankful that he was witnessing such great asceticism and love among the brothers, devoted himself to more severe practices in the monastic life.[8]

(3) Those who had heard it from his mouth swore to us that once during the night a demon knocked on the door of his cell and said: "Get up, Abba Macarius, and let us go to the gathering,[9] where the brothers are assembled to celebrate vigils." Being full of God's grace, however, he could not be deceived. He recognized that this was the devil's ruse and said: "You liar and enemy of the truth![10] What business, what association do you have with the gathering and meeting of the saints?" The demon replied: "Macarius, are you forgetting that without us there *is* no gathering or meeting of the monks? Come, and you will see our handiwork there." At that point Macarius said: "The Lord rebuke you, foul demon!"[11]

Devoting himself to prayer, he asked God to show him wheth-

7. Cf. Phil 2.4; 1 Cor 10.24.
8. Cyril of Scythopolis (*v. Sab.* pp. 88–89 Schwartz) similarly tells of how Sabas once, while working in the monastery garden, was seized with a desire to eat a plump, prematurely ripe apple but he exercised self-control (ἐγκράτεια) and, reasoning that this was the fruit through which Adam fell from grace, vowed never again to eat apples.
9. Lat. *collecta*. The *collecta* was a formal gathering of monks for the purpose of corporate prayer and worship; see B. Capelle, "*Collecta*," *RBén* 42 (1930): 197–204.
10. Cf. Acts 13.10.
11. Jude 9. Macarius quotes the archangel Michael's rebuke of Satan when Satan tried to resist his attempt to move Moses's corpse to another location. For a reconstruction of this story and Jude's possible sources for it, see R. Bauckham, *Jude, 2 Peter* (Dallas: Word, 1983), 65–76.

er the demon's boast was true. He departed for the gathering at which the vigils were being celebrated by the brothers, and he again beseeched the Lord in prayer to reveal to him whether this claim was true. Lo and behold, he saw what appeared to be little black Ethiopian boys[12] all throughout the church running about and being whisked around as if in flight. Now, it was the custom, while all were seated there, for the psalm to be recited by one while the rest either listened or chanted in response.[13] While each and every one was sitting down, the little Ethiopian boys ran about and frolicked mischievously. If they covered anyone's eyes with two little fingers, he immediately fell asleep, and if they inserted a finger into anyone's mouth, they made him yawn.

After the psalmody the brothers prostrated themselves to pray, and the little boys kept whirling past each of them. To one who lay prostrate in prayer they assumed the form of a woman, while to another they appeared as if they were building or carrying something and being engaged in any number of occupations. Whatever things the demons had concocted through their trickery, the brothers turned their thoughts to these while praying. When, however, they had begun to stir up trouble like this, they were driven back by some of the monks as if by force and were knocked down headlong, such that they did not dare even to stand or pass in front of these monks, yet they would play on the necks and backs of others.

12. In monastic hagiography the devil and demons occasionally appear to monks as black boys (e.g., Athanasius, *v. Ant.* 6.1; Palladius, *hist. Laus.* 16.4). Oftentimes, as in the story recounted above, demons are specifically designated as Ethiopians (Evagrius, *antirr.* 4.34; John Cassian, *coll.* 1.21, 2.13, 9.6; *AP* Heraclides 1; *APsys* 5.27; *APanon* 426; Anon., *v. Sym. Styl. iun.* 124), thereby playing on the early Christian (monastic) objectification of Ethiopians as demons. See D. Brakke, "Ethiopian Demons: Male Sexuality, the Black-Skinned Other, and the Monastic Self," *JHSex* 10 (2001): 501–35; A. Nugent, "Black Demons in the Desert," *ABR* 49 (1998): 209–21; cf. P. Frost, "Attitudes towards Blacks in the Early Christian Era," *SecCent* 8 (1991): 1–11; F. Snowden, *Blacks in Antiquity: Ethiopians in the Greco-Roman Experience* (Cambridge, MA: Harvard University Press, 1970).

13. The Psalter was the core prayer text in fourth-century desert monasticism. See A. Davril, "La Psalmodie chez les pères du désert," *CollCist* 49 (1987): 132–39; J.W. McKinnon, "Desert Monasticism and the Later Fourth-Century Psalmodic Movement," *M&L* 75 (1994): 505–21.

(4) When holy Macarius saw this, he groaned deeply and poured forth tears and said to the Lord: "Pay attention, Lord, and do not stay silent or be gentle. God, rise up so that your enemies may be scattered and flee from your presence, for our soul is filled with illusions."[14] After the prayer, in order to find out the truth, he called aside each of the brothers before whom he had seen demons playing tricks under diverse guises and in a variety of forms. He interrogated them to see if during prayer they entertained thoughts about building or taking a trip or any of the various things he had seen represented to each monk by demons. Every single one of them confessed that what he disclosed had been in their hearts. At that point it was recognized that all the vain and futile thoughts that each of them mulled during psalmody and prayer originate from the demons' deceptive trickery. Moreover, the foul Ethiopians were driven off by those who "kept control of their hearts with all watchfulness."[15] For a heart that is joined to God and focused on him, especially during prayer, receives into itself nothing foreign and nothing futile.

He also mentioned something much more horrifying, which he had witnessed when the brothers were coming up for the Eucharist. When they stretched out their hands to receive it, Ethiopians came first and placed coal in the hands of some, and the Host which was seen being carried in the priest's hands returned to the altar. But as others, whose greater merits protected them, reached out their hands toward the altar, the demons drew back at a distance and fled in tremendous fear.[16] For Macarius noticed an angel of God standing beside the altar who placed his own hand over the priest's hand during the distribution of the Eucharist.[17] From that time on, there remained with him a God-given grace: to discern whether any brother during

---

14. Macarius's prayer is an amalgamation of three different versicules from the Psalms (37.8; 67.2; 82.2).

15. Prv 4.23.

16. Demons' fear of believers is a *topos* of patristic literature; see, e.g., Tertullian, *apol.* 27; Athanasius, *v. Ant.* 43.3. Cf. A. Cain, "Antony's Onocentaur: The Symbolism of a Mythological Curiosity (Athanasius, *Vita Antonii* 53.1–3)," *WS* 133 (2020): forthcoming.

17. On angels administering the Eucharist, see Palladius, *hist. Laus.* 18.25.

the psalmody vigils or time of prayer had pondered any thought
inspired by the demons' trickery, and to be privy to either the
unworthiness or the merits of those approaching the altar.

(5) One time both Macarii,[18] men of God, were on a journey
to visit a certain brother. They boarded a large ferry customarily used for crossing the river.[19] On it there also were some
tribunes, wealthy and very powerful men, who had with them
a great many horses, slaves, and an extensive military escort.[20]
When one of them caught sight of the monks sitting in a far corner of the ferry clad in cheap clothing and free of all earthly en-
tanglements, he addressed them: "Blessed[21] are you for mocking
this world and not seeking anything from it except the cheapest
clothing and the sparest provisions." Then one of the Macarii
replied to him: "As you say, truly indeed do those who follow
God mock the world. We, however, have pity on you because
the world mocks you." He was struck by compunction at this remark. As soon as he got home, he relinquished and liquidated
all he had and gave the proceeds to the poor, and he started
following God and was eager to take up monastic practices.

As I have said, many other amazing things are related about
the deeds of holy Macarius,[22] and the inquisitive reader will
find some of them reported in the eleventh book of the *Ecclesiastical History.*[23]

18. I.e., Macarius the Egyptian and Macarius of Alexandria.

19. I.e., the Nile River.

20. The *GHM* (23.2) specifies that there were two tribunes and that their
horses were fitted with golden bridles and their servants wore golden belts
and collars. As is suggested by D. Woods, "An Imperial Embassy in the *Historia
monachorum,*" *JThS* n.s. 48 (1997): 133–36 (135–36), these tribunes may have
been on an official embassy sent by the emperor Theodosius to consult the
monk John of Lycopolis in c.387/88.

21. Lat. *beati.* Rufinus is unable here to preserve a pun found in the *GHM*
(23.3), whereby the tribune salutes both Macarii as being *makarioi* ("blessed").
For the same pun made (though in Coptic) on the name of another Macarius (fifth-century bishop of Tkôw), who also was on a ship, see D. W. Johnson,
trans., *A Panegyric on Macarius, Bishop of Tkôw, Attributed to Dioscorus of Alexandria* (Louvain: Peeters, 1980), 14.

22. For a slightly later source of stories about Macarius of Alexandria, see
Palladius, *hist. Laus.* 18.1–29.

23. Rufinus references his own *Historia ecclesiastica* (11.4).

CHAPTER 30
AMOUN OF NITRIA

HEY SAY THAT the monastic settlement at Nitria was founded by a certain Amoun,[1] whose soul holy Antony saw borne up to heaven after it had left his body, just as the writing describing Antony's life relates.[2] This Amoun was born of noble parents, who forced him to marry against his will. Since he had been unable to overcome his parents' heavy-handedness, he married a virgin bride.[3] After they had come together in their conjugal bed-chamber and were afforded the quiet privacy of a bedroom, he began talking to the girl about chastity and exhorting her to preserve her virginity: "Corruption assuredly will possess corruption, but incorruption looks forward to incorruption.[4] It is much better if both of us remain virgins than if one is corrupted by the other." The virgin agreed, and the vessel of incorruption took the veil in silence. For a long while they were content to have God alone as their witness. They were more closely connected to God than to flesh and blood, but after the death of his parents he withdrew to this part of the nearby desert, whereas the virgin resided in

1. Amoun, who built two cells for himself at Nitria as early as c.315 and as late as c.325–c.330, is believed to have been the first monk to settle there. Over the next several decades monks from all over Egypt flocked there to live; see Evelyn-White, *The Monasteries of the Wadi 'n Natrûn*, 45–59.

2. See Athanasius, *v. Ant.* 60.1–2, 11; cf. Palladius, *hist. Laus.* 7.6. "The writing describing Antony's life" is of course Athanasius's *Life of Antony.*

3. Among the upper classes in Roman antiquity, a bride marrying for the first time was expected to have a reputation for chastity and in fact to be a virgin; see K. Hersch, *The Roman Wedding: Ritual and Meaning in Antiquity* (Cambridge: Cambridge University Press, 2010), 61.

4. Cf. 1 Cor 15.50.

their house for a short time, and she gathered around herself large numbers of virgins, and he, large numbers of monks.

(2) While he was living as a recluse in the desert, a certain young man who went mad after being bitten by a rabid dog was brought to him bound in multiple layers of chains, as his parents accompanied him and made petitions on his behalf. Amoun said: "Why are you bothering me, people? What you are asking for is beyond my merits. Nevertheless, I can tell you this: his health is in your hands. Give back to the widow the ox you stole from her, and your son will be restored to you in pristine health." They were petrified that what was perpetrated in secret did not escape the notice of the man of God. Yet they did rejoice that he showed them the way of salvation, and as soon as they returned the stolen goods, the man of God prayed, and the youth had his health restored.

(3) On another occasion when some people had come to see him, Amoun, wanting to test their inner disposition, said he needed a large jar to store water for visitors. After they had promised to bring it, one of them changed his mind and figured that his camel could be put at significant risk if he loaded such a heavy weight onto it. He said to the other: "If you are willing or able, take the jar back. As for myself, I am sparing my camel so that it does not die." The other said: "As you yourself know, I have an ass, not a camel. Surely an ass cannot carry what a camel cannot carry?"[5] He said: "Do what you want. You'll see what happens. I will not put my camel in harm's way." Then the other said: "I will load onto my ass the weight you say is onerous for your camel, and the merits of the man of God will make the impossible possible." He strapped the jar onto the ass and brought it all the way to the man of God's monastery without the ass feeling itself carrying any of the weight. When Amoun saw him, he said: "You have done well in using

5. Asses (or donkeys) are able to carry up to a third of their body weight without flinching; see D. B. Dill, *The Hot Life of Man and Beast* (Springfield, IL: C. C. Thomas Publisher, 1985), 93–102. Their impressive load-bearing capacity as well as the fact that they are cheap to feed and easy to maintain made them ideal for agricultural work and transport throughout Greco-Roman antiquity; see C. Adams, *Land Transport in Roman Egypt* (Oxford: Oxford University Press, 2007), 49–90.

the ass to carry the jar, for your friend's camel is dead." He returned and discovered that this had happened as the servant of God had predicted.

(4) The Lord displayed many other signs through him. For example, when he was wanting to cross the Nile River and was ashamed to get undressed [for swimming], he is said to have been whisked suddenly to the opposite shore by God's miraculous power.[6] Furthermore, it has been passed down that the blessed Antony held Amoun's righteous life and spiritual virtues in the highest regard.

---

6. See Athanasius, *v. Ant.* 60.5–10. Cf. Palladius, *hist. Laus.* 8.6, who specifies that Amoun crossed the Lycus, which according to Sozomen (*hist. eccl.* 1.14) was a canal branching out from the Nile, possibly at Lycopolis in Upper Egypt.

CHAPTER 31
PAUL THE SIMPLE

MONG THE disciples of Antony was a certain man named Paul, called "the Simple."[1] This is how his conversion came about.[2] With his own eyes he saw his wife sleeping with another man but said nothing to anyone and left the house. Beside himself with grief, he went off to the desert, where he wandered about in a distressed state of mind. He came upon Antony's hermitage, and there he formulated a plan of action based on the penitential ambience of the place and the timeliness of his finding it. He approached Antony to ask him about the path to salvation, and Antony, staring intently at this man with a simple nature, replied that he would be saved in the end if he complied with what he said. Then Paul answered that he would do all of whatever Antony instructed.

(2) In order to put Paul's promise to the test, Antony told him as he was standing at the door of his cell: "Wait here for me and pray until I come out." After going in Antony remained inside all day and all night. Even still, numerous times he furtively peered through the window and saw Paul praying without ceasing and not budging an inch but standing still in the daytime heat and the nighttime dew, remembering the command not to move even a step. After coming out the next day, Antony

---

1. See Palladius, *hist. Laus.* 22; Sozomen, *hist. eccl.* 1.13. Paul, a rustic herdsman and farmer, was surnamed "the Simple" on account of his lack of education.

2. In the *LHM* "salvation" has a monastic connotation: it is an ongoing quest for spiritual perfection, which is achieved by degrees through ascetic self-discipline over the course of a lifetime. It begins with a point of conversion (*conversio*), but this conversion, like "salvation" itself, is a process, as we see in this story about Paul.

began training and teaching him about specifics, namely how to quell his sense of loneliness through manual labor and how to perform his earthly labor with the limbs of the body but to perform the things of God with mental deliberation and spiritual resolve. He also instructed Paul to eat in the evening but to make sure that he never arrived at satiety, especially in drinking [water], and he affirmed that an abundance of water causes fantasies to occur in the soul just as much as wine causes the body's heat level to rise. After he gave him comprehensive guidance about how to act in specific circumstances, Antony set up a cell nearby, about three miles away, and ordered Paul to put into practice what he had taught him. Antony nevertheless frequently visited him and was gratified to see him persevering in what he had learned with whole-hearted resolve and unflagging conscientiousness.

(3) One day, some highly esteemed brothers and perfected men had come to see holy Antony, and Paul happened to be there with them. When the conversation turned to ethereal and mystical matters and much discussion ensued about the prophets and the Savior, Paul inquired out of the simplicity of his spirit who was superior to the other, Christ or the prophets. The blessed Antony all but blushed out of embarrassment at the absurdity of Paul's question, and with a gentle motion of his hand (the kind he was accustomed to use with simpler folk) he ordered him to be quiet and leave. Because Paul had resolved to abide by everything Antony said as if it were God's commandment, he departed for his cell and, seeing that he had received an order, resolved to maintain silence and not say a single word.

After discovering this, Antony began to marvel at how this obedience, which he knew he had not demanded of Paul, was agreeable to him. After he had ordered him to speak and explain why he was quiet, Paul said: "You told me to be on my way and stay quiet." Antony was stunned that the words he had spoken casually were heeded by Paul, and he said: "May this man put us all to shame. For although we do not hear the Lord when he speaks to us from heaven, anything whatsoever that comes out of my mouth is heeded by this man."

(4) In any event, holy Antony, intent upon teaching him many things, had gotten into the habit of exacting obedience from him even when no reason or justification called for it, so that his spirit could be shown worthy in matters relating to obedience. For instance, Antony once ordered Paul to draw water from a well and to pour it onto the ground for an entire day, to take apart woven baskets and then weave them again, to unstitch his cloak and sew it back together and then take it apart again.[3] Paul is said to have had a great many tasks like these foisted upon him by Antony so that he would learn not to utter a word in protest, not even in cases when the tasks imposed seemed to defy logic. After a short period of being trained through all these experiences, he achieved [spiritual] perfection.

On the basis of Paul's example, blessed Antony would teach that if anyone desired to achieve [spiritual] perfection in swift fashion, he should not be his own master nor obey his own desires, even if what he wants seems right to him. Rather, there should be adherence to the Savior's commandment: "Above all, let each person deny himself and renounce his own desires."[4] For the Savior himself says: "I have come not to do my own will but the will of him who sent me."[5] To be sure, Christ's will was not contrary to the will of the Father, but would the one who had come to teach obedience not be deemed disobedient if he did his own will? How much more disobedient, then, will we be reckoned if we do our own wills?

(5) In summary, the aforementioned Paul is an example for us: by virtue of his obedience and simplicity he rose to such a lofty height of spiritual gifts that God performed many more powerful miracles through him than he did through holy Antony. On account of the richness of his gifts, many people would flock to him from all corners of the earth to be healed by him. The blessed Antony accordingly feared that annoyance at the crowds would discomfit him, and so he made Paul stay in the

---

3. Cf. the three trials that Venus forced Psyche to endure (Apuleius, *met.* 6.20–21).

4. Cf. Mt 16.24.

5. Jn 6.38.

inner desert, where nobody could have easy access to him, meaning that Antony was the one in a better position to welcome visitors. But those he could not cure he would send to Paul, who had a more prolific gift of healing, and they would be cured by him.

They say that Paul had earned so much respect from God for his simplicity that one time when a madman was acting like a rabid dog and ripping into everyone who had dared to approach him or had been brought near him, Paul devoted himself to prayer in order to expel the demon that was oppressing the man. But when there was a delay and the desired result did not come right away,[6] he became indignant as children do, and it is related that he said to the Lord: "Truly, I will not eat today if you do not heal him." Right away the Lord's tender little boy (so to speak) had his request divinely granted, and at once the madman was cured.[7]

6. Instantaneous exorcisms are by no means unheard of in the literary sources; the monk Posidonius, for example, drives a demon out of a pregnant woman after genuflecting in prayer only twice (Palladius, *hist. Laus.* 36.4; cf. Cyril of Scythopolis, *v. Sab.* p. 164 Schwartz). More often than not, however, we hear about ones of longer duration, whether two hours (Gregory of Tours, *lib. mir. Mart.* 2.37.1), several hours on end (Palladius, *hist. Laus.* 44.4), a few days (Cyril of Scythopolis, *v. Euth.* p. 76 Schwartz; Anon., *v. Sym. Styl. iun.* 43), forty days (Callinicus, *v. Hyp.* 40.7), or even an entire year (Callinicus, *v. Hyp.* 44.20–22); in the case of Paul the Simple, Rufinus does not tell us how much time elapses between Paul's prayer and his childish temper tantrum. Cf. Minucius Felix, *Oct.* 27.7, who says that when demons are exorcised from their human hosts, they either leap out at once or vanish gradually (*vel exsiliunt statim vel evanescunt gradatim*).

7. The story recounted in this paragraph, which simultaneously humanizes Paul by showing his potential for petulant outbursts and emphasizes God's attentiveness to his (indignant) requests, is absent from the *GHM*.

CHAPTER 32
PIAMMON (PIAMMONAS)

IT DOES NOT SEEM appropriate to me to pass over in silence the inhabitants of the desert that borders on the Parthenian Sea and the town of Diolcos.[1] We saw there a wonderful priest named Piammon,[2] a man who was full of humility and kindness. He also had the gift of receiving revelations. For example, once when he was offering sacrifices to the Lord,[3] he saw an angel of God standing by the altar and writing down the names of the monks approaching the altar in a book that he held in his hands; yet he did not write down some of their names. The elder carefully took note of whose names the angel did not write down. After Communion was over, he called each one to the side and interrogated him about any sin he had committed in secret, and he discovered from their confessions that each one of them was guilty of mortal sin. He then admonished them to repent. He prostrated himself, along with them, before the Lord day and night as if he himself had been implicated in their sins. He wept and persevered with them in repentance and tears until he again saw the same angel standing by the altar and writing down the names of those coming up. After he wrote down the names of all, Piammon saw him calling them by name and inviting them to be reconciled at the altar. When the elder saw this, he realized that their repen-

---

1. Diolcos was a harbor town situated between the Sebennytic and Phatnic mouths of the Nile and on the shore of the Mediterranean Sea. Cf. *APanon* 614 (Wortley, *Anonymous Sayings,* 493) for an anecdote about some unnamed monks who settled on a mountain near Diolcos.

2. See John Cassian, *coll.* 17.24; Sozomen, *hist. eccl.* 6.29. Cassian devotes his eighteenth *Conference* to Piammon.

3. I.e., when he was celebrating the Eucharist.

tance had been accepted, and he restored them to the altar with immense rejoicing.

(2) They also related that one time he had been beaten by demons so badly that he could not so much as stand or budge.[4] When Sunday came and the sacrifice needed to be offered, he gave instructions that he be carried to the altar by the brothers' hands. After he had lain there in prayer, he suddenly saw before him the angel who was accustomed to standing by the altar, and the angel extended his hand to him and lifted him from the ground. All of his suffering immediately went away and he was made healthier than usual.

4. Cf. Athanasius, *v. Ant.* 9.2: Antony is beaten so badly by a band of demons that he does not have the strength to stand up. Cf. also Palladius, *hist. Laus.* 18.9, where a demon pounds Moses the Ethiopian with a cudgel so hard that he nearly dies, and it takes him a year to recover fully from his injuries. According to the *First Greek Life of Pachomius* (20), Pachomius often was assaulted during the night by demons, and the bruises would be visible in the morning.

CHAPTER 33
JOHN OF DIOLCOS

N THOSE parts[1] there was a holy man named John who was completely full of grace. He had such a powerful gift of offering comfort that a soul, after receiving a few words from him, would be filled with cheer and joy, no matter the dejection or depression that had been oppressing it. God also bestowed upon him a significant gift of healing [the body].[2]

---

1. I.e., the desert outside the town of Diolcos, where the visionary priest Piammon, profiled in the previous chapter, lived.

2. The entry on John in the *GHM* (26.1) reads differently in several respects: "We also visited another John in Diolcos, who was the father of hermitages. He, too, was endowed with much grace. He looked like Abraham and had a beard like Aaron's. He had performed many miracles and cures and was especially successful at healing people afflicted with paralysis and gout."

EPILOGUE

N SCORES of other parts of Egypt, too, we visited saints of God who were completely full of his grace performing many miracles and wonders, but I have recalled only a few out of many because it is beyond my capacity to detail them all. As for those who are said to live in the Upper Thebaid around Syene, we only heard that they are regarded as being more eminent and more magnificent than virtually all the ones we saw. We were unable to make our way to them on account of the peril of the journey, for even though all the areas of that region are infested with highway robbers, the ones beyond the city of Lyco are plagued by barbarians. We had no way of getting to them, and indeed it was not without peril that we saw the men I recalled earlier. During the journey we were in danger of losing our lives seven times, but "the eighth time trouble did not touch us,"[1] as God protected us through it all.

(2) The first time we were traveling through the desert for five days and nights and almost died of thirst and fatigue.[2]

The second time we wandered into an area with a ravine

---

1. Cf. Jb 5.19: "[God] will deliver you from six troubles; in seven no evil shall touch you." Both Rufinus and the anonymous author of the *GHM* retouch this Scriptural intertext, adding one to the number of Job's "troubles" in order to accommodate the circumstances of the seven monks' journey.

2. Similiarly, Sabas, when traversing the desert with two monastic companions, fainted and nearly died of dehydration (Cyril of Scythopolis, *v. Sab.* p. 94 Schwartz). In Theodoret's *Religious History* (2.7), the noble youth Asterius almost dies of thirst in the desert, but the ascetic Julian saves him from dehydration by causing a spring to well up from the sand. Not all desert travelers fare as well as Sabas and Asterius in the hagiographic literature: for instance, in Athanasius's *Life of Antony* (59.1), one of two unnamed monks coming to see Antony dies after their supply of water has been depleted.

which produces a briny liquid that the sun's heat concentrates into salt (just as winter snow hardens into ice) and causes sharp spikes to be formed out of the salt. This whole area is so rugged that the salt-thorns can prick and lacerate not only bare feet (as it did ours) but also feet protected by sandals. At any rate, we had found ourselves in great danger and barely escaped.

The third time we were venturing through the desert and wandered into low-lying terrain which also produced briny liquid, though it did not reduce down to hardened salt. Intent upon walking on ground which was loose and packed with foul-smelling mud, we sank up to our waists. As we were on the verge of being submerged, we cried out to the Lord and uttered the Psalmist's words: "Save me, Lord, for the waters have flooded my soul. I have sunk in the slime of the deep and there is no ability to stand."[3]

(3) We endured the fourth danger in waters which had remained after the flooding of the Nile. After having been stuck in them for three straight days, we barely were able to escape.

The fifth danger came to us in the form of highway robbers when we were making our way along the road by the sea.[4] They pursued us for ten miles and were unable to harm us with weapons but made us almost die from exhaustion during the chase.

We faced the sixth hardship on the Nile itself, when we were sailing on it and almost drowned.

The seventh danger occurred on Lake Mariut.[5] We were driven onto an island by a strong wind, and a severe rainstorm

3. Ps 68.1–2. The psalmist is taken out of context: the mire and water from which he seeks deliverance are metaphorical.

4. The seven monks had left Alexandria and were following the coastal road eastward to the harbor town of Diolcos. Even though their brush with highway robbers occurred near the end of their Egyptian travels, this event is placed near the middle of the list of the eight hardships.

5. The monks were headed north to Alexandria and took a ferry across Lake Mariut (Mareotis). Under normal circumstances this trip would take a day and a half (so Palladius, *hist. Laus.* 7.1). Rufinus omits a detail found in the corresponding place in the *GHM* (Epil. 10), that they were stranded on the lake for three days and three nights. Rufinus also does not translate the anonymous Greek author's aside here that papyrus was sourced from this lake (ἐν ᾗ ὁ χάρτης γεννᾶται); on Mariut as a source of papyrus, see Leontius, *Life of John the Almsgiver* 8.

poured down on us. This was during the season of Epiphany.⁶ (4) The eighth danger occurred when we arrived at the monasteries of Nitria. We chanced upon a place where flood-water from the Nile had gathered and formed a pond. There were a great many wild animals and especially crocodiles in it. After they had gotten out to warm themselves in the sun, they lay around the edge of the pond so perfectly still that, to us who knew no different, they seemed dead. We approached to inspect and admire the massive size of the beasts we presumed were dead. As soon as they heard footsteps, they were stirred from their slumber and began lunging at us and chasing us. We, however, called upon the name of Christ the Lord with a loud shout and in fear. His mercy came to our aid, and the beasts that had risen up against us were driven back at once into the pond, as if repelled by an angel.

We quickly headed straight for the monasteries and gave thanks to our God, who saved us from such great dangers and showed us such amazing things. To him be glory and honor forever.⁷ Amen.

6. Schulz-Flügel printed *sperabantur* here (*Erat enim tempus, quo Epifaniorum sperabantur dies*), with this verb implying that Epiphany was approaching but not yet there. I have followed instead one of her textual variants, *celebrabantur*, which better preserves the sense of the Greek (ἦν γὰρ ὁ καιρὸς τῶν ἐπιφανειῶν) in specifying that this event occurred during the season of Epiphany. This dominical feast day was established to celebrate the baptism of Jesus; see R. Wilken, "The Interpretation of the Baptism of Jesus in the Later Fathers," *StudPatr* 11 (1967): 268–77 (274–76). Its origins in fourth-century Egypt probably were in the pagan festival, celebrated on the evening of the winter solstice (January 6), in honor of the sun god Aion's birth from the virgin Kore; see R. G. Coquin, "Les origines de l'Epiphanie en Égypte," *LO* 47 (1967): 139–70. In late fourth-century eastern churches, the Feast of Epiphany was celebrated on January 6.

7. This doxology was inspired by Paul: cf. Rom 11.36; Gal 1.5; Phil 4.20; 1 Tm 1.17; 2 Tm 4.18. After Athanasius (*v. Ant.* 94.2), it became conventional for Greek and Latin hagiographers to bring their works to a close with the doxology used here; cf. Theodoret, *hist. rel.* 30.8; Cyril of Scythopolis, *v. Euth.* p. 85 Schwartz.

INDICES

GENERAL INDEX

INDEX OF HOLY SCRIPTURE

INDEX OF GREEK AND LATIN WORDS
AND PHRASES

INDEX OF OTHER ANCIENT SOURCES

RECENT VOLUMES IN THE FATHERS
OF THE CHURCH SERIES

ST. CYRIL OF ALEXANDRIA, *Glaphyra on the Pentateuch, Volume 2: Exodus through Deuteronomy,* translated by Nicholas P. Lunn, Volume 138 (2019)

ST. CYRIL OF ALEXANDRIA, *Glaphyra on the Pentateuch, Volume 1: Genesis,* translated by Nicholas P. Lunn, with introduction by Gregory K. Hillis, Volume 137 (2018)

ST. MAXIMOS THE CONFESSOR, *On Difficulties in Sacred Scripture: The Responses to Thalassios,* translated by Fr. Maximos Constas, Volume 136 (2018)

EUSEBIUS OF CAESAREA, *Against Marcellus and On Ecclesiastical Theology,* translated by Kelley McCarthy Spoerl and Markus Vinzent, Volume 135 (2017)

TYCONIUS, *Exposition of the Apocalypse,* translated by Francis X. Gumerlock, with introduction and notes by David C. Robinson, Volume 134 (2017)

RUFINUS OF AQUILEIA, *History of the Church,* translated by Philip R. Amidon, SJ, Volume 133 (2016)

DIDYMUS THE BLIND, *Commentary on Genesis,* translated by Robert C. Hill, Volume 132 (2016)

ST. GREGORY OF NYSSA, *Anti-Apollinarian Writings,* translated by Robin Orton, Volume 131 (2015)

ST. EPHREM THE SYRIAN, *The Hymns on Faith,* translated by Jeffrey T. Wickes, Volume 130 (2015)

ST. CYRIL OF ALEXANDRIA, *Three Christological Treatises,* translated by Daniel King, Volume 129 (2014)

ST. EPIPHANIUS OF CYPRUS, *Ancoratus,* translated by Young Richard Kim, Volume 128 (2014)

WORKS OF RUFINUS OF AQUILEIA IN THIS SERIES

History of the Church, translated by Philip R. Amidon, SJ, Fathers of the Church 133 (2016)

Inquiry about the Monks in Egypt, translated by Andrew Cain, Fathers of the Church 139 (2019)